Of Dogs and Cats and Bear

Jenny Melmoth

Jenny Melmoth

Illustrated by

France Bauduin

France Bauduin

Author's Note: While every effort has been made to ensure that the information given in this book is correct the author does not accept responsibility for any inaccuracy.

To protect people's privacy some names have been changed.

Cover design – Jaz Singh
Cover Illustration – France Bauduin
Artwork – France Bauduin
Photographs with *Bear* – Becca Thornton
Pre-press – Jen Darling (*Alfresco Books*)
Printer – Ellesmere Press Ltd

For my family

especially our grandchildren

CONTENTS

Poems

Prose Pieces

Chapter One

Dogs and Doodlebugs

'Rrrruff !' It was the first proper word I ever uttered, according to my mother, and was directed with the 'r' fully rolled from the pulpit of my highchair at my grandparents' large, affable liver-and-white springer spaniel, who was a family favourite for many years. He must have been the imprint for my love of dogs and indeed the basis for my affection and respect for all animals.

I was born Jennifer Mary Banning in Sevenoaks, Kent, in March 1942, my parents living in a rented ground floor flat, and my maternal grandparents a few minutes walk away along a footpath which dipped up and down through the fields to such an extent that it was known locally as The Switchback. If I think of it, I see the vivid green of early summer grass and a tall haze of white which I take to be cow parsley as viewed from the safe seat of my pushchair.

It was wartime. My father was away in the army manning search lights, with only the occasional leave. My grandfather, George Harrison, had served his war from 1914-1918, emerging handsome and unscathed. His son, my young Uncle John, found himself to his dismay in a reserved occupation that kept him living at home in Sevenoaks for the full length of World War Two, frustrated because he wanted to be in the navy defending our shipping lanes or helping to convey essential cargoes like his West Mersea sailing friend John Connaught, who was the first great love of my life. My grandfather, with his bright blue eyes and dark hair, was an affectionate, kindly man with a jolly whistle or song when shaving, and Uncle John was fun and a bit of a tease, so that between them and the occasional glimpses of the flame haired and much adored John Connaught in his naval uniform, my early impressions of men were favourable – easy and relaxed. And I do not remember feeling betrayed when, later on, John Connaught did not fulfil my small child's dream of marital bliss with its heartfelt plea of 'Wait for me to grow up, John'.

Since they lived nearby I must have seen my grandparents, whom I called Pop and Nanny, almost daily when I was small, then for a time my mother and I were actually living with them at their home 'Oswald'. And if it was there that my love of dogs was established, so also was my fear of spiders, for I can remember sitting on the Persian style carpet in my grandmother's breakfast room, at a stage when I could not so much as crawl (at least that is my memory of it) and Nanny suddenly shrieking, 'Oh Jenny look, a great big spider!' And there was this hairy monster not far short of the size of Shelob* cantering towards me at speed across the floor. Terrified, not by the spider itself in all probability, but by the adult reaction to it, I was snatched to the safety of Nanny's arms in floods of frightened tears and have been trying ever since to conquer my fear of big spiders, which as we all know is ridiculous, for even the largest of their number must be so much more scared of us with our gargantuan proportions. However, pitting grown-up common sense against an early implanted fear is a tussle hard to win, and I have every sympathy for people who have been unfortunate enough to learn from bad early experience to fear dogs, or other animals, before they were able to establish the habit of loving them.

Rather more dangerous than spiders were the flying bombs, buzz bombs or doodlebugs as they were unaffectionately called, which the Germans were sending us towards the end of the war. These V-1 flying bombs were an early form of remote control rocket whose forté was to keep coming over until, without warning, their mechanism cut out and they fell from the sky, exploding on some unfortunate target – except that they were far from accurate. They could also be brought down and, whenever possible, our fighter planes would take them out in an area of sky where they could do least harm. But this was war and there was no guarantee that they could be put out of action safely. They could fall to the ground inflicting considerably more damage than the proverbial arrow and, as a very little girl, I was to experience something less enchanting than fairies flying through the air at the bottom of our garden.

I was at the toddling stage, so probably around 18 months old. I can remember running across the room laughing, with one sock on, the other in my hand. My mother was laughing too as she chased me. I remember reaching up to touch the round and shiny brass door handle. I remember the feel of my mother coming up close behind me and the knowledge that she was bending down to pick me up. That is all I remember, but the next second the large window at the far side of the room blew in, throwing us both to the floor with much of the ceiling on top of us. A doodlebug had been brought down and chosen to land, mercifully, just beyond the big trees bordering the garden. These trees must have absorbed some of the impact, but my mother's hair was prickled with fragments of glass, as was the protective back of her quilted dressing gown. Her body, in turn, protected me, so that we both escaped with minimal physical injury. Had the window blown in a moment or two later, when my mother had turned back into the room, facing the blast with me in her arms, it would have been a much sadder story.

The rescue services were soon on the scene, coping with us in our shocked state and enquiring whether there was anyone else in the flat who should be helped to safety. It was only then that my mother remembered our dog, Paulette, who had been in her basket in the kitchen at the moment of the doodlebug's impact. Some kindly person in a tin hat went off to search, returning both bemused and amused with the dog, whom he had found sleeping unconcerned in her bed under a pile of ceiling rubble.

Ah, Paulette, the little dog I was to know till I was well into my teens. Hers was no ordinary story; born into a world where the norm was pounding artillery, the rattle of machine-gun fire and the threat of strafing aircraft, no wonder that, for her, the mere patter of a collapsing ceiling did not disturb a good sleep. The miracle of Dunkirk took place over a few days from 26th May to 4th June 1940, when over 338,000 defeated French, British and Canadian soldiers were lifted from the bombarded beaches; large ships were nobly aided by about 700 smaller vessels, transforming the dismal defeat of Allied Forces into some kind of victory by the courage of so many people, many of whom were non-combatants. Some of the craft that joined the rescue fleet were very small indeed, one of them a mere 15-footer; pleasure boats, fishing boats and RNLI lifeboats made the hazardous journey across the channel – some more than once – rescuing thousands of men, so that this desperate army could re-form and continue the fight until, at last, many of these same men returned on D-Day for the final Allied push to liberate France.

One of the soldiers rescued from the Dunkirk beaches had a small dog tucked under his greatcoat. Whether she had been with him just that day or for a while we don't know, but that soldier was determined not to leave her behind to be blown to bits. So Paulette went aboard the rescue vessel with her Tommy friend, thus travelling across to the relative safety of Britain.

Unsurprisingly, no one was looking too hard at the quarantine laws at this time, so Paulette, as a puppy or very young dog, moved seamlessly on to Sevenoaks, Kent, where (because he had to return to active service) the soldier gave her into the care of some married friends of his. Here the plot goes more than a little hazy, but it seems that the husband (in a reserved occupation) was jealous of his wife's relationship with the soldier and, because the little dog was associated with his erstwhile friend, he took out his feelings on the innocent party of Paulette. I think it was my Uncle John, working in his own reserved occupation as a mechanic in a garage, who heard about the situation and told my mother. Very soon afterwards Paulette moved yet again, this time to a much more welcoming and kindly home – with us.

She was pretty and dainty as a fawn. Her exact parentage was uncertain but there was whippet and probably fox terrier in there, with perhaps a dash of papillon. She was also the gentlest of creatures and my best friend. I was an only child until I was seven, so Paulette was a substitute brother or sister, a playmate and confidante who was never bored by my imaginings which led to long involved games. Sometimes the fire screen laid flat on the floor became a raft on which she and I would escape shipwreck, sailing over the silvery sea of the carpet before landing on the sofa which was, of course, a romantic desert island. Another time she and I were captive in the curved turret of an armchair waiting for our prince to come.

But Paulette had a very different side to her nature. She was a true hunting dog, as my father soon discovered when he began taking her out rough shooting. He was astounded to find that she was so fleet of foot, and so intelligent that, not content with putting up a rabbit and chasing it into a tangle of brambles, she was fast enough to be round the other side to catch and kill it if it were foolish enough to emerge. We all admired her skills and, though I never liked the idea of killing anything, even when very young I could somehow differentiate between the kind of kill that an animal will make in response to instinct, and that of a human being out with a gun.

I was always upset by the latter, never mind if that person was my own father or my much adored grandfather or uncle. Both Pop and Uncle John would go wildfowling and it always made me sad to see the results; such beautiful feathered beings, hanging limp and lifeless when they could be flying the skies. It puzzled me that people whom I loved very much could want to spend time reducing wildlife, in which they were so interested, to this grim state.

However, hanging pigs' corpses in butchers' shops always upset me too, so that I would dread going into these shops with my mother. Fishmongers were no better – all those poor dead eyes looking up at me from the white icy slabs, silver scales dulled, on bodies that should have been ribbonning gracefully through water, now lying there pathetically rigid.

After the Day of the Doodlebug my mother and I stayed for a short while with my grandparents. I still have a small scar on the inside of my left leg by my knee, and have a vague memory of a piece of glass being gently extracted while I sat on my mother's lap after being rescued. My mother had fragments of glass in her hair, but her dressing gown had protected her back, so we were hardly physically hurt at all, but of course shock is in itself dangerous. My grandmother (Nanny) in a way experienced the worst of it, for she would have heard the explosion and known that it came from our direction. She then had the agony of not knowing what had happened but, fearing the worst, had to negotiate the ups and downs of The Switchback before arriving to find us emerging shaken, exceedingly dusty but fundamentally unhurt. Many strong, sweet cups of tea must have defied rationing to restore nerves that day and, not surprisingly, in the ensuing weeks I would get very distressed every time I heard a plane going over or any other sound that reminded me of when my world collapsed around me. To help me cope after such a trauma it was decided that my mother would take me down to Mersea Island in Essex, far away from the noise of the war.

She was able to rent a pretty little cottage called Othona in the place that my mother loved best all her life. My grandparents and other members of the family had all had holiday homes there since my mother had been a child. It had not been a true island for many a long year as a road had been built across the short distance from the mainland to the marshes of Mersea, but when there are spring tides the sea still rises over the road sufficiently to prevent traffic crossing for an hour or two. In line with its half island status it had then a gentle wildness about it; wide skies and marshes were decorated with patterns of tiny creeks and, in summer, these were enhanced by the misted blue of sea lavender and the small green tangy spears of samphire – edible if you like very salty crisp plants. Inland, there were meadows of long grass where buttercups, campion, sorrel and delicate blue scabious grew, as if Monet had dropped by to flourish his brush across the landscape with background music provided by the song of larks ascending.

The seawall, a much needed defence against the tides, provided good walks and a superb vantage point from which to watch the sailing boats on the Blackwater Estuary, and high above it geese flew in fluid formation dark against the sky. The tides on this part of the coast sweep out almost to the horizon, then lap in across thick black oozy mud – Mersea mud. Many is the mariner alighting from a dinghy who has sunk to his or her hocks, emerging with weird sucking noises apparently wearing thick black rugger socks. However, along some stretches of the shoreline there are some sandy beaches. During the war these were protected against the danger of possible invasion by coils of barbed wire but it was still possible to paddle on the edge of the beach at high tide and for a little girl to be taken onto the beach to play.

On one occasion this beach trip with me was undertaken by Thelma and her friend, both of whom were Jewish refugees my mother had befriended. These two young women understandably had a great deal to talk about and, of course, were doing so in their native German. By now I was around three-years-old and quite able to decide when I was bored by an incomprehensible conversation that excluded me. But, being a very polite little girl, brought up not to interrupt grown-ups when they were talking, I simply decided to go home, which did not seem unreasonable, except, of course, I did not actually know the way. I was found an hour or so later (while much panic was ensuing on the beach) by a kindly lady who lived a mile or so away in an area known as Hilly Brooms. Like much of Mersea this has since been over-developed for housing, but at that time consisted of a rough track winding through country meadows with a house dotted here and there. It was a hot afternoon so I had sensibly taken off my bathing costume and was discovered trailing it in the dirt quietly crying to myself, for my bold decision to go home was by then marred by the realisation that I was lost.

Do I truly remember my small self in that situation or do I only think I do because I have often heard the tale retold? With these early memories it is hard to know, but I am sure I can remember sitting in a friendly kitchen, which had a huge painted dresser

In wartime, on the beach at Mersea with my mother.

with cups hanging on hooks, and a smiling woman who gave me a drink of orange and a biscuit while she gently tried to discover who I was and where I lived. Of precisely what happened next and how I was returned safely home I have no recollection, but the relief to my poor mother and her friends must have equalled that of surviving an exploding doodlebug.

The experience did not put me off the German language. In fact it may explain why I have been trying ever since – on and off and rather unsuccessfully – to learn it. Certainly in later life I have come to find it fine and attractive, especially when sung, as in Schubert *Lieder*. Neither did my escapade curb my wanderlust for, soon afterwards, I was invited to the birthday party of a little boy who lived in the next road, about half-a-mile away. Having deposited me there safely my mother was somewhat amazed to find me half-an-hour later trundling up the path to home, proudly ensconced on my host's brand new tricycle. Having carefully explained to me that this was not the usual way to repay hospitality, I was escorted back to the party, where I was later to vanish a second time, to be found eventually by the worried mother of the small boy, happily chatting with the conjurer behind the scenes as he prepared his show.

From the vantage point of the 21st century one has to ask why my mother did not stay at the party with me. She was a conscientious, caring mother after all, but perhaps children were expected to be a little more independent earlier on than they are now? So much has changed in my lifetime, and not all for the worse, despite our tendency to grumble and grump about life today.

I was, in effect, an only child for my formative years, my sister being more than seven years younger than me. This probably made me more reliant both on adult company and on my own imagination and resources. It certainly led me to a close relationship with Paulette and, as I grew older, we would go for long walks together, not considered in those days to be a dangerous pastime for a child. I was proud of her French ancestry and would solemnly tell people, 'Our dog came from France you know and she barks in French'. My early bonding with a dog must explain why I have always loved them and felt easy in their company, and home would not be home without one.

You might also have thought, though, that I would have had several favourite dolls who were my imaginary companions, but I never liked them much, and still don't. I find classic dolls, even now, faintly sinister – hard and dead yet with the threat of coming suddenly to life with a dangerous flashing of their glassy eyes. There were just two dolls I ever took to, and they were certainly not of the classic variety. The first was a soft, raggitty 'Red Indian' which a friend of my mother's gave me when I was very small, saying, 'I thought Jenny might like this. I won it in a raffle'. I did like this fellow and took him everywhere with me for a long time, displaying an early feel for imaginative language for, when asked his name, I replied without hesitation, 'Wunnit'.

The only other doll I ever liked came a year or two later. She was a small, rather pathetic, bald number made of a cracked rubbery substance, which adults found hideous as it looked as if she was suffering from some form of dry skin dermatitis, but

12

she was soft and squidgy, and it was this unsuitable 'baby' that I insisted should grace the luxurious interior of my longed for doll's pram, a post-war Christmas present from my grandparents with a lining of palest blue, which I swear smelt of expensive leather. Apart from the unbeautiful but adored Amelia, the only other occupants I ever took for a ride were my teddy bear and three brilliantly coloured feather dusters – one yellow, one pink, one green – which I considered exquisite for their bright, friendly softness.

The end of the war did not bring an end to austerity and it must have also brought new problems to many families as they had to get to know each other again. After all, some wives and husbands had been separated for many years during which time the women had grown much more independent, while the men might have suffered who knows what, either in battle or as prisoners of war. Some children, conceived before their fathers went away, had never known Dad about the place and resented this stranger suddenly coming into the home and taking up slices of Mum's attention. It cannot have been easy.

In our case I had seen my father on sporadic leaves throughout the war as he was not serving abroad. On one infamous occasion my mother awoke on a summer's night to hear someone moving about downstairs. Understandably she was very frightened, after all it could have been an invading German! She crept to my room which was at the front of the cottage, thus ensuring that I was as safe as she could make me, then through the open window she screamed down the long garden path to some people passing by, 'Help! Help! There's a man in the house!' The passers-by responded swiftly, rushing through the gate towards the door. But meanwhile a sheepish cry of, 'It's all right, it's only me darling,' had wafted up the stairs to my mother who, in a rare moment of uncool, screamed out again, but this time with more venom, 'You bloody fool, you frightened the life out of me!' The passers-by made a tactical withdrawal, leaving the young couple to reconciliation. Trying not to disturb his wife, my father had crept indoors like the proverbial thief. Paulette was a good house dog but of course had not barked at a family member, greeting him quietly – flaunting neither her native French nor her newly acquired English voice.

Paulette with me in about 1948.

13

Chapter Two

Bananas, Mars and Blackheath

I do not remember feeling deprived as a small child. On the whole children don't if that is the way of things at the time and everyone is in a similar boat. I am sure I never went hungry but there was strict rationing of many foods including, of course, sweets and certain fruit. Apparently when my father came home on leave I always greeted him with the question, 'Dadda bring orange'? I have retained my love of a juicy orange and, much later in childhood when sugar was back, enjoyed nothing more than sinking a sugar cube deep into the flesh through a small hole then sucking that space with disgusting slurpy noises. When I read Mrs Gaskell's *Cranford* in my teens at school one of the few passages I found interesting was the eating of oranges, for each sister had to retire to her room to enjoy the sucking of the fruit in private. Not even your own sister should witness such an uncouth occupation. I am afraid that in our house there could be a veritable chamber orchestra of slurp and suck.

Though I was excited by the prospect of wartime oranges the promise of a 'banana one day' was dangled before me as being the ultimate treat. They had become unobtainable but were billed as the most delicious experience to come, like so many things 'when the war is over.' I think this was the first time I consciously felt let down by grown-ups, for one of my early disappointments in life was my first taste of this much vaunted fruit. I watched the long yellow fingers of skin peeled slowly back for my delectation, then the banana was handed to me with much adult anticipation of my reaction. This was not as expected, for my face must have reflected the experience of biting into a squidgy uninteresting texture with a marked lack of flavour. Compared to an orange this was indeed a poor cousin and I was not impressed. I am still not over keen on bananas, probably never having forgiven them for disappointing that small child but then I fear I don't have highly developed taste buds and will never make a reliable gourmet. More talented friends can find all kinds of refined, subtle flavours in their eating and drinking which totally pass me by. Truffles, for example, do they taste of *anything*? There are, of course, compensations for such insensitivity; a friend who has super-efficient taste buds cannot enjoy goat's cheese, apparently being able to taste the pungent smell of goat in it, which she finds nauseating, while someone else rejects courgettes as being 'too bitter'. Both these items are among my favourites, so I sometimes consider my more sensitive friends to be the ones deprived.

Bananas may have let me down, but the discovery of the *Mars Bar* in post-war Britain was indeed a trip to another planet, as was our move to suburban London from the rural and seaside setting of West Mersea. Othona, our home there, was a child's classic drawing of a little house – a long garden path up to a front door exactly in the middle of the building, four windows, one either side of the door and two more above those. The chimney was set bang in the centre above the doorway and I think it must have been Othona that I drew for my first teacher (Miss Brown) with smoke puffing happily in two directions at once – to left and right. Miss Brown was much amused but I was puzzled by her questioning the phenomenon, not seeing anything at all peculiar in it myself. One wonders what a psychologist and interpreter of *Rorschach Blots* might have made of my picture . . .

This child shows the ability to see more than one possibility in any given situation but may, therefore, experience difficulty with decision making. She shows the ability to absorb the full gestalt but is ambivalent about the idea of 'home'.

I had never thought the latter to be true. Whenever I have thought or written the word 'home' I have always had the warm feeling that Dorothy held to her heart all through her adventures in the Land of Oz. However, this may have been because my mother worked so hard to make it so. She was warm, affectionate and always there for me. I was no latchkey child. My father on the other hand was a difficult man, troubled with depression, brought up not to show his softer feelings and not knowing how to express his affections. He was often bad-tempered and somewhat aggressive in his behaviour, swearing and banging things about and slamming doors, though not, I hasten to add, physically violent to his wife, my sister or me. He was the product of an upbringing by a Victorian style father who decreed that his son should be a lawyer when John Banning wanted to be an engineer. He seems to have adored his father nonetheless and followed his lead when a little sister was born. My grandfather sulked for days because Stella was not a boy, never seemed to love her, and encouraged my father to bully her, though he did pay for her to go to Oxford University – so long as she studied classics and not veterinary science as she wanted to do.

It sounds a strange upbringing but perhaps was not so unusual for its time. My father's mother, my grandmother – or Banny as we called her – was a gentle ineffectual sort of person who needed a rest after lunch everyday. She would become ill if the news on the wireless was bad and would have to retire to bed. She did not have to cook because there was the splendid Mrs Girlock and the children were mainly cared for by kindly Nanny Blythe for whom both my father and aunt retained huge affection till the end of her long life. It was Nanny Blythe whom they loved, always being rather negative

My father's mother, Mabel (Banny) with her children, my father and Stella.

15

about Banny whom they saw as a hopeless mother. For whatever reasons my father tended to have a pejorative view of women and, in his turn, sulked when I was born. Allegedly, I was a particularly pretty baby with no new-born redness or wrinkles, but in answer to the question from my maternal grandmother, 'Well John, what is the baby like?' the reply came to his indignant mother-in-law, 'A rat!'

My father found this view hard to uphold as I began to develop. Apparently he soon forgave me for being a girl, so much so that when my sister arrived in 1949, far from having a negative reaction to her, he said that if she turned out to be like Jenny he would be more than satisfied. Sheila, of course, has always been her own person and arrived with a relatively dark skin and a shock of black hair. The Korean War was raging at the time and my father, who was good at coining phrases (often with a punning content) was soon referring to her as 'Daddy's Korea girl'.

Thinking again about that 'child's eye' drawing of a house with the chimneys smoking simultaneously in two directions, perhaps the subconscious signals were not so far out after all; in adult life, if I need to make a rushed decision between two enticing purchases, it is not unknown for me to take both. Moreover, life post-war may well have made me more ambivalent to the idea of home, for it was not all roses round the door. By the end of the conflict I had experienced several changes which I think I took in my stride only because of the loving and stable presence of my mother. The post-war years meant huge adjustments for many families and we were no exception. Men being demobbed now had to look for work and my father was to become a solicitor working for a firm in Leicester Square, defending motorists for the AA. There was a shortage of houses to buy so my parents were lucky to find one conveniently located in Beckenham, Kent. 21 Clockhouse Road was a late Victorian suburban semi-detached, only a few minutes walk from the station.

This new setting must have been a severe change, not only for my parents and me but also for Paulette, who had grown used to the rabbit strewn countryside, and she must have found the suburban pavements of Beckenham a poor swap. Kelsey Park, with its lake, pretty gardens and waterfall, was not too far away but to go there meant a road walk of about 20 minutes. We did, however, have a pretty garden with a pond in it, which was a fascination for me, if not the dog. It was not deep enough to be considered dangerous and was probably only something like six feet by four in size, but it was here I learnt to observe frogs, tadpoles – and then more frogs. I was also thrilled to meet another amphibian with the graceful beauty of a little 'water lizard' – the newt. Winters were exceptionally hard in those years after the war and 1947 was one of the worst of the century. The pond, of course, froze over but at some stage I was able to break off some ice and, to my mother's horror, told her I had eaten it. I was nonplussed by her concern since I had conscientiously run it under the cold tap before consuming it. My innocent, 'It's all right Mummy I washed it first,' may not have convinced my mother but my child's faith must have paid off as I had no ill effects.

To be honest I do not remember the extreme cold, the shortages of fuel and the general dispirited feeling in the nation at the austerity of the post-war 1940s. I do remember, however, wearing a liberty bodice as well as my vest. The latter garment was worn over the vest so that it added another warm layer underneath a blouse or dress, with a cardigan or jumper on top to complete the outfit. Given that long socks and large bloomers were the order of the day – for school these had to be navy blue of course – I was well wrapped up against the cold. Generally, no one had central heating so ice patterns on the bedroom windows were the norm, but I only remember how intricately pretty they were not how cold that bedroom must have been. Ironically, I do remember being cold in later years, for one of my father's many eccentricities was his dislike of a roaring fire. Coming home from work he would barge into the sitting-room where my mother, sister and I would be chatting happily by a cheerful blaze, glare at the flames and exclaim, 'Phew it's hot in here!' He would then proceed to remedy all this unsatisfactory heat production by smothering the flame with coal dust or, better still, damp leaves, so that a miserable single curl of smoke could just about escape from burial to show that the fire was fighting for its life.

3 Orchard Drive, Blackheath, was where my father was mainly brought up and where he met my mother, who was the girl next-door. It is a large detached Edwardian house on a shallow crescent facing the heath. By the time I visited it as a little girl the kitchen was to the right of the front door, but the house had been constructed with the kitchen and scullery 'below stairs' and attic accommodation for servants. The rooms were large and high ceilinged and the fires (according to my mother) were small and inadequate so that my father had been brought up to withstand the cold. Tonbridge School, where he spent his latter schooldays, no doubt completed the conditioning. I don't remember the cold when I stayed with my grandparents but the memorable 15 watt light bulb on the main landing created a miserable gloomy effect, for my grandparents were curiously mean with their money, on one occasion telling my frustrated mother when she was desperate for a lick of paint and new wallpaper in her own home, 'Oh but Marjorie, decorations are a luxury'. Servants, on the other hand, were apparently not.

With their careful consumption of electricity my grandparents might now be seen as early Greens, though I hardly think that was part of their rationale. On the other side of those 'green' scales, my grandfather, a good golfer, would practise putting on his immaculate lawn, making war on the innocent and, as we now know, beneficial earthworms.

Strangely, for one who allegedly so disapproved of girls, he was always very kind to me and I was fond of him. He would encourage me to try my hand at putting and tell me the names of the flowers which came into glorious bloom in borders either side of his long lawn in late summer. Here I would play with the little wire-haired fox terrier called Hamish, the last in their long line of dogs. Papa Banny would also spend many hours in his study, now in the 'below stairs' location. When I was about ten I was told that my grandfather wanted to see me in this sanctuary. This was unusual and I wondered if I had done something wrong.

Henry Druce Banning, my grandfather

I was a nauseatingly well-behaved little girl so went down the short stairway with trepidation. As I entered the room Papa Banny rose to greet me and came to stand by the oval table in the middle of the room, on which was placed a large, highly polished wooden box. 'Your grandmother and I wondered if you would like to have this,' he said, opening it to reveal an exquisite, beautifully equipped Victorian lady's travelling box with silver scent bottles, a needle case, a place for letters in a green silk pocket set in the lid, and the added charm of a secret jewel drawer in the base. My ten-year-old eyes came out on stalks and I was struck speechless with thrilled disbelief at being given something so wonderful. I suppose we all have five star moments in our lives which always stay with us and this was certainly one of mine.

I loved the big house with its many nooks and crannies, tucked away stairways and the lavatories (always the proper word in that household) with heavy, wide mahogany seats. There was more antique furniture in that house than in my other grandparents' and I enjoyed its smooth patina and graceful shapes. The only experience I did not enjoy was sitting down for a meal on the dining chairs at the large, elegant, round table, for the seats stuffed with horsehair scratched and tickled my bare legs so that I found it hard to sit still. However, my grandparents seemed to make all kinds of allowances for me that they would never have made for their own children and I was very happy staying with them. My grandmother devoted her days to me. We would walk to Blackheath village together or across the heath to Greenwich Park, where she showed me the mass of crocuses in spring and the Queen's House* down near the river. Banny would often play long imaginary games with me, in which I was usually a princess.

Banny also taught me to play matador which is so much more interesting than dominoes, on a pretty, little, folding black-lacquered table, which now resides in our own drawing-room. The domino pieces themselves lived in a special wooden box and were made of ivory and ebony, so they were a heavy, smooth delight to hold, and so old that some were worn away with curves made by many previous players' fingers. I have these dominoes too, and have begun playing matador with my own granddaughters who, like me, love the feel of the pieces, their gliding on the surface of the table and the music of their clicking when they touch:

Starting with seven dominoes each, the aim of the game is to go out leaving your opponent with the highest possible number of points against him or her. A player who cannot go, must pick up from the pool. Unlike dominoes, however, you do not match but make connections that add up to seven. The matadors are the three dominoes that total seven within themselves – one-six, two-five and three-four. There is a fourth one, which is double blank. The matadors may be played at either end and either way round. They are essential to open the game up again where a blank has closed it off, as below, where five-blank has been played but is then overcome by a matador.

Of course I feel much less comfortable about ivory today, even though it comes from long-ago elephants for whom the conservation warning bell had not yet rung. Sadly, alongside the lamentable way we humans often treat each other, our abusive treatment of the natural world, and our relations with the animal kingdom, is hardly a record to be proud of either – from the huge bloodbaths of the Roman arenas to the horrific cat persecution of medieval times, the bull baiting, the near extinction of the North American bison and the blue whale, then the actual extinction of numerous species, the rape of fish stocks, the killings for fashion fur and the harrowing waste of so many horses in World War One. The list is both dismal and endless. However, although far too belatedly, attitudes have begun to change and continue to do so. Alongside modern day wanton cruelty, greed, thoughtlessness and killing with kindness, there are people putting themselves in the front line to conserve, save, heal and rescue. Fortunately this list is also a long one and, on the domestic scene, much has improved since my childhood; in the bigger scheme of things only a flea bite perhaps, but the control of those self-same itch-making creatures is now effective and considered essential, whereas I can remember it being cheerfully accepted that cats and dogs had fleas. So what? There might have been a sprinkling of rather doubtful white powder from time to time but there would also be many moments of rummaging through the animals' coats trying to catch the little beggars yourself. I would frequently get bitten but my parents did not seem to worry about it. I was also a primary target for mosquitoes when we were at Mersea and my parents seemed to put fleas in the same category – an inevitable nuisance. Veterinary science in Britain today is not only so much more skilled, with drugs, surgery and specialised diets, but also takes a gentler, more kindly line. It is now a matter of course that castration for male kittens, for example, is treated as a minor operation. They are properly anaesthetized rather than being *done* on the kitchen table, while the docking of puppies' tails has become more or less illegal in Britain.

It is also worth remembering that, for all those bad stories through the centuries, there are also a few good ones of heartwarming, affectionate bonds between humans and animals. The respected writer Mary Renault, in *The Nature of Alexander,* tells of the great conqueror's favourite dog, Peritas, that he hand-reared from a puppy and after whom he named a city. But it was Alexander's devotion to his horse, Bucephalas, which really catches the imagination. Only the king rode him and they must have made a daunting team in battle. When, in well earned retirement, his old friend was stolen, Alexander, endearingly distraught and also something of a power in the region, threatened to unleash all kinds of hell unless Bucephalas was safely returned:

The King's Horse

The word went hushed around the camp, an anxious whispering,
Bucephalas was stolen, gone, and who should tell the King?
He was Great King and conqueror, the world shook with his deeds,
But he gave trust for loyalty; he loved his ageing steed.

Bucephalas, his boyhood friend, whom only he could ride,
The warhorse who had saved his life, now sold for meat and hide?
Young squires attended on the King, his horses were their care,
The thieves had caught them unprepared, their shame a scar to bear.

The King's grey eyes hurled javelins when he had heard their tale;
The man who'd won the Persian Crown would make Hyrcania quail,
'I'll lay this land to blackened waste, I'll devastate and burn!
Send out the ultimatum for my old friend's safe return!'

The heralds' horses' hooves raised dust, their message billowed plain,
The chieftain of the Mardians weighed swiftly loss with gain.
He made his luckless thieves draw lots and each man held his breath,
Two men must act as sacrifice and dice a ride with death.

The King was restless all that day, he went to bed but late,
His mind was charged with memories and not affairs of state.
Then word went murmured round the camp, a cheer was gathering;
Bucephalas, with equine pride, returning to his King.

Then Alexander's warm relief swept him to horse for joy,
There rode once more upon that back a Macedonian boy.
He rode among his cheering men, the thieves stood under guard
Until at length the King drew rein; his gaze ran through them hard.

Then Alexander laughed and said, 'No harm deserves no sword,'
And to their dazed astonishment he tossed them a reward.
He was Great King and conqueror, the world shook with his deeds,
But he gave trust for loyalty; he loved his ageing steed.

Chapter Three

Who's Afraid?

Mary Renault was thorough and based her research on ancient sources. Even if the story is part legend it is powerful, and those of us brought up on the old fairy tales know how they can become embedded in the psyche. They certainly made a deep impression on me; I still especially enjoy books, films and plays that have a strong story line and, as a child, one particular fairy tale gave rise to a recurring nightmare . . .

At the far end of our garden in Clockhouse Road was a large workshop. It ran the full width of the garden. This was a sanctuary for my father – a glorified version of Man's Essential Shed – where he could potter about spending his time on a big workbench, using a treasure trove of hoarded tools, developing his talent for making useful, but curious looking, implements from unlikely source material such as a shot-down Messerschmitt*, which provided a venerable fish slice. Then there were two brass ashtrays fashioned from a bicycle bell, a petrol lighter from a five-inch, spent brass shell, and a long-handled dustpan for gardening converted from half a battered petrol can attached to an old broom handle. Years later, when my sister was married and living in Woodham Mortimer in Essex, there was a designer 'spider swiper' to help her cope with the large arachnids which favoured her country cottage.

Although he had to wear a suit for the office and for appearing in court to defend AA motorists, this was not how my father felt comfortable. He much preferred his oldest, scruffiest garments, which he called his 'ratting clothes', and in which he would go joyfully poking about in any old rubbish he could find, in the hope of discovering gems of junk which might yield the potential for developing one of his inventions. Other people's fly-tipping was my father's playground.

I liked the workshop, not for any fascination with the junk, or indeed the inventions which came out of it, but because it had a huge chestnut tree growing through the middle which, for me became *The Magic Faraway Tree* of the Enid Blyton stories. I could imagine that, way up in the branches above the roof, lived the little fairy folk, Saucepan, Moonface and Silky, whilst in the topmost branches would arrive the magic lands which the children in the stories so loved to visit. But beyond the workshop and the cosiness of these phantasies lay something much more threatening, for our garden backed on to a railway goods yard. At night the steam trains would shunt up and down with a clank and a clang before beginning a slow, steady 'ch, ch, ch' rhythm, as they gradually built up speed until they sped into the distance.

My bedroom was at the back of the house so I could hear all these sounds very clearly and they would fill my sleeping head, bringing with them my recurring dream, always the same and borne on the influence of *Little Red Riding Hood* and *The Three Little Pigs*. Enter the Big Bad Wolf, for the steady 'ch, ch, ch' of the train became the rhythmic 'pad, pad, pad' of a wolf chasing me, starting slowly so that I could run ahead of him, but always growing faster and closer so that I ran on with increasing terror, knowing that soon he would catch and devour me. But this *was* a dream and, just at the last tormented moment, when the slavering jaws of red-eyed ferocity were about to envelop me, I escaped by flying and, looking back over my airborne shoulder, would see the wolf still snarling but safely grounded. It was at this moment that I would wake up, my heart thumping, still terrified, and would call to my mother to comfort me.

There were other sources to perpetuate the myth of the wolf as a savage little girl-eater. At school there was a game (not unlike *Grandmother's Footsteps*) but called *'What's the Time Mr Wolf?'* in which one child would play the wolf, standing ahead of the class while the others crept up towards him, or her, continually asking the time; for the aim was to touch the wolf's back before he or she could turn and catch someone. The response would come 'three o'clock' or 'ten o'clock' or 'six o'clock', as the question was repeated and the children crept closer, until the answer 'dinnertime' provoked squeals of excitement as the wolf turned to chase us. Each child who was 'caught' would then join the wolf pack, helping in each subsequent chase.

There were sinister wolves in John Masefield's *Box of Delights* too and they figured as servants to the White Witch in Narnia, so it was some time before I began to think differently about them and hear more kindly stories. Roman legend gave me Romulus and Remus, the twins who founded Rome but, as babies, were left abandoned to die. Found by wolves they were raised to young boys before being taken up by humans again. Unfortunately, they showed their gratitude to everyone by managing to fall out very badly and had a fight in which Romulus killed his brother. One up to the wolves for better behaviour, especially as Romulus went on to be responsible for the raping of the Sabine women!

Then, of course, there is Rudyard Kipling's *Jungle Book* in which the little Mowgli is cared for by wolves, Mother Wolf and Father Wolf, and the pack leader (the alpha male) is called Akela. Lord Baden Powell was a friend of Kipling and, in founding a section for the younger children of his Scout movement, chose to use some ideas from his *Jungle Book*. The boys were called wolf cubs and formed into packs, the adult leader being known as Akela. Much later on, many countries changed the terminology to cub scouts, but since the term 'cub' is retained, the origin still shows and should be a salute to the truer nature of the wolf, which must be one of the world's least understood and most persecuted animals. Gradually, I came to doubt my own image of the red-eyed child-devouring monster, becoming more and more convinced that this was not the true story and, in recent years, I have become interested in the research being done to try to conserve this marvellous creature, with its family bonding patterns not so far removed from our own. Long extinct everywhere in Britain, there have even been tentative plans to try to reintroduce the wolf to Scotland under strict controls. The wolf, once the largest predator at the top of our medieval food chain, would have kept down the deer numbers naturally, whereas they now have to be culled to prevent starvation over the winter months. Not surprisingly, however, any such idea of reintroduction has run into heavy opposition, both from those who still subscribe to the erroneous fairy story image of the wolf, and, with much better reason, farmers who have sheep or cattle which might fall prey to them.

In 2009 I visited the Combe Martin Wildlife Park in Devon where Shaun Ellis was working with a wolf pack. As someone with a passion for wolves and a commitment to try to make life tenable for them in the wild, Shaun had taken the view that the only way forward was to live among this captive pack as one of them, finding his own role or position within that pack and, among other things, exploring the significance of the howl – not the sinister portent of werewolves to come but a complex system of sounds helping the bonding within a pack and signalling various messages to other wolves, for example, 'Territory taken, pack complete. Keep out!' or 'We are some females in search of an alpha male. Are you a lone wolf ? Could you fill the bill?'

Shaun's research has shown wolves to be highly intelligent, capable of disabling electric fencing and able to defeat any other form of protection farmers might provide for their livestock, short of locking them up in barns. But if wolves can be convinced that another pack is already in possession of the territory where that livestock is kept, then they will simply move on and revert to hunting wild game in the forest. The trick is to record a howl which gives out the right message and then play it back, very loudly, from the farmstead to the outlying area. This has been tried successfully in Poland, saving cattle and hence the lives of wolves which would otherwise have been shot. In Poland children often have to walk through the forest to school and it is neither bears nor wolves they fear, but wild boar and elk. Bang goes another myth. Slavering wolves licking ravenous chops do not stalk children in order to eat them. Their capacity for scenting is 100,000 times larger than ours so they will certainly be aware of us at a distance, but the scent of any human is likely to make them fade in another direction, avoiding all contact whenever possible. In fact, in his book *The Wolf Talk* Shaun makes the point that the wolf still honours a truce made with the Native American people who were also driven nearly to extinction; it would seem that the wolf is the only large carnivore which, in its natural environment, does *not* attack man.

My friend and illustrator, France Bauduin, has experienced wolves round a cabin in the wilds of her native Canada, and says that she has never felt threatened. She, like Shaun, says that wolves' eyes do not glow red at night, they are green. Moreover, the legends and stories of wolves caring for lost or abandoned babies and children are rooted in fact. I was pleased to have all this confirmed as my adult interest in wolves was reawakened by a brief news item back in the winter of 1977-78. It was reported that a little girl was lost in the snows of a remote wilderness of what was then the USSR. Her despairing parents were convinced she must have perished overnight but, next morning, her father went looking for her again and, to his amazed relief, found that she had not only survived but had an astonishing and heartwarming story to tell . . .

Who's Afraid?

'Mama, the snow cut on the wind, the silence cold ice blown,
I called, 'Papa' I cried, afraid, for I was lost, alone.
I huddled in the blanket white, tears frozen on my cheek,
The chill crept with the dark that grew, as life dimmed in me, weak.

I sensed amid my slumbering, which drew me close to death,
An anxious, panting, whining touch that stirred me with its breath.
And when I peeped, I saw the dog, his tongue a licking flame,
He huffed and puffed his comforting; life kindled in my frame.

I rubbed my fingers in his coat, and it was thick and rough,
I spoke to him and he grinned back, his hot jade eyes enough
To light me through that big bare night, until the dawning sky
Brought Papa's voice and the grey dog ran, fading on a sigh.'

'My sweet, there are no kindly dogs to roam that bitter waste,
But Papa found the careful marks fresh all around you traced:
Swift as wild your comforter, who warmed your fear away,
Out in the far bleak forest land, some wolves run gentle grey.'

Chapter Four

Stitches in Time

I s memory a patchwork quilt? Or perhaps it is the cloth on which the patches are sewn, sometimes spread singly, sometimes in groups that form a larger pattern. Each of us tends to remember things differently, or with a different emphasis on the same events of any given moment, keeping our own, unique experience of something apparently shared. Thus, my sister Sheila and I have memories of childhood seen from the different perspectives of a seven year gap in age. Besides the obvious point that she could not share in my memories until she was at least a toddler, as Sheila herself grew, she can sometimes remember experiences which she says we shared, but of which I have no recollection and the same is true in reverse. Or, on Sheila's quilt, a memory patch may match one on my own, but appear very different in colour. She may also have been told information by a parent or other family member which never came to me, for example she has it firmly in her head that she was about six months old when we left Clockhouse Road. Since it is unlikely to be a first-hand memory, my mother must have told her this, as she certainly did not get it from me, for I was vague about exactly when we moved, until Sheila told me.

On other occasions I have searched for a memory, feeling sure that such a patch on the quilt must exist, but where I think it ought to be is only the outline of an empty space. It is as frustrating as the email with the photo attachment that will not open, or some enchanting little video on U-tube that refuses to play. Then there are those patches badly sewn onto the quilt, cobbled together so that they merge, defying logic, for these pieces of one's life could not possibly have occurred exactly as remembered. And yet, if that is the memory, the only memory, does it have some claim to being true?

A good example of this is our settling in at Clockhouse Road – post-war, thus late 1945 or early 1946. My memory has this coinciding with my starting school just turned five – too old for Miss Barnard and the Kindergarten, therefore going straight to Transition and Miss Brown, a tall, gentle stooped lady with thick glasses and delicately waved grey hair, who rode a bicycle. This is fine until you realise that even by spring 1946 I would only have been four, whereas for the above memory to fit I could not have begun school until the summer of 1947 at the earliest. However, it seems inevitable that life must have taken a good while to settle down to any kind of normality after the end of the war, thus my mother and I may have stayed on in Mersea for a time, whilst my father searched for a job, and the hunt for a permanent new home was instigated. It could also be that, because of all the moving around we had done, and the relative trauma of the previous years, my parents decided not to send me to school until the law actually required it.

Whatever the real timings of the start of my school career, I was very lucky to attend Woodbrook, a small private school run in a large Victorian house by Miss Elgin and Miss Meade. Miss Elgin, who taught the older pupils, was an elegant intellectual, quietly spoken, with her brown hair in a neat bun. Miss Meade, even to my small self, was tiny, resembling nothing so much as a pin, for she had bright, white hair, shiny as a pin's head, atop twinkling blue eyes. Misled by her prematurely white hair I thought she was a little old lady but she was probably not a day over 40. She always wore a straight dress and held herself erect as a guardsman, but far from a sergeant major's bellow she spoke in a tiny, squeaky voice in which she would impart kindly home truths:

Apart from the ever present dictum of the day of 'putting others before ourselves' and forever being told to 'be kind to those less fortunate than ourselves', two little pieces of Miss Meade's wisdom have stayed with me. Teaching us five-year-olds to read, she explained that an 'e' on the end of a word was like a fairy with a magic wand who can touch the letter in the middle of that word and thus make it say its name – thus, 'gap' becomes 'gape' pronounced 'gayp', 'hop' becomes 'hope' pronounced 'hohp'. Of course, the English language is a minefield of exceptions and she did not explain why 'came' is pronounced 'caym' while 'come' is pronounced 'cumm' not ' cohm'. However, it was not a bad rule of thumb. Miss Meade made reading and writing fun, but the influence of her magic wand theory may explain my grumpy abhorrence of the modern habit of writing café without its accent, turning it into *caif*.

Her other little gem, which I think defies exception, was, 'There are three ways to enjoy something – looking forward to it before it happens, the pleasure of the actual moment, then the memory of it afterwards.' Dear Miss Meade, what she did not tell us, at a stage in our lives where we believed that the natural order was for good always to triumph over evil, was that the above scenario can also hold true for negative experiences, but what the heck? We had just won World War Two, defeating the evil of Hitler. It was a time to think positively.

These were days when many people did not, apparently, have Christian names. Our friendly next-door-neighbour was always known as Mrs Trill. I doubt if my parents ever knew her first name, or she, theirs. It was also a time when milk and bread were delivered by horse and cart. When, soon after starting school, I contracted chicken pox, one of the comforting sounds of the day as I lay there feeling sorry for my itchy self was the jingle of harness and the clip clop of large hooves. I would worry about the horses out in all weathers pulling their heavy loads, but missed them desperately when, all too soon, the music of their harness gave way to the anodyne hum of an electric milk float and the tootle of a baker's van.

Heavy Horses

I remember heavy horses

Leather blinkers on mild eyes,

In the dark-light early morning

When my ears were open wide.

And I heard the heavy horses

From the child-depth of my bed,

Bring the safety of their hoof-clop

With the milk and then the bread.

I remember heavy horses

With the nosebag smell of oats,

And yellow teeth on sugar

From my hand held out tiptoes,

And I saw the heavy horses

Draw the seagulls with the plough

To blend the kind of furrow

That could fall from memory now.

But I remember heavy horses

By the water, on the path,

As they pulled the boats with flowers

With their slow chests through the grass.

And the medals on their harness

With the brass of music shone,

I will look back down the pathway . . .

Have the heavy horses gone?

A year or so after the end of the war my mother's parents decided to move from Sevenoaks and come to Chislehurst, partly to be nearer the family building business, but probably also to be nearer to us in Beckenham. Neither Nanny nor my mother was a sufficiently modern woman to be a driver so, although we soon acquired a dashing black Ford Eight car – APM 199 – capable of speeds akin to 35 miles an hour, it was the little, bright red, single decker 227 bus, which ran from the nether reaches of Penge through to the leafiness of Chislehurst Common, that provided easy transport for my mother and me in one direction, and Nanny in the other. This proved to be a vital service, for the latter half of the 1940s saw a huge epidemic of poliomyelitis, or infantile paralysis. It was a very serious illness from which people died or suffered permanent paralysis, some of them staying in an 'iron lung' for months and years to enable them to breathe at all. Horrible! I believe it was in the summer of 1947 that I went down with the high fever and bad headache which could signal the onset of polio, but it developed into nothing worse, except that it was mooted that I may have had an abortive form of the illness, while giving the fuller version to my father. He had to be hospitalised for several weeks and I went to stay with my grandparents during the crisis.

Nanny came to take me there using the 227 bus, and I hurtled down the pavement towards her approaching figure, tripping over my feet in my excitement, sprawling myself in a grazed heap across the flagstones and spilling the contents of a small brown attaché case in a colourful stream of little figures – a Disney style Snow White, the Prince, the Dwarves, a tiny tree, rabbits, Bambi, a small clockwork engine, some pretty beads, a bracelet and probably a good fairy or two. Nanny successfully scooped me and my treasures into her comforting arms and conveyed me and them on the 227 bus back to Chislehurst, where I stayed happily for several weeks. (This episode may help to explain why I think I was turned five before I started school.)

Nanny and Pop's new home was jauntily called The Shanty, tongue in cheek we think, for anything less like shanty town would have been hard to find. It was an attractive, friendly house, with four bedrooms and three bathrooms, and was surrounded by a huge garden. Two brothers had had it built to their particular specification in the late 1920s or early 1930s, on their return from working abroad for many years in Africa or the Far East. I can still see the layout of both the garden and the house clearly in my head. It was a light and airy dwelling, with a split stairway; at the far end of one landing was my grandmother's en suite bedroom (unusual in the 1940s) and, at the other end of the house, was my grandfather's. Of course it never entered my head to wonder why they had separate sleeping arrangements, but therein hung many a tale, for theirs was not an easy marriage and Pop had an eye for pretty women. When the marital storms blew too fiercely he would retreat for days or weeks 'to Chesham' and 'Mrs Williams'. You could be forgiven for thinking that these were euphemistic expressions to cover the latest philandering. Perhaps they sometimes were, but he really did have a wooden bungalow retreat in a wooded area he had bought in Chesham, Buckinghamshire, and there really was a Mrs Williams, who seemed unlikely mistress material. I know, because in later years I met her, with Graham, when we were setting up our own home and went to collect furniture that she had been storing for my grandfather. Kindly as

My grandfather (Pop) and my grandmother (Nanny) with my mother (Marjorie) and Uncle John, in the garden at Cadeby, the family holiday home on Mersea Island, Essex. Circa 1925.

ever, he was giving it to us, including the bed we still sleep on – a bed which had seen, along with the other pieces, more exciting days – for all the furniture came from a flat which my grandfather had set up for a 'best belovéd' who was not my grandmother. To add a further piquancy to the story there is a strong family rumour that this mysterious lover was, in fact, my grandmother's youngest sister. Ouch, shame and scandal, only redeemed by her having had the grace to die young. But what depths of emotions must have wracked such an unhappy triangle. Moreover, my mother once told me that her father had confessed to her that he had felt trapped into marrying my grandmother, Doff as she was known, even going so far as to say that he was not sure that she, my mother, was really his daughter, but that he was very fond of her anyway. Oh well, that was all right then!

The spare room at The Shanty, my room, had a double bed with a feather mattress into which I could sink deliciously and, in the folds of its valley, could dream deep dreams, unthreatened by shunting trains, but sometimes woken at first light by a curious rattling and clunking. With a delighted squeal I would then leap from bed and bounce up onto the ledge which filled the bay of the window. Tweaking the curtain carefully, lest he look up and see me, I would gaze out on the magical spectacle of Smokey Joe, a legendary, if somewhat unwashed, tramp who travelled with his bicycle so overladen with old pots and pans and other paraphernalia that there could never be any hope of him riding it. Indeed, it may have been the prototype pushbike. He would trundle past in the early light of summer mornings, heading for goodness knows where, and the story went that, come the chill of autumn, Smokey Joe would commit some petty larceny, just sufficient to send him to the warmth of prison for the duration of the cold months of the year. It was a good story, which I believed, admiring his ingenuity.

The garden of The Shanty was very large. The grounds were adjacent to Chislehurst Caves, which had sheltered people during the war and were now open to the public, though I don't think there was much of interest to be seen down there. Above ground, however, on our side of the paling fence, was wonderland for a small child, a fascinating mix of levels, styles and landscape. The house sat, like an island with a sea of land around it, perhaps as much as two acres. There was woodland on a high slope, an orchard, pond and croquet lawn. But my favourite haunt was a grassy hillock hidden by wild roses set under a massive wych elm. The grass here was soft and welcoming. It was my secret den, except that I called it the Gypsy Encampment, where adults were only allowed if prepared to join in one of my imaginary games which kept me occupied for many happy hours.

The contrast between my two grandmothers was marked. They were like two different kinds of flowers. Banny (still living at Blackheath) was a rather faded, mauve coloured, old-fashioned rose. Nanny, on the other hand, was a little, frothy Mrs Sinkins pink (*dianthus*) like the sweetly scented, dainty, white flowers edging The Shanty's June borders with their fragrance.

Nanny was full of energy and bustle, a lover of pretty things including clothes, music and jewellery. She was also house-proud and a hard worker, but full of fun with lots of amusing anecdotes to tell about her younger days and family entertainments. She would regale me with stories of her much loved brother Charles, who had a strong dramatic talent, then of everyone singing along with Pop, whom she accompanied on the piano, describing this activity in her own mysterious terms as 'playing the lum'.

Nanny was also a very good cook, making simple food taste delicious. To this day, when in need of a tummy filler at bedtime, I will make myself sleep-inducing bread and milk after her style, and no one could scramble an egg better than Nanny. I still do it her way, using butter, slow and gentle till just setting. She must have had many culinary secrets, but those are two of the ones I remember best, and her Christmas Day spread was second to none as she calmly produced, not only the massive lunch, but also Christmas tea then, perhaps best of all, that cold turkey supper in the evening. Moreover, my sister and I both remember a curious, but very tasty, baked suet pudding that Nanny always served with roast lamb. If Yorkshire pudding used to be given so that people required less beef, perhaps this was an equivalent once common with lamb, but neither Sheila nor I have ever come across it elsewhere.

Although Pop and Nanny never had servants in the same way as my other grandparents, who were their next-door neighbours at Blackheath, Nanny had help from the splendid Mrs Tansy but, after the family left to go to Sevenoaks, she more or less coped alone, for the war effort must have meant few people were available for domestic work any more. Nanny took housework very seriously and had a definite system. Monday was washday, for which she refused the newfangled gadget of a washing machine, resolutely hand-washing then squeezing the water from the clothes by putting them through the menacing rollers of her trusty old mangle – turning the handle with the energy of a bargee opening a lock. Tuesday was ironing day and Wednesday was cleaning the brass and silver, of which there was a lot. I would enjoy helping with all these tasks, particularly the latter one, sitting in The Shanty's cosy breakfast room at the oval gate-leg table, feet dangling over the same Persian carpet that had hosted the galloping spider. Rag in hand, I delighted in the shine returning to a jug or kettle that had been smeared grey with *Duraglit*, while we listened to *Housewives' Choice* or maybe *Music While You Work* on the BBC's Light Programme.

Nanny never allowed work to go on for too long. She told me she had once made herself a promise that she would always be washed and changed from her older working clothes 'just for mornings', into her smarter clothes by eleven o'clock, and she always was. In a pretty dress, or a crisp, white, frilly blouse, complemented with make-up and earrings, she was ready to go shopping, to meet a friend for coffee, or face whatever crisis the day might hold.

I ought to remember that Ruff was alongside us during this time at The Shanty but I don't, which leads me to think that he was no longer there, for something unbearably sad happened when my parents were looking after him at Clockhouse Road, while Nanny and Pop were away on holiday. My father had taken Ruff and Paulette for a walk one evening, without leads, as people often did then. Father was a great one for stopping to chat to people and became absorbed in a conversation which took his eye off the dogs. When he eventually looked for them Ruff had disappeared and, despite all the efforts made to find him, was never seen again. My mother found it hard to forgive my father for his stupidity but I think my parents must have tried to protect me from the immediate upset by reassuring me that one day Ruff would be found. However, I guess that I picked up on my mother's underlying desperate distress, which made a lasting impression on me, for I experience irrational panic if any of my animals are missing, even for an hour. Was Ruff stolen? Was he trying to get back home? We shall never know. My grandparents were so upset that they did not have another dog for a long time and, when they did, it was not another springer for there could never be another Ruff. The new puppy was a golden cocker called Bill, who was probably inbred, as he was wild and silly and not a huge success. When he passed on, relatively young, my grandparents gave up on pedigrees and offered a home to a chirpy, rather scruffy, black, white and tan little mongrel called Peter – an affectionate, easy-going ordinary sort of dog of whom we all grew fond, but who held no threat to the memory of Ruff.

I have a second cousin Pam, who is a few years older than me. She remembers Ruff clearly and says that he was the most intelligent dog she has ever known. When she visited Uncle George and Auntie Doff (as she called my grandparents) Ruff would play a form of hide-and-seek with her. She would give him an item to sniff, then go and hide it well out of his vision. Ruff would rush off to find whatever it was and return full of good humour at his own success. He was a very special dog and his spirit lingers on for, although my grandparents never had another springer spaniel themselves, once my Uncle John left home, married and had children and dogs of his own, he never had any other breed, and the same is still true of his son, my cousin Paul and his family.

Ruff

Chapter Five

'Children's Hour' and the Search for Romany

Family life settled down in Clockhouse Road. We coped with the intense cold of 1947, one of the worst winters of the 20th century; it boasted snow cover from January to March and must have taken its toll on the vulnerable. The summer of 1947 saw my father succumb to polio but he was relatively lucky, any permanent damage being confined to a very slight limp and occasional pains in his hip and down his leg – nothing serious enough to prevent him riding a bike or playing tennis when he had a mind to, but enough to make him attend massage with the revered Miss Lynnie who had for years provided an early form of alternative therapy to the residents of Blackheath. My father started work as a solicitor in London, while my mother began playing a lot of tennis and ran a steady, if not altogether happy, good ship Home, a ship in which I could sail contentedly and securely enough, for though I was not close to my father he was not unkind to me and I had the familiar reassurance of my mother and Paulette to hold on to, while exploring new friends and school.

Part of the rhythm of the school day, following the 20 minute walk home with my mother and the dog, was having tea while listening to *Children's Hour* on the BBC Home Service – a magical wonderland of voices that became friends in their skilled story telling. There was, of course, Uncle Mac (Derek McCulloch) with his memorable end of programme goodbye – 'Goodnight children (big pause) everywhere' – plus a bank of actors who would appear in different roles according to the piece – Wilfred Babbage, Norman Shelley, Violet Carson and Mary O'Farrell. But if I were to pick a radio voice for the 20th century it would be that of David Davis, soothing as a light breeze on a summer's day, comforting as melted chocolate, a feather bed, or an affectionate caress through your hair. 'Uncle' David also played the piano and would sometimes be the announcer in place of Uncle Mac. Both of them would play parts in the various dramatised stories, or act as the narrator in these programmes that allowed a free range to the child's imagination. In later years someone once said to me that they preferred dramas on the radio because the scenery was better than on television.

Children's Hour finally bowed out to the tempting visuals of Children's Television on good Friday 1964, but it had run for 42 years, benefiting numerous generations of youngsters. The American poet, Henry Wadsworth Longfellow, best known for his *Hiawatha*, had kindly provided the programme's title in a poem called *The Children's Hour* which begins . . .

Between the dark and the daylight,
When the night is beginning to lower,
Comes a pause in the day's occupation
That is known as the Children's Hour.

The poem is 19th century of course and harks back to an era when there was only a small space allowed in the daily routine for wealthier parents to meet their children and enjoy their company as, for the most part, they were cared for by a nanny or nursery maid. My own mother, a classic housewife of her time, was there for me all the time anyway, but she would enjoy listening to the programmes, deriving from them as much pleasure as I did – her own enjoyment probably enhanced by my captivated reactions. We would discuss the stories and characters, and develop catch phrases from our favourites: Mr Grouser in *Toytown*, Pooh Bear in *The House at Pooh Corner* and the boys in *Jennings at School*. Jennings must have been a Saturday broadcast as I can remember my father chuckling at it with us.

Children's Hour was such an important part of my own childhood that I had thought this would be true for my contemporaries, so I made enquiries around family, friends and acquaintances but, to my surprise, with a few notable exceptions, the feedback was disappointing. One writer friend, for example, was forbidden to listen to anything so frivolous as 'the wireless'. My husband's memories are hazy and my sister can only remember *Listen with Mother*, for that seven year gap between us sometimes takes on canyon like proportions and, by the time she might have joined me sitting by the radio I was turned 12 and moving on to other interests, while Children's Television was rapidly growing in popularity.

The full list of programmes I can remember (along with one other which will merit a special mention later) runs something like: *Winnie the Pooh* with Norman Shelley playing Pooh, *The Wind in the Willows* with the same actor playing Toad, *Toytown* with Uncle Mac as Larry the Lamb, whose friend was Denis the affable Dachsund – 'Larry my frent I can with a jolly German äccent und vord order English speak.' Then there was Nöel Streatfield's *Ballet Shoes*, Pamela Brown's *The Swish of the Curtain* and an exciting adventure story called *The Green Dolphin* set in Rye. My introduction to Narnia was listening to *The Lion, the Witch and the Wardrobe* narrated by the incomparable David Davis. There were the exciting adventures of the boy detectives Norman and Henry Bones (both played I think by women, one of whom was Patricia Hayes) and *Jennings* and *Just William* had us in stitches of merriment. The last programme to make an impact, when I was a little older, was Rosemary Sutcliff's *Eagle of the Ninth* which featured an orphaned wolf cub brought up to be the centurion hero's companion. It was also my introduction to the historical novel, leading me to many others, including those by Mary Renault.

Of course this is nothing like the complete list of programmes broadcast over the years, nor is it indeed all those I would have listened to, for there were also music, quiz and nature programmes, but those named above are the ones that especially lodged with me. However, there is one *Children's Hour* character, mentioned to me in recent years by one or two friends (notably Keith Littlechild*) which aroused my curiosity and created a puzzle, namely Romany, his nature walks and his vardo. It became a challenge to track this programme down, as I was mystified as to why I had no memory of it myself.

The information on *Children's Hour* that came in (mainly by email) was carefully sifted and those people actually quoted are named, but I am indebted to everyone who took the trouble to search their own childhood memories and reply to my enquiries. The responses show *Toytown* to be the clear favourite, indeed it is sometimes the only programme that people remember. Some replies made for joyous reading, even though they had nothing to say about *Children's Hour*, for example Derek McBryde* conjures up his Northern Ireland childhood with a memory of 'whipping tops in the street, my red pedal racing car and the telephones we made out of baked bean cans and a piece of string.' These images are only outshone by the unlikely phrase 'playing cricket with my grannie's violin'. It transpires that the violin had long out-lived its owner, but my initial picture was of an instrument enjoying a double life, with a despairing grannie trying to coax *Danny Boy* from a triumphantly out-of-tune violin, still resounding with the hits of the afternoon's winning sixes.

David Griffiths* mentions other programmes not heard on *Children's Hour* but having a resonance of their own – *The Billy Cotton Band Show*, *Educating Archie* and *Hancock's Half Hour*. His evocation of the physical presence of the wireless itself includes memories of *Journey into Space*, broadcast, I think, at 7.30 in the evening. My father, mother and I would listen to this exciting adventure together, sitting by our radio the size of a polished wood washing machine, in front of a mouldering fire while playing ludo. Though neither David nor I can remember the plot, one scene in *Journey into Space* stands out in my memory – the moment when the spacemen first see the aliens, reacting with revulsion at their appearance, only to realise that it is not appearances that count, it is behaviour. The alien beings prove kindly and helpful, not to be feared at all. A lesson for life which has stayed with me.

Though unable to help trace Romany, despite having all the right interests, Peter Walton* evokes his early experiences as a birder:

'where Worcestshire rubs shoulders with the Birmingham conurbation. House-building was still prohibited; motorways were not yet on the horizon . . . on hearing a bird call or song . . . I would track it to its source . . . so that the link between sound and sight were mine for life.'

Small wonder that Peter's favourite *Children's Hour* programme was *Nature Parliament*, 'the panel comprised some of the luminaries of their day – the content adult by modern standards'. Among the naturalists were bird experts Peter Scott and James Fisher.

The view that *Children's Hour* did not 'dumb down' to the young listeners was one shared by several contributors, but not by Jan Shirley*, whose view of the programme was rather different:

'No . . . I didn't often listen. I think I felt annoyed by the condescending voices of grown-up people. There was also a sneaking awareness that my mother thought the programme would be Good For Me and I didn't want to be done good to. Oh dear. I would always rather bury myself in a book or go outside and climb a tree.'

These feisty comments bring a refreshingly tart flavour to some of our other, more sugary memories. At the time I never felt in the least condescended to, only cared for, but having recently obtained a recording of a few *Children's Hour* programmes, in some of them I take her point. What a perceptive child she must have been. But then comes Ian Slater*, remembering as I do, the comfort factor as a backdrop to *Children's Hour:*

> '. . . a teapot under a tea cosy, teacakes, jam sandwiches (sometimes tuna) oh and there was always a dish of tinned fruit and evaporated milk; they were such warm comfortable days . . .'

You would not dream from reading the above that the late 1940s are charted in other places as being among the most austere, cold and miserable years of the 20th century. I know my mother remembered them as being worse than the war itself. It says much for our inner glow of security and happiness that some of us remember that time as we do, and it stresses once again how hard it is to pin truth about life's experiences.

However informative they might be, none of these memories were of any help in my quest to track down Romany. So far there was only Brenda Perridge* who, besides recollecting many *Children's Hour* programmes, including *Nature Parliament*, also recalls 'nature walks with Romany and his dog, when he took children into the countryside and pointed out interesting things on the way.' He seems to have been hugely popular and I found it very puzzling that I had no memory of him at all, especially as his countryside rambles were accompanied by a cocker spaniel called Raq, and his caravan or vardo (a Romany word) was pulled by a horse called Comma – because she never quite came to a full stop! I felt sure I would have found the programme irresistible.

But at last I found the right contact, the helpful Olive Ambrose of the *Romany Society* which flourishes in our area of Cheshire. Thus, I was able to visit the vardo, claimed to be the smallest tourist attraction in the country, on one of its open days, in its Wilmslow home. In so doing I was able to lay the Romany mystery to rest:

Romany's mother was a true gypsy and he was born George Bramwell Evens in 1884. There is an endearing story of him as a youngster when, returning to boarding school he would send a homing pigeon to inform his parents of his safe arrival. Shades of Harry Potter and Hedwig*. Later he became a minister of the Methodist Church but, in 1921, bought his own vardo in Cumbria and made journeys round the countryside with it.

Then, in 1932/3, he began making the broadcasts for which he became famous. Loved by 'children everywhere' he sold thousands of books, some of which are still obtainable through the *Romany Society*. He was the first ever natural history broadcaster and is said to have been an influence on both David Attenborough and David Bellamy. Romany's last broadcast was made in 1943, just six weeks before he died. However, far from the recordings from those ten years being saved and replayed for the next generation of children (of whom I was one) the large metal reels on which the programmes were recorded were sent, along with many others, plus railings and cooking pots, to help the war effort. Let's hope they really did do some good, for much valuable recorded material was lost. Looking back it seems a huge sacrifice for the BBC to have made.

Thus the puzzle of why I had never heard of Romany was solved for unless, like Keith, the books had been put your way, you would have to be over a certain age even to have heard of him. However, there is some better news too. A recording of his very last programme did survive – the only piece to have come to light so far. I was, therefore, able to buy the CD and sat down to listen, wondering if any of the magic would still live. Would the attempted effect of a spontaneous nature ramble in the countryside be convincing, or would it sound unbearably stilted? Remember, these were programmes from the studio, not on location. Scripted by Romany himself they were unrehearsed, partly improvised, broadcast and recorded live. This would be enough to give any seasoned radio personality the jitters.

There are no sound effects, no wind or rain or birds singing, only the voices of Romany and the children, Muriel and Doris, to create the illusion that they are exploring the countryside together. I found the dialogue completely convincing, though the voices of the girls (played by adult women actors) sound strange to the modern ear as the speech is the clipped English which requires 'that' to be pronounced 'thet'. Thus Raq becomes 'Req'. Romany himself is entrancing. Speaking with a soft northern accent his mellow voice could never date. From an obvious fund of deep knowledge he explains to the girls the sights they see along their walk, in a way that is totally accessible without ever being patronising, and it all unfolds so naturally that I found it hard to be convinced that they were only in a studio. No wonder Romany captivated so many children, and what a loss to the rest of us that, from years of his programmes, only this fragment survives.

Subsequently, a Stockport friend has told me that she remembers her mother, who was a bus conductress, being thrilled to have Romany travel on her bus sometimes. But if you want to capture the essence of Romany and understand what he meant to some of that generation of children who saw the outbreak of World War Two in 1939, you could not ask for better than the following excursion back into childhood . . .

A Sunday Morning in September

by Pennant Roberts*

I didn't want my mother and father coming to sit under the kitchen table with me. It was my special place, and if my sister was allowed to be there as well she'd make fun of me. She was older than me and always telling me she knew better than I did. She already knew, from watching me playing, that when I was crouched between its big legs it became my Romany caravan, my vardo. She laughed out loud when she overheard me talking to myself when I was out in the country flicking the reins of Comma the horse and stroking the head of Raq the cocker spaniel. From beneath the cover of the table I would look out to see – even hear – the birds in the trees and hedgerows, and watch across the open fields hoping to catch sight of a hare.

But I knew somehow that if another big war broke out what I wanted wouldn't matter at all. If the worst did happen, all four of us would be sheltering under the table together, the wooden leaves pulled out to stop the bombs falling on our heads. Perhaps I might never listen to *Children's Hour* on the wireless again. I felt sad about that. When I was under the table the voice of Romany had brought me close to where Plume the woodcock lived and Flash the fox.

My mother had been sewing curtains every evening after supper. She went on after my sister and I were in bed, treadling away at the blackout material that didn't allow light to shine through it.

My father had been shouting about dangerous people called Germans who were very angry. He knew because he had been in the trenches fighting against them in France. He said they were angry because they had been promised an Ar-miss-tis – or something like that.

I had heard the air raid sirens being tried out. I had listened carefully to them and knew the difference between the *Alert* and the *All Clear*. The *All Clear* was like a dog whining and the *Alert* like a dog groaning with pain. I knew if they sounded like a dog in pain my father and mother and my sister with her big legs would come to sit with me under the table in the dark that would last forever. There were all kinds of bombs to listen out for too. It must be true because the man with ARP written on his helmet had said so.

Now my father was sitting next to the wireless. I couldn't see why they called it a wireless because there were lots of wires sticking out of the back of it. It had four big knobs on the front and when it was switched on a voice as dark as chocolate cake spoke from behind a piece of netting hanging inside two rings of bakelite. It was called the Ecko Radio and my father was in charge of it.

There was a smell of meat cooking coming from the kitchen and drifting through the house. I knew the wireless was going to tell us whether the Germans were coming to bomb us or not. If the wireless gave the wrong news it meant the world would be in darkness. That was what the man with ARP on his helmet had said was going to happen. There would be German aeroplanes, he said, that would drop bombs on us if they saw a light shining.

I imagined if there was to be no sunshine ever again there would be no countryside either ... no Fletcher's Farm ... and every bird and animal would go to sleep like Hotchi the hedgehog did in winter.

My father shouted for us to keep quiet. The voice on the wireless sounded as if it was talking down one of those kazoos they had on the toy counter at Woolworths. There was a humming sound and a buzzing but I made out some of the words, 'I'm speaking to you from 10 Downing Street' said the voice. I think his name was Mister Chilblain. He was talking about another man called Adolfickler.

Without us noticing my mother had brought our gas masks into the room. They had arrived a few days ago. She had taken them out of their cardboard boxes and lined them up on top of the sideboard. They looked like the heads of four black pigs staring into the room, looking as if they were listening to the wireless too.

I picked up some of the words Mister Chilblain was saying, '... that unless we heard from them by eleven o'clock ...' The wireless crackled and my father looked at my mother and made a swear word with his mouth.

I looked out of the window. The sun was shining in the garden. I knew I had to be out-of-doors throwing a tennis ball against the wall. There might not be sunshine ever again. Then I heard the tinny voice on the wireless saying ... 'I have to tell you no such undertaking has been received.'

I ran from the house into the garden. I didn't understand the next word I heard. It sounded like con-sick-went-ly, but the last thing Mister Chilblain said was quite clear '... this country is at war with Germany.' As I bounced my tennis ball hard against the side of the house a siren was sounding the *Alert*. Later the ARP man said it had only been a test to see if it was all working. But my mother had come rushing out of the house to find me.

The worst had happened. The next moment all four of us were sitting under the table – in my caravan – and I was wearing a gas mask over my face.

Chapter Six

'Said the Cat . . .'

Miss Meade, with her tiny voice, did not hold the record for the smallest adult in my young life. This accolade went to Auntie Gertie, who was, I believe, my great, great aunt. By coincidence she lived like us in Clockhouse Road, with her niece May, who was another of Nanny's sisters, and a World War One widow. 'Auntie' and 'Uncle' were terms loosely used in this era which could apply to anyone from the straightforward real aunt or uncle, to great uncles and aunts, great, great ones or indeed people who were no relation at all but were sufficiently close friends of parents not to necessitate being called Mr or Mrs.

Family legend has it that Auntie Gertie was only four foot two in height (127 centimetres). Certainly I remember her as being hardly any bigger than me. She had cotton-wool wavy hair and a rosy gentle face. She gave me a ring – my first piece of proper jewellery. It was Victorian, a single garnet in a pretty, gold, circular setting and was so small it transferred from her hand to mine in a perfect fit.

I hold a few images of the aunties' home – a brightly burning coal fire, a round table covered in a dark green chenille cloth with fringing that tickled, an Art Deco milk jug with a heavily beaded lace cover that clinked and jingled whenever lifted, and a cheery plump canary in a cage. Here was Tweetie Pie indeed, but no Sylvester! No Sylvester here, no Sylvester at my grandparents' nor at any of my mother's friends. I can remember no contact with cats whatsoever in my early years apart from a stunning black cuddly toy, almost life-size, which had a musical box at its base that played *Jingle Bells*. I came by this through the first love of my life, John Connaught, who had a millionaire friend in London, and I was invited to a children's party in this man's smart home. I can remember nothing about the occasion except the whispering rustle of my pale blue, taffeta party dress, and then the thrill of coming home with Sooty, who lived on the end of my bed for many years, often encouraged to play his one tune. Although I loved Sooty very much, even he was a poor swap for the warm fur of the real thing. But there was antipathy on both sides of the family to cats. My father always said he hated them as did Nanny, though I have a feeling that Banny in Blackheath did like cats, but they had never had one because my grandfather disliked them. So, when and how was my first introduction to the wonder that is a cat?

From an early age I enjoyed stories featuring animals, and there was a family connection with the *Little Grey Rabbit* books by Alison Uttley, for the charming illustrations were by Margaret Tempest, whom I knew as Cousin Margaret since she and Banny were first cousins. I can vaguely remember this (to me) famous cousin, a small, quiet lady in her huge Ipswich house, her studio with the easel, and the little wooden figures of Hare, Squirrel and Little Grey Rabbit, which had limbs she could move, presumably to facilitate the task of drawing and painting the illustrations. We would take tea in the cathedral-like proportions of the sitting room, for it seemed that our whole house would have fitted easily inside this one room. Cousin Margaret was looked after by the indefatigable Doris, who tottered into that vast space, semi-invisible under a tray heavy with scones.

Sometimes, when a new book came out Cousin Margaret was kind enough to send a signed copy for my sister and me. She also wrote illustrated stories herself and must have enjoyed creating these books which were entirely hers, for she and Alison Uttley were not bosom pals and frequently fell out. Published in tiny books measuring a mere four by four inches Cousin Margaret's own 'babies' fitted snugly in a child's hand, with enchanting pictures of Pinkie Mouse and latterly Curly Cobbler. One of these stories featured a Pekinese called Koko, with an injured paw carefully tended by the kindly Pinkie Mouse.

From 'Pinkie Mouse and Koko', artistic impression by France Bauduin of the original colour illustration by Margaret Tempest.

However, no cats here. No cats anywhere when I search early memories. Possibly from family loyalty to Margaret Tempest, Beatrix Potter hardly featured in my young reading and I only discovered Tom Kitten and Mrs Tabitha Twitchit years later when the books appeared *en français* in the school French library.

I had shown an early interest in drama when, aged five, wearing a red velvet dress with a white lace collar, I recited a poem about a busy bee at a school concert. By six I was a rabbit in *Snow White* and by eight I was starring as the princess in the *Tinder Box*, which gave me the chance to befriend three dogs. Still no cats but, thanks to my mother's father, Pop, who would take me on outings, not only to London Zoo and the

Me starring as the princess in 'The Tinderbox'.

Natural History Museum, but also to suitable films and live shows, I was introduced to professional theatre, where I encountered Dick Whittington. He and his cat made a big impression on me, so much so that I tried to put on my own show in which I played our hero. Unfortunately Dick's adventures were somewhat conflated to a hesitant march around the room with a walking stick slung over my shoulder sporting a forlorn hanky, coupled with occasional encouraging exclamations of 'Come on Puss'. My audience was hardly wowed!

Then, somewhere in my enthusiastic listening to *Children's Hour* came the programme I loved best of all – *Said the Cat to the Dog*. Few people seem to remember it but it featured a cat called Mompty and a dog called Peckham. The animals were family pets living with 'Mum' and 'Dad', the stories being told entirely from the perspective of the cat and the dog. This was radio, but Mompty and Peckham were vivid characters. I had no doubt that the dog was a large good-natured liver-and-white springer spaniel, who thought that Mompty was far too hard on Mum and Dad for, in Peckham's view, they could do no wrong. In contrast, Mompty was sleek and black, with long whiskers, a flicking tail and an infallible capacity for being right. In true feline attitude she always put her own needs first. I can't remember any of the actual story lines but the impression of the style remains strong . . .

Sound of key in lock

Peckham: *There, you see Mompty, they're back. I told you there was no need to worry. Mum and Dad never leave us for long.*

Mompty: *Oow Peckham, that's all very well, but I don't see why they had to go and leave us in the first place. They know I don't like it. It upsets me. So you can make a big silly fuss of them but I shall just sit here, flick my tail and ignore them.*

I lapped up this feline way of looking at life, finding it totally endearing, and it has forever been associated in my mind with 'cat think'. Of course I have subsequently learned that no two cats are ever alike, but nonetheless, the gulf between a cat's eye view of humans and that of dogs was forever clearly defined in this programme, and I am convinced that this is where I began to develop my strong feel for cats.

Haiku – for animal companions

Says the Dog

You are wonderful.

I adore and worship you

even when you're wrong.

Says the Cat

I am wonderful.

I adore and worship me.

I am never wrong.

Chapter Seven

The Queen and the Schoolgirls

Early in 1950, when my sister was about six months old, we moved from the semi-detached house in Clockhouse Road (and thus away from an area of Beckenham dangerously close to the much maligned Penge) to settle closer to Bromley, in Shortlands, at 13 Bromley Grove, which was detached, with a bigger garden and apparently no history of being unlucky. So far as I remember, on moving day, after standing outside Number 21 to say goodbye, I walked to school on my own and, in the afternoon, brought myself home on the now familiar 227 bus, to our new house, with a six or seven minute walk at either end of that bus ride. From then on, at eight-years-old, I travelled to and from school solo, though my mother may sometimes have walked with me to the bus or met me with Paulette, and my sister in the pram, on the way home. Whatever the case it all seemed perfectly safe and normal.

Opposite our new home was a row of very large terraced houses which had been turned into flats, and in one of these lived Mrs Farell, a lively and charming widow, who, although she had no children herself, had a very good understanding of them. She also loved music and cats, and had a large, friendly ginger tom-cat called Rufus. Mrs Farrell became a good friend to the family. My father would help her out with any odd jobs that needed doing and I would love visiting her, exploring her extensive collection of records, where I believe I may have been introduced to opera. She treated me very much like a grown-up, respecting my ideas and encouraging both my friendship with Rufus and then my wish to have a cat of my own. It was not long before my mother was softening, saying that she did like ginger cats and perhaps one day . . . but my father was adamantly against the idea, which may explain why my parents gave in to my having a rabbit.

We would go back to Mersea for our holidays, renting a cottage, or sometimes more excitingly a houseboat. One of the traditional holiday pastimes which never failed to entice all children was 'crabbing'. This involved staking a claim on the causeway, where patient yachtsmen dodged round us while trying to embark or disembark their dinghies, while we crabbers, armed with a bucket, a piece of weighted string and some bacon rind, would dangle our sophisticated fishing gear down into the dark green, or grey, shallows of the North Sea until, at the third or fourth attempt, the line would be hauled in, gripped by a soon-to-be-indignant smallish crab which had to take up forced residence in the bucket. It was subsequently joined by various compadres amidst excited competition among the children, to see who could catch the most of these grumpy, little sea dwellers, which were, of course, not edible. At some given signal, such as lunch or teatime, or maybe just an overloaded bucket, the prisoners would be released onto the causeway, each crabber counting his or her own catch as the crabs thankfully made their sideways scuttle back to their natural habitat – I hope none the worse for the experience.

It was on one of these crabbing trips that I met a boy called Arthur, and was impressed because he said he was going to be an actor and was already appearing in a professional stage show by Ivor Novello, in which he played the boy king – a small, silent role as it turned out. But for him to have been on a proper stage filled me with wonder, even if, as I fear, that performance may have proved to be both his debut and his swan-song. Arthur and I shared crabbing experiences and he had rabbits! He had baby rabbits and, since I was not allowed a cat, my parents were persuaded. Thus Flopsy came into the family. She was a Flemish Giant, which is a breed not unlike the wild rabbit in colour, but larger. While she was a baby I took her about with me and spent a lot of time with her, but then I had to return to school and, looking back, I think her life must have been a lonely one in her hutch at the end of the garden. I know I wanted my father to make her a run on the lawn but it never happened. My parents were probably afraid of Paulette's hunting instincts. Occasionally, when the dog was secured indoors, we let Flopsy loose to have an adventure in the garden. Not surprisingly, once tasting freedom she was difficult to catch again and this gave rise to anxiety, and the chasing around must have been frightening for her. So, after a while, this garden activity was abandoned. All in all it was not the most glorious episode in the family's pet owning history.

Meanwhile, my sister was rapidly growing from babyhood into a chatty and amusing little girl, whose company I began to enjoy much more, for I was never one to go gooey-eyed over babies. We became devoted friends, though she must have sometimes felt, as she grew up, that she was caught in my shadow. However, in the early years there was only admiration, and one of the several personae that she insisted on adopting was that of 'a big schoolgirl, like Jenny'. Even at the age of three Sheila could be very determined and woe betide any of us who failed to call her by my name. This led to some confusion, till my father hit on the idea of calling me by my second name –Mary. For my father this stuck, my middle name becoming his pet name for me, even surviving the period when our imaginative family member became Mother Mary, with a doll which she called Jesus. Sheila famously embarrassed our own mother one day when, returning from kindergarten on the bus, the doll slipped from my sister's knee to land on the floor, and a reproving shrill voice sang out, 'Oh Jesus!' the words reverberating down the full length of the 227.

In 1953 it was the Queen's coronation and we went to watch the great events of the day on a friend's television, for it would be a year or two before we succumbed to having such advanced technology ourselves. My sister was besotted with the glamour of the whole affair and, overnight, became 'The Queen', with our mother, of course, becoming the Queen Mother. With the impeccable logic of a small child she made me the Queen Sister, and my father the Queen Father. To his dying day my father would talk of my sister as 'The Queen' and address her as Queenie.

When I was ten I left Woodbrook to go to the junior department of Sydenham High School, which was part of the Girls' Public Day School Trust and a considerably longer journey on our old friend the 227 bus. Under the kindly eye of Miss Howell, the junior school headmistress, I sat the Eleven Plus exam with the idea of my winning a free place to the senior school. Unfortunately, I managed to fail this test and could have been taken away from Sydenham High to go to a Secondary Modern School, but my parents covered their disappointment well and knuckled down to many more years of school fees so that I could move seamlessly onward with my education.

However, it was not altogether seamless, as it was interrupted, with some drama, in the summer term of my first year at the senior school. Black, flapping gowns were worn by the teachers and the atmosphere, though not unkind, was strict and work focused. The headmistress, Miss Yarmsley, had the dryness and deep brown eyes of a tortoise and was inclined to make remarks at assembly which somehow failed to terrify such as, 'Girls, I am deeply grieved, for it has come to my attention that some of you are not wearing your school hats all the way home!' There was only one crime worse than this, and that was to be seen, in school uniform, eating in the street. Miss Yarmsley could hardly survive the deep grief that such a report would bring. She did, however, command respect and, to this day, I worry that I failed to understand the huge nugget of wisdom imparted when, as eighteen-year-olds, we left her school to go out into the challenges of the real world – 'Girls I want you always to remember when sending letters to use envelopes which match your writing paper.' Could there be some vital metaphorical meaning to this instruction, a hidden mantra for conducting oneself? Even now, should I find myself short of an exactly matching envelope, I have a twinge of guilt as I slip the letter into the offending piece of stationery, wondering what Miss Yarmsley would have had to say about such a solecism.

Poor Miss Yarmsley, she was taken horrifically aback, indeed I am sure the whole school was shaken to its conventional roots, by my behaviour one summer's afternoon. During that morning I had had a dull ache in my stomach and, somewhat reluctantly (surely the child is making an unnecessary fuss) I was allowed to sit out and watch our gym lesson, rather than taking part. As the morning went on the pain grew worse and I took myself to the office and thence the sickroom, where I was given a hot water bottle for an hour or so, and was then asked if I could not eat a little light lunch of soup, ryvita and cheese? 'Otherwise, Jennifer, you will not be able to stay in school this afternoon.' To the school secretary the nightmare scenario of a girl having to miss afternoon school was unthinkable. So, with my white face, which impressed my peers with its ghostly glow, I struggled back down to the gym, where lunch was served, and ate a little of my privileged meal in a quietish corner of the room.

It was a Tuesday, and the afternoon's big event was Miss Yarmsley's weekly English Grammar lesson. My desk was near the back of the room and, as we rose to greet the great woman I was feeling decidedly groggy, but what can an obedient eleven-year-old do in those circumstances? I swayed at my desk, turning, I imagine, from white to a ghoulish green, feeling hotter and sicker, until obedience did not come into it. One hand waving desperately in the air to attract Miss Yarmsley's attention, the other clapped to my erupting mouth, I vomited over myself and a large portion of the classroom. This did, successfully, get Miss Yarmsley's attention. I was whisked away and my mother received a shocked and solemn phone call from the school secretary, 'Mrs Banning we think you had better come and collect Jennifer, she is not at all well and has been sick in Miss Yarmsley's English Grammar lesson!'

Once home, rescued from school by my mother with help from a neighbour and his car, our much loved Dr Finer was called to visit, and diagnosed threatening peritonitis. By late evening I was in theatre. I made a good recovery and enjoyed my convalescence, especially as I missed the end of term exams. However, my parents were much more aware than I was of how seriously ill I had been, and probably felt that they could have been close to losing me. For whatever reason, they finally gave in to my plea for a cat.

Someday a cat . . .

Chapter Eight

At Last – A Cat

Simba   Here was my first adventure into kitten, the family's first experience of a little blue-eyed seducer, ginger-and-white, still fluffy with babyhood, so small, so agile. That tiny mew, that throbbing big purr, the mad chase of ping-pong ball across the floor or toes under the covers, that little trusting face. How could we not fall in love with this little creature skittering through our affections so irresistibly? We had been concerned about Paulette's reaction to a small feline intruder, after all she had never been discouraged from chasing small furry things, but we need not have worried; when presented with a small, arched, furry spit of a kitten, glaring at her from a safe height, she looked questioningly at Simba, then at us, then back to him again. With gentle encouragement to be friendly towards him, that was precisely the stance she took; it did not take long for dog and small cat to settle down to an amicable relationship.

My father, the man who hated cats, had succumbed within a day, and I could only wonder that we had waited so long. Moreover, kittens are so easy compared with puppies; there is no house-training since they use a tray, and once they feel secure they don't mind being left alone for an hour or three, with no chewing or damage to worry about. There are no needle sharp bitings to hands or legs, and their baby claws are only able to inflict pinpricks.

This is a time to cherish, for the snag with both kittens and puppies is that they grow too fast and, as they grow, they naturally change character to a lesser or greater extent. Approaching adolescence, independence arrives, 'I'm a big teenager, I know everything and I will do my own thing!' This development comes with cats and dogs as well as with children. Simba was no exception. He started being out more and was harder to attract back indoors. When he was six months old he was castrated, this being done on the kitchen table. I was upstairs at the time but heard Simba cry out. It now seems barbaric but at the time was the way things were done, even with a trusted vet.

Perhaps because of this trauma – and who could blame him after such a betrayal of his trust in us – Simba wandered further and was away longer. One day he did not come back at all and we were frantic with worry. He was missing for 48 hours and we were miserable without him. Maybe the anxiety of his loss brought on the bad cold which laid me up in bed, when my mother, having set out to do the daily shop, returned after only ten minutes with a big smile and an armful of purring ginger-and-white cat. She had found him walking along the top of a fence on her way down to the shops. Simba seemed as pleased to see us as we were to have him back, and we all hoped he had learned from his experience and would never do it again. But it seemed that the call of the far away was too strong for him and, a few weeks later, he disappeared again. Again the waiting, the hoping, the imagining of what had befallen him. Is there anything worse than this 'not knowing'? Yet I was still of an age to believe in happy endings and my mother would have kept hope alive as long as she could. I cannot now remember these empty, anxiety filled weeks, and guess that my subconscious has successfully buried them, but I think I was scarred by the experience for, as an adult, though generally not bad in most crises, I become an irrational neurotic if one of our cats cannot be found, even if only for a few hours.

One day many weeks later, I came home from school to a happy surprise. A gentle, smiling, white cat, marked with large, ginger splodges was purring contentedly in the kitchen. My mother had received a call from the RSPCA to say that a ginger cat had been brought in. Would she like to see if it was ours?

She was there as fast as bus and feet could carry her, but her first reaction on walking into the room was disappointment. It was not Simba. It was, however, a friendly young charmer. Kneading the table with ecstatic paws he was obviously thrilled to be in safe hands. No one had claimed him. Would my mother consider offering him a home? The considering did not take long and she was soon carrying the prize of her new-found friend back to Bromley Grove.

The moment I saw the newcomer a flutter of deep affection stirred through me. He lifted not only his smile to me but one of his paws, as if so happy that he could not keep his feet on the ground. I stroked him, he chirruped. Simba had never been very vocal. I picked up this bundle of contentment and he nestled his head, with its purring engine, into my neck. It was love at first sight. I have never been skilled with my hands but, from an obliging cardboard box, I made our new friend a bed with a roof, painted the outside carefully with poster paint and labelled it *Piedy's House* for I decided Piedy was a good name for him, suiting what I thought were his piebald markings. They were no such thing of course, for a piebald horse is black-and-white. In reality, our Piedy was skewbald, so should have been called Skewy, but it would hardly have had the same ring and, by the time we realised the mistake, Piedy was so well established in our hearts that Piedy was the name and the name was the cat.

If I had had more experience with cats I would have known that people who go to great lengths, and sometimes much expense, to provide their beloved pet with the most comfortable of beds, baskets or cosy igloos, are often open to disappointment. The cat will take a cursory look and say, 'Why on earth would I want to go in that when I can sprawl on the sofa, your bed, lie on the clean washing or squash myself into a box or drawer three times too small for me?' The rejected comfort zone is recycled to the charity shop, or passed to a friend to offer to the next feline personage, who will probably take a similarly disdainful view. However, I did not know any of this and my naive enthusiasm carried the day. Piedy responded by being delighted with his special 'house' and would obligingly sit in it, contentedly smiling at us from the triangle formed under its painted eaves.

We were going to keep our new cat indoors for at least a week but, after a day or two, he caused great alarm by getting out. The next thing we knew he was sighted two gardens away sitting on top of a large aviary. My mother and I were worried, thinking that despite Piedy's apparent delight at finding us, the urge to roam had kicked in and we would lose him to the wanderlust that had taken Simba. I stood at our back door, whence I could plainly see Piedy's fascinated budgerigar-watch. He had a perfect vantage point on top of their large caged space. He was busy doing cat things. It was unlikely he would respond even if he was intending to return home later, so it was with faint hope but strong trepidation that I let loose with my best cat calling voice – one I was to use over the years in many another crisis. At once Piedy looked up and, with hardly a second's hesitation, leapt from the aviary to the fence and down into next-door's garden. In a moment he was in my arms and our relationship was cemented.

Paulette readily accepted this new and definite family fixture. Piedy would rub against her chest just as he would rub against our legs. He loved everyone, but I was his special person. The only time we ever saw him alarmed with people was when we took him to the vet for a routine check. He became very distressed in the surgery, so much so that the kindly vet remarked, 'He's very wild'. We were indignant as this was the last adjective we would have applied to our gentle Piedy. It is a reminder though, that when cats are sufficiently nervous, for whatever reason, their wilder instincts – always there somewhere beneath a cuddly exterior – will show themselves. You can never take a cat's good nature for granted.

Piedy

Piedy was my special friend. He would follow me around and sit in my lap while I was doing homework. Sitting upright, he had the distinctive habit of kneading the surface on which he was sitting, lifting first one paw and then the other in the air, while gazing up adoringly and even drooling in ecstasy. He would always want to be nearby, being an invaluable and sympathetic comforter when parents either caused, or failed to understand, adolescent trauma and storms. There were not many of these, for I was never much of a rebel even during my teenage years, but any teenager has emotional ups and downs. At night-time it was especially reassuring to have Piedy's non-judgmental purr, and the familiar weight of Paulette, with me on the bed, almost as if they were extensions of myself. If ever I was away from home I would find the excitement of new people and new experiences compensated for my parents and sister, it was the animal companionship I missed.

One such foray away from home was with Miss Crowne, one of the fine young teachers at Sydenham High School. She taught geography and, with never a note, would hold her classes rapt. I suspect she was something of an innovator too, and that it caused a flurry in the more academic dovecotes when she organised a field-trip to Derbyshire. How daring! Had anything like it ever been attempted before? To venture fearlessly on a train with a troupe of 13-year-old girls, not merely north of Watford Junction but into the realms of that remote city called Sheffield, surely this could not be wise? I, for one, had never been north of London, nor seen anything more hilly than the South Downs. There was a general feeling of 'outward bound' as we boarded the train with our pristine rucksacks like tortoise shells on our backs. We were headed for the pretty village of Castleton in the Peak District, with its stone-built cottages and its Blue John Mine. We stayed in the youth hostel there. This too was a new experience, but it was the scenery which captivated me – the rocks, the caves, the rivers and little streams, and the ruggedness of the hills compared with southern England. I felt instantly at home and enjoyed every moment of the week's walking and exploring. I was so full of it when I got back to Bromley Grove that, the following summer, my father was persuaded away from Mersea (Essex) or Pevensey (Sussex) and we went to North Wales for our family holiday. There I excelled myself by suddenly seeing a large shape on top of a high craggy ridge and proclaiming it a cow. Next moment the unlikely bovine spread its wings and soared into the sky, proving itself to be a golden eagle. My feeling silly was a small price to pay for the luck of seeing something so rare and wonderful. Some 50 years later I wrote a quirky little poem for a cat-loving French friend, which probably has its roots as much in that Welsh cow-eagle as in the old nursery rhyme . . .

The Cat and the Cow

The cat and the cow were dancing one night,

Said the cat, 'You are heavy while I'm a delight,

See how I'm dainty and gracefully leap,

While you are a lumbering, cumbersome heap.'

The cow softly smiled to herself on her hoof,

'Well now my dear, the pudding's the proof.'

How gentle her tone – a mellowing croon

As with effortless ease she jumped over the moon!

Chapter Nine

The French Connection

At the age of 14 I was introduced to 'abroad'. Family holidays with my parents had only just begun to venture further than Sussex, with that wild excursion into North Wales the previous summer, so crossing the Channel would have been considered reckless. Now I was to make an exchange with a French girl, staying on my own for three weeks with Catherine and her French family just outside Paris. Though fuddy duddy in many respects, our school had excellent French teachers, and exchanges of this kind were encouraged and often set up as this one was, through established friendships that the teachers themselves had with various families. Catherine came to stay with us for three weeks, then it was my turn to travel to France. She was a young 13 and, on that first stay, related as well to my sister as to me, but she revelled in the relative freedom teenagers enjoyed in the UK, compared with the parental strait jackets imposed on them at that time in France.

When I arrived at Catherine's home in Le Raincy I was enthusiastically welcomed by her family, who took their responsibilities of showing me the sights and teaching me the language very seriously. Most of the time only French was spoken, but occasionally, meaning to be kind, Papa would try out his English, partly to give me a break and partly, I suspect, to demonstrate his skill in another language. Unfortunately, while he certainly spoke English after a fashion, it was his own idiosyncratic fashion, with a very strong accent and some eccentric usage, so that when he solicitously enquired '' 'ave you spleen?' I was totally nonplussed. I think I would still find difficulty today in knowing that he thought he was asking, 'Are you homesick?' I came to dread his launches into my mother tongue for, embarrassingly, I found them much more difficult to understand than French which, if geared to my level, I found I could cope with quite well, though on that first visit I tended to clam up when required to speak it myself.

There was much in France to find different. The family dog was called Strolch and was a German hunting dog, or short-haired pointer, with an easy-going affectionate nature despite living much of his time in a small enclosure in a corner of the large garden. He had a good kennel and plenty of food and water. For much of the day he was loose in the garden and very occasionally was taken for a walk, but I don't remember ever seeing him in the house. This seemed strange to me but, on the other hand, the dog was not unhappy, he was used to this and would have been in his element in the hunting season. However, my teenage self thought that such a friendly chap deserved better.

In fact he did have better, for I have subsequently found out that, in the winter months, he came into the kitchen and nestled against the radiator along with one of the cats, which only goes to show that my schoolgirl impressions were not altogether reliable. During my visits to France I experienced a few incidents which seemed to me then to indicate that the French were more callous in their treatment of animals than the

Strolch

British. But teenagers tend to see life without its shades of grey, and my views modified as I grew older, coming to think that perhaps the French are just less hypocritical than we are. I have also become much more cynical about seeing Britain as 'a nation of animal lovers'.

Like many French people, not least the writer Colette, Catherine was very fond of cats and there were two at the house, a brother and sister, though I can only remember Lily clearly. She was very much Catherine's cat as Piedy was mine; this tender bonding with a pet was one of many things she and I shared. Lily was the typical French feline – a small slender tabby. She adored both Catherine and Strolch. Everyone else she could take or leave. She was highly intelligent and, at night, she would somehow manage to climb onto the roof of the salon. From there she would miaow till Catherine opened, first the shutters, then the window, for her to come in and snuggle down on the bed beside her best friend.

Catherine, just like me, would always stop to talk to any feline person we met when out. My impression was that French cats were inclined to be tabby and smaller than their British cousins and I soon learnt, when speaking to them, that the proper mode of address was *Bonjour minou*.

I knew I was there to absorb France, its language and the French way of doing things. I tried very hard to fit in and ate everything that was put in front of me, including snails which were palatable by virtue of their garlic butter, and oysters (those 'vile jellies'*) which I managed – just – to slip down on life rafts of crusty bread, heavily bandaged with butter. My hosts, who were kind and solicitous, assured me that there would be no horse meat for the duration of my stay since they understood the *Anglais* to be weirdly illogical, happily eating cows but distressed at doing the same with horses.

Ironically, my worst moment came, not with meat or fish, but with an artichoke. A total unknown to me, I was confronted with this large green acorn of leaves and dutifully peeled one off and attempted to chew it, causing much merriment round the lunch table, before having it explained to me that one should merely strim the flesh from the base of each leaf, having first dipped it into a tasty dressing. It takes a good while to dissect an artichoke in this way, so it is a helpful aid to the philosophical discussion at which the French excel, particularly when enjoying a meal.

The French home was very different from that of the English. Central heating was the norm so the main focus in the living area was not the fireplace but the large rectangular dining table upon which delicious food was miraculously conjured from a small, inconvenient kitchen worked stalwartly by Grand'mère – a tiny, wizened, Belgian widow, who wore the black of her station with a kindliness that never allowed her a bad word for, or about, anyone. She had been a cook by profession and could work magic with the simplest of dishes. For example, from the hens she looked after in the garden she would collect freshly laid eggs, then bake them in the oven with cream, butter and a little salt, turning them to nectar with the talent of her wrinkled hands.

I was fascinated by the French use of shutters which, because they were outside the windows, required the windows themselves to open into the room. Shutters seem so sensible as they protect the house from both bad weather and strong sunlight. Moreover, since most French people close them when they are not at home they also prevent the nosy or the dishonest from peering into the house. The shutters, coupled with high walls and the clanging gates that guarded the typical French house, made me begin to wonder however, whether it was really the Englishman whose home was his castle.

Brought up on lino and then fitted carpets, I was impressed by the quality and practicality of French floors, which were far less often carpeted than back home. Downstairs, the floors were either good quality tiles or polished wood, while the best room or salon – only used for state occasions – had an Aubusson rug set on gleaming parquet, with elegant gold-painted furniture which could have been awaiting the arrival of Madame de Pompadour. What did not strike me at the time, was the lack of any easy-chairs for anyone to relax in. The family did their relaxing on straight-backed dining chairs while conversing over their meals. Once the table was cleared people sat on those same chairs to continue the evening. There was, of course, no television.

The room I loved best in the house was my bedroom. On the first floor landing was a small door which opened onto a little, wooden stairway curving up to the attic with its sloping walls and ceilings, which were papered all over in grey and white 18th century pastoral scenes. The bedspread matched these, as did the curtains hung to screen my clothes on the rail set under the slope of the ceiling at one side of the room. I had never seen anything so pretty and was enchanted. Because the house was tall and stood on a hill, with the shutters flung wide you could see for many miles, right across Paris to a distant skyline, where the Eiffel Tower and Sacré Coeur were clearly visible. The view was even better at night-time with the twinkling lights of Paris and those two familiar shapes illuminated. With the shutters closed overnight the early morning was kept well at bay, so that I would almost certainly have slept late except for the crowing of the cockerel strutting his stuff in one of the gardens down the hill on the quiet road below. The sound of a cock crowing still makes me think of France.

Visits to my French family were always in summer, so I would not have remarked on the convenience of the central heating, but I was surprised at the inconvenience of the only WC I ever discovered, for this was situated downstairs off the hall. Presumably Maman and Papa had their own bathroom off their bedroom, but the one I shared with Catherine and her sister was en suite with their room and was a good size. It boasted a bath, basin and bidet but no loo. The logic of this still eludes me but was typical of French houses at the time.

During my first visit I remained tongue-tied but the experience of being in France was invaluable and, in subsequent years, my French developed to a passable fluency that took me easily through French 'A' level. Fortunately, for good relations with the family, summer is the close season so they were not going hunting – their wintertime passion. How I would have coped with a day *à la chasse* with bodies falling from the sky I do not like to think. At home, my father would sometimes take his rifle up to a bedroom window to make war on the wood pigeons that liked to visit and devour our vegetable garden. He would come downstairs again puzzled that the birds always seemed to sense him there and fly away before the gun could be fired. Little did he know that, down below, his devious daughter was frantically flapping the kitchen curtains in order to frighten them to safety. Had it been the hunting season in France when I was there I fear my French hosts would have found me a far less amenable *Anglaise*. As it was I responded with enthusiasm to everything my committed chauffeur and guides showed me. I was given an extensive tour of the Parisian tourist attractions, including luscious stores like Galeries Lafayette, and we visited Versailles and Chartres, Compiègne and several of the Loire chateaux.

Like many French families mine only rented their main residence but owned a seaside holiday home. Theirs was on Île d'Oléron, which lies off the Atlantic coast just south of La Rochelle. The place was a little one-storey house, gleaming white with dark green shutters. For some reason I can never quite fathom, one would never describe such a dwelling as a 'bungalow' for that term (despite its origins in India) seems to smack of middle class English suburbia or seaside.

So *Le Rayon Vert* was a house, a modern house but in a fairy-tale setting. I fell in love with it. It nestled in a sunny forest glade at the end of a sandy track and the beach was a short stroll through the pine-scented woods until you reached the rush of the Atlantic, the pleasures of *la plage*, and the evening magnificence of sunsets which, on

Hollyhocks and French cat

rare occasions, would apparently throw out a ray of green light as the sun disappeared below the saucer rim of the horizon. The house was named after this phenomenon which I am still waiting to experience.

Previously, I had never liked cycling, viewing it merely as a faster way of getting from A to B rather than by my preferred Shanks's pony. It was on the Île d'Oléron that I first really enjoyed riding a bike, exploring the flat, yet fast-changing terrain, from harbour to oyster beds, from beach to forest, from marshland to white painted cottages, where choruses of hollyhocks flaunted their pink, red, and cream laden stems, pampering the already pretty walls of the little houses.

In her turn Catherine enjoyed Mersea, which had some similarities with Oléron, and our respective stays with each other's families established a strong, warm friendship, making us respectively anglophile and francophile.,

During my teenage visits to France however, I missed the animals very much. After all, I was used to a dog and a purring cat asleep on my bed. For obvious reasons we had never known Paulette's exact age, but she was older than me in real time and, in dog years, was becoming an elderly lady when I was in my early teens. She aged gracefully, growing deaf and then losing her sight but retaining her sense of smell which guided her seamlessly around her familiar territory. When the time came to say goodbye my parents took her to the vet together and came back red-eyed. We all cried, feeling we had lost a best friend and, in my case, a life-long companion. Yet Paulette had had such a full, happy life it is surely only for ourselves that we weep in such circumstances, not for that brave little spirit released from any suffering.

It was early January and, as it happened, was a Saturday. My father, in one of his more inspired moments, suggested we all went to the pantomime at Streatham Hill to cheer ourselves up. He managed to get last-minute tickets and, although I can remember feeling horribly bruised as I settled into my seat, the sheer silliness of panto and its colourful brightness began to work its magic. I believe it was *Aladdin*. Of course there was a Dame and this Widow Twanky had a beguiling pet. In reality a feather boa, it had been adapted for its stage debut on some sort of wiring device. Long, pale pink and fluffy, it whizzed about the stage and up and down walls – 'It's behind you!' – at demented speed. Widow Twanky was devoted to her pet which, she explained to the audience, was called a Woofapoof and, of course, we had to shout out every time we saw it flash past. It was this character which made the most impression on all of us and, on the way home, as we talked about the loss of Paulette and what we should do next, my father suggested we get a Woofapoof!

Chapter Ten

Towards a Woofapoof

A house that has always had a dog in it no longer feels like home when that presence is gone. Paulette had been a faithful friend all my life and had been the least demanding of animals even as her faculties faded and her kind brown eyes turned to milky green. She had slept on my bed and I never minded having my sleep broken to let her out into the garden if she needed to go outside in the early hours. It was empty without her though Piedy did his best to comfort us. We would surely never find another dog to match Paulette. This being so, the decision was taken to give some poor, needy animal a good home. None of us felt we could bear the heartache of going to Battersea Dogs Home and being unable to help them all. Our beloved Piedy had come through the RSPCA so why should we not find a dog through the same route? These dogs in need of homes were still with their owners who could no longer keep them for whatever reason. The RSPCA acted as brokers, the deal being that you had the animal to stay for a few days' trial to see if he or she would fit in with the family's lifestyle. If not, then it could go back to the original owner with no questions asked.

I am not sure why my usually cautious parents thought it was a good idea to try Kerry, but try Kerry the foxhound we did. She was young, healthy, beautiful, affectionate and strong, strong in both mind and body. As part of the testing process Sheila and I attempted to take her for a walk, and I flew behind her several inches off the ground on the end of the lead while she took me where she wanted to go. Kerry was certainly not a dog dangerously out of control, rather a dog dangerously in control! Of course, the contrast with Paulette was like comparing a lamb with a lion, but was hardly Kerry's fault. She had been bred for the chase and any attempts by her owners to calm down this aspect of her nature while she was a puppy had obviously failed.

Kerry

It was bad enough that she launched herself on the streets of Shortlands as if in search of John Peel 'and the fox from his lair', but much worse was her reaction when she saw Piedy. Fortunately she was on a lead but, with Kerry baying at full throttle, I was flown up the stairs and along the landing in reluctant pursuit of my terrified darling, who took leaping refuge on top of a wardrobe. I am afraid that was it as far as we were all concerned. To have Piedy so frightened, never mind in actual peril of his life, was something not to be countenanced and, if it had been thought through properly before we tried her, poor Kerry would never have come to us. She had to go back.

Once bitten we were very shy but my father had good memories of his parents' wire-haired fox terrier, Hamish. So, when we heard of a Lakeland terrier living in a flat in Chelsea who was finding her London life too confining, we thought this could be the answer. At least she would be small and manageable. We began to have some doubts when Debbie's doctor owner handed over, not only a smallish dog but also a large packet of bromide tablets 'for her nerves'. I am not sure we ever got as far as trying to take her out for a walk or introducing her to the cat. Almost as soon as her guilt-stricken owner had departed and we were chatting to Debbie in the living-room, thinking she was quite a sweet little thing, our one and only telephone rang in the next room. Debbie was transformed into a snarling, yelping, whirling dervish, attacking the door of the living-room and threatening anyone who dared to attempt an exit by that route. The phone could not be answered. Calm was restored once the instrument had given up on us, but this did not augur well and soon chaos erupted again as a friend of mine from a few doors up the road, who had heard that we were trying a new little dog, called to meet her. Said friend made the mistake of ringing the front door bell and the Hound from Hell was again let loose amongst us. We looked helplessly at each other, not knowing who was at the front door but agreeing that it would be the normal response to answer it. In a moment of inspiration I volunteered to climb out through the window while the dog was distracted, entrenched in her campanological warfare which made the whole world her enemy. Poor Debbie, probably inbred and certainly too hypersensitive for anybody's good, she was not for us either.

Two attempts at rescue dogs did not encourage any of us to try third time lucky, but neither was it an option to remain for much longer without a dog. Thus it was decided to start all over again, but this time to find a puppy who would be more tailored to our family's needs. Shandy duly arrived at about eight weeks old. He had no pedigree but was a sound mixture of collie and Labrador or retriever, with the good humour of the latter and the intelligence of the former. He was a glorious golden colour (reminding my father of a favourite tipple) with a white tip to his tail and a star on his forehead. When he came to us he was at the puppy-fat cuddly stage. Of course he was mischievous and needed house-training, but what a relief to have an animal of a size and temperament we could enjoy. He bounced around Piedy, wanting him to play, and the cat responded with a gentle biff on the nose. That was their relationship sorted. The cat was boss but would tolerate a fair bit of cheek from this harmless small newcomer, who amused us by his attempts to travel the stairs, wiggling up them on his short little legs in a fashion reminiscent of a caterpillar or indeed a Woofapoof. My father was quick to spot the resemblance and, within days of his arrival, Shandy had an established nickname. He was known as Woofah, the Woofah or just Woofie. Of course to most people it was merely a rather unoriginal pet name relating to barking, but we of the inner circle knew differently, the more so as Shandy proved to be something of a comedian and would have done well in panto.

It was not long before his rotund, small shape gave way to a more gangling long legged one. He could run fast, of course, but with nothing like the grace and speed of Paulette, and his hunting instincts seemed to be confined to chasing trains in the park or, to be more accurate, racing alongside them as they whizzed along the track on the safe side of the fencing. It is one of the endearing quirks of the English language that we talk about 'going to catch' a train or a bus, which conjures up for me a picture of someone with a huge butterfly net in frantic pursuit of very large prey. So, whereas we could say with some accuracy of Paulette, 'she's going to catch a rabbit', it became family parlance to refer to a walk in the park as 'taking Shandy to catch a train'. He could also give a good passing imitation of a kangaroo when he was in very long grass, as he would leap a considerable height above it as he sprang around with his laughing head popping up first here, then there, as he travelled, making us laugh too with his virtuoso performance in the 'hoppity grass'.

Shandy had something of the Labrador's devotion to food, but was not a thief. He did not need to be for he devised a much more subtle approach to having his way with us. At our meal-times he would pick up his own food dish and solemnly bring it to each family member in turn, holding it out for food parcels. It was against many a principle of dog training but impossible to resist this self-taught trick of the begging bowl, which always entertained visitors and earned the bowl bearer satisfying rewards.

Shandy

Shandy was a resounding success. We all loved him, but my relationship with him was a very different one from that which I had had with Paulette. After all, she had been the companion of my early childhood, a companion to an only child until I was turned seven. Shandy was very much the whole family's friend, and much as I loved him, my sister was probably closer to him than I was. I was busy growing towards young adulthood and, anyway, I had pole position with Piedy, from whom I learned so much.

My sister, meanwhile, was also devoted to her tortoise. Tina had a hole in her shell through which a string was attached so she could not get lost (I hope this was not cruel) and was carefully put to bed each winter. My sister was so fond of Tina that, for one of her birthdays, I bought Sheila three china tortoises, ranging from small to tiny, the idea being that they would keep her company while Tina was in hibernation. Not content to wrap them up and present them as gifts I hit on the idea of putting them in a neat row in the slow wake of the wandering Tina, then calling excitedly to my sister that it looked as if Tina had had babies in the night. Sheila's face was a picture of surprised disbelief as she looked down from her bedroom window onto this new grouping on the lawn. But her face did not change to a delighted smile as I had expected, far from it, she was horrified, apparently thinking these three small creatures were some sort of parasitic threat to her Tina Tortoise. So, with extreme caution and armed with a stick, out she went to confront these dangerous aliens. She crept up on them till the reality of the little ornaments was obvious. Then there was relief, wry amusement and some considerable annoyance at having been conned by her big sister, and who could blame her?

My sister was not the only one I conned. I was always a little afraid of my father and his irascible temper but, more than once, I found a way of getting what I wanted by being devious. The most famous time was when I grew desperate to have my bedroom redecorated. It really was very frowsy but I was well aware that there was no hope of persuading my father to spend the necessary money on such frivolous luxury. However, he had the Achilles' heel of being neurotic about the dangers of woodworm – quite overblown for, as we now know, woodworm can be swiftly and efficiently eradicated with little expense. With the connivance of my mother and sister I launched an unscrupulous plan. Taking one of my father's drills from the garage I carefully chose a drill bit* that would match the size of a hole left by the offending insects. Then, climbing on a chair, I went round my bedroom leaving a trail of little holes in the picture rail for my father to find, for I knew that, every so often, he checked a room to convince himself that the woodworm peril had not arrived. I was fairly sure that he had not yet had a good peer round my own room and patiently waited for this to happen. When it did so, a week or two later, I was amazed that he was so completely taken in. 'Rounder than round they are. You couldn't drill a hole as round as that if you tried,' he said. 'Come and have a look Mary.' Mary duly went to view and was suitably impressed with the general roundness of the holes! She then tentatively asked what he thought we should do about it. There was to be no messing about. Down with the infected picture rail and, since that would leave an unsightly mark all round the room, it would have to be redecorated, so I had better think what wallpaper I would like. Game, set and match. I could hardly believe my luck. I had only a slight twinge of conscience, for my bedroom certainly needed its refurbishment.

I was usually an honest and very truthful girl but, in this instance, I decided that mum was definitely the word, and neither my little sister nor my own mum were going to spill any beans. I was thrilled with my new look bedroom but, from a safe distance in time after all this had happened, my conscience finally pricked me into confessing the truth to my father. However, he was not having it, 'No, no, Mary, those holes were rounder than round.' He was totally convinced that the holes had been genuine and, if not all of them, then at least some of them, certainly enough to justify the major overhaul of that room. I knew very well that there had never been a hole in sight before

I wielded that drill but it was hardly worthwhile labouring the point. I had committed the perfect crime, so perfect that even when I confessed to it I still got away with it. I suppose it might have given me ideas for a career as a con artist, but all those years of school assemblies with their Do As You Would Be Done By messages had worked too powerfully upon me. As a criminal I had peaked too early and never struck gold again.

Tina Tortoise and her babies!

Chapter 11

Lessons and Loss

My schooldays were drawing to a close with the two most enjoyable years of my secondary education; farewell to the misery of mysterious maths, here was concentration on the three subjects at which I was best and which I liked the most - English, French and History. During these two years I also played a lead role in the school play, bringing my French and my acting talents together, for the school in its wisdom had chosen to perform *Le Barbier de Seville* by Beaumarchais. Being Goody Two-Shoes*, I was learning my words for my role as Rosine during my summer sojourn in France, to the delighted amusement of my French family, so that I was word perfect for the first rehearsal. As a cast we had fun putting on this play, but for the audience, trying to follow the twists and turns of a plot which is complicated enough in translation, let alone performed in the original French, it must have been challenging to the point of boredom, if not extreme torture. It says much for my own family's loyalty that they managed to appear enthusiastic, and I was left on that glorious high that actors feel on the wings of a successful performance, only dampened by the sense of anti-climax at the end of a run which in this case was a mere three days.

Of more enduring use to me, than this brief pinnacle of dramatic experience, were the weekly sessions in the sixth form on the appreciation of both Art and Music. The classes formed the basis for what little knowledge I have in these subjects and I was also involved in some self-help. With my friend Anne, I would catch the number 12 bus up to London, go straight to the Old Vic where we would book gallery seats for whatever Shakespeare was playing that afternoon, and then spend two or three hours exploring London sights and visiting a gallery or two. Another friend was studying Music for 'A' level and she was my operatic mentor. She and I would go to Sadlers Wells, where *Eugene Onegin* made a huge impression on me and it has remained a favourite opera ever since. It also provided a salutary lesson about life in the grown-up world, for I had always assumed that my teachers - having that ultimately impressive qualification of 'A Degree' - must know all there was to know (and quite a lot more) about their chosen subjects. So it was an astonishing revelation to hear our excellent Music teacher say, when telling us about current musical events in London, that she knew nothing about the opera *Eugene Onegin*. My friend and I exchanged surprised but smug glances.

My parents and my teachers had opposing views as to what should happen when I left school. My mother could see no point in my going to university, thinking I should train as a shorthand typist and become secretary to someone important - presumably a man. She had allegedly trained in this way herself, but I never saw her use a typewriter or make a shorthand note. Perhaps she was now trying to relive her own lost opportunity through me. My father was strangely quiet about my future career path, and seemed content to follow my mother's thinking. Miss Yarmsley of course wanted me to get a good degree and to become a schoolteacher. Left to my own devices I would have chosen to go to drama school, but here the joint forces of parents and school were ranged against me, so St James's Secretarial College in London it was for about three months, when I did finally rebel. I became bored witless with the endless pounding at a typewriter, and was quite unable to take the finer points of touch-typing seriously enough - it seemed such a fuss about nothing. I enjoyed the shorthand more, as that was akin to learning a language, but I began to feel I needed to spread both mind and wings, and wondered if working with 'those less fortunate than ourselves' would be an opening for me. In those days it was not done to take a year out between school and university so in many people's eyes I was 'wasting' a year by delaying university. There was a way round this, as I could take a two year certificate in Social Administration and then follow it up with a post graduate Diploma in Social Studies, thus being fully qualified in three years rather than four. My parents must have wondered what had hit them as their usually pliable daughter turned her life round, leaving St James's and gaining a place at Queen's College Dundee (then part of St Andrew's University). My view was that if I was going to leave home to study I might as well do it in style, and Scotland had a certain ring to it.

Once the university place was mine, there were several months of the year to fill before the term began in the autumn, and it seemed a good idea to gain different sorts of experience before settling down to academic study. I spent a week or two at the sharp end of social work at the Peckham Settlement in south London, and then had two or three temporary jobs. It was while I was fumbling towards competence as a waitress in the big Bromley department store of Medhursts, that Piedy became ill; a large lump came up on his throat and the vet diagnosed cancer. The vet, Mr Rutheridge, knew only too well what this meant, as he himself was a victim of throat cancer - his voice being produced by a kind of burping through a hole in his neck. There was no escaping the bitter truth; at a mere eight or nine years old, it was a death sentence for Piedy. He would have only a week or two before he began to be very uncomfortable, and in those days there was no veterinary surgery or treatment that could help him.

Piedy himself was unaware of the menace looming over him and remained his angelic purring self. While at work, I could (just about) shut the pain away, but when I came home to Piedy's usual delighted welcome, the tears welled up and I would spend much of the evening with him on my knee, stroking him, talking to him, loving him and - I suppose - both saying goodbye and preparing myself for that final parting. It seemed strange that on the evening I came home knowing he would not be there, despite my mother's tearful face, I felt little emotion. This in itself upset me as I thought there was something wrong with me, but later in my social work training I learnt about anticipatory grieving, how grieving in advance of the event prepares your emotions for the shock of parting, so that when it comes it is easier to cope.

There was another lesson drawn from losing Piedy. My mother did not tell me till months later that she would never be able to forget the look on our cat's face as she left him at the vet's. Mr Rutheridge, meaning to be kind had said he would see to everything, there was no need for her to stay, but afterwards my mother bitterly regretted not having insisted on being with Piedy at the end. I was eighteen. No one had suggested that I should have been there, and I suppose I still felt enough of my mother's little girl to feel the need for some protection from such hard reality. I don't think it occurred to any of us that such a grown-up thing should be expected of me, but my mother's words had a lasting effect. She told me that she had made a promise to herself that day - never again would an animal in her care be left feeling abandoned and betrayed at the end. I took this to my heart, thinking how right she was, promising myself that I, too, would always endeavour to honour that code in the future. Piedy was a cat who knew both how to give and to receive love. He knew nothing but kindness and affection in his life with us, except for that one moment at the end, which we so much regretted. However, it was his legacy to me and to all the animals I have loved since, that (barring accidents) I have enjoyed quality time with them towards the end of their lives and been with them to offer comfort at the last . . .

Another Sleep

How many times have I caressed your head

or touched the warm relax of fur

or watched you sleep

your paw across your nose?

And this is but another sleep,

where I am here to hold you through,

until you float into the stars

or some eternal garden.

Chapter 12

A Prince By Any Other Name . . .

Perhaps it was fortunate for me that the loss of Piedy more or less coincided with my leaving home for the summer, to work in the office of a holiday camp near Bognor Regis, thus filling the time before I packed my bags for university, to begin my training for social work in the September. Thus it fell to my mother and sister to find another cat, and my sister very much wanted a kitten this time. A friend of my mother's knew of some 'lovely kittens' and, on this recommendation, a tiny fluffy tabby bundle arrived. I had the honour of giving the new baby her name. She reminded me so much of all those little French cats I had learnt to address as *Minou* so I suggested this possibility. Everyone liked it and thought it a pretty name which suited her. Minou may have been young and small but she knew how to puff herself up to three times her true size and spit ferociously at Shandy when he approached her, causing him to back off gingerly and treat her with respect thereafter. They were not close friends but they lived together amicably enough and my sister has a recollection on the memory quilt which totally eludes me, that they would sometimes work in concert, Shandy apparently chasing some hapless squirrel under the large garden shed (actually more of a garden playroom or summer house) and Minou pouncing on the creature, killing it as it emerged at the other side. None of that sounds very likely to me; why on earth would any self-respecting squirrel dive under a shed rather than escaping up a tree or fence? But my sister saw it happen and knows it to be true so who am I to argue? She also remembers the resourceful Minou raiding the cooking pot on the stove and tossing down tasty morsels to Shandy. I am afraid I don't remember this either but we certainly had something similar happen between a cat and dog when I had a home of my own.

Minou was always nervous and never fully outgrew her near feral ancestry, but my sister was very fond of her, and Minou in her turn coped with Shandy while making a best friend of the rabbit, Toby Bun. He was a large, black and white Dutch, who had come to us from some friend of Sheila's who could no longer keep him. He was a star rabbit and had a much happier life than my poor Flopsy. Shandy was no threat to him, so Toby wore a little collar and was on a long leash on the lawn, where he could hop about at will all day, enjoy the taste of fresh grass and the company of his feline friend, for Minou and Toby were really close buddies. They would sit side by side for hours and even have play fights. Shandy would trot over once in a while to make it a threesome – a harmonious trio.

Minou and Toby Bun

I was very much on the edge of these events as my university career had begun and I was busy falling in love with Scotland (while in Dundee) and then Northumberland (while in Newcastle) – not to mention the relationship with my first fiancé. I emerged, as planned, a qualified social worker after three years. I was appointed to the Family Welfare Association in south London, working at its Lewisham office and once more residing in the family home, now an attractive house in Ashmere Avenue, about a mile from where we had lived before, my parents having moved while I was in Dundee.

It was while I was working for FWA that Prince entered our lives. I first met him in a rather grotty council flat in Deptford. He was a pretty dog, black-and-tan with an enquiring look in his bright eyes. He was about the same size as Shandy but with a fluffier coat. He was of course a 'mix up' but, because of the deep tan colour and a few purple spots on his tongue, we thought he might have chow in him. Prince had been brought home by the son of the family, who had rescued him from some unpleasant situation or other. Both dog and family were delighted with their new friendship but, unfortunately, the council was not, as dogs were not permitted in blocks of flats. So Prince had to go. I was as upset by this as was the family, especially as the dog adored me and made a huge fuss whenever I visited. I said I would see what I could do to get him happily rehomed. The Blue Cross were very helpful, but made the not unreasonable point that if Prince went to them he would become their responsibility and, although they would guarantee to do their best for him, it was not their practice to allow people parting with a dog to have follow-up information. I was not comfortable with this and I knew the family would not be either. So I suggested I try to rehome Prince somewhere local to Beckenham so that I could keep in touch with the new owner and hear how he was getting on. This may not have been wise, nor very professional, but this was a dog several of us had come to love.

The detail is hazy here but, so far as I remember, in response to my advertisement a very pleasant woman and her daughter got in touch, and I collected Prince one Saturday morning from the tearful family in Deptford and took him to his potential new home. This gave me the chance to check on the sort of people they were and that they had a dog-proofed garden. In their turn they could meet Prince and see if they thought they liked him. This 'interview' went very well. The two women thought Prince was a lovely, friendly dog, he liked them and they were more than happy to stay in touch to report on how things were going. The understanding was that the dog would be with them for a week 'on approval' before anyone was totally committed. I left the house congratulating myself on a job well done.

The job felt a little less well done when, three hours later, the telephone rang to say that Prince had gone frantic after I left, was leaping over the fence out of the garden and that it was a miracle that they had managed to recapture him. He was now secure, but most unhappy in the house, and would I please come and collect him! There was no arguing with this. Thank goodness Prince had not bolted, never to be seen again. He was rapturous to see me of course and there was a touching reunion with his family back in Deptford. However, the problem was not solved.

I gave my clients what reassurance I could that all would yet be well and came home somewhat depressed, to my own family setting. I was not driving at this time so it may be that my father had been helping with the ferrying that day. Even if my parents had not, at this stage, met Prince, they certainly knew all about him and the issues involved. In certain kinds of crises my parents could be wonderfully supportive and this was one of them. They suggested that we experiment to see if Shandy would accept Prince and that, if the two animals got on, we should become a two dog household.

Meanwhile, my love life had become something of a three, if not a four, horse race. To keep my dramatic leanings satisfied, when I came back to live at home I had joined a local amateur society called Parklangley Players, where one of the members was a particularly handsome and attractive young man. I was not immune to his charms and it made me realise that what I was feeling for my then fiancé was not enough to justify marriage. I suppose many of us have these emotional muddles in our lives and, if we are lucky, it happens while we are young and we then emerge with the right partner for a stable long-lasting relationship. This was certainly what happened to me. I agonised for weeks, was upset, guilty but ultimately determined. I broke off my engagement and began going out with the aforesaid Dish of Delights, who my mother thought was a much more suitable proposition than my erstwhile fiancé.

But then there was Graham, who was on the casting committee for the first play I was in and later played Clarence Whiteheart (clean hands and clean heart) to my Arabella in a spoof melodrama. Then he was the father to my daughter in *His Excellency*. Much of this on-stage activity was happening under heart-rending circumstances for Graham as, off-stage, I was messing him about horribly. For the other members of Parklangley Players it must have been better than a soap opera, watching the shifting romantic patterns. At one stage The Dish ditched me, leaving me forlorn, so that I accepted a date from Graham, and it was during this phase that he too met Prince for the first time and was very helpful. However, The Dish then reappeared and swept me off for a few more months, even coming with me to spend a weekend on Mersea, staying with my grandparents (Pop and Nanny) who by then had left marital storms behind them and found their Darby and Joan* haven in Cadeby, the house which had been their holiday home before the war. Like many second homes theirs had been requisitioned by the army for much of the conflict, been sadly abused during that time then had taken several years to be returned to its owners in the early fifties, in a more than sorry state. However, my grandparents had soon made it a comfortable place to live in again and I had loved visiting them over the years. They were always pleased to see me and, in this instance, also gave a handsome welcome to The Dish.

What with the Mersea weekend, then an idyllic one in a hotel in the Malvern Hills, I was in heaven until he proposed to me. This proposal, which surely was what I had been hoping for, frightened me silly. It was as if my eyes suddenly sprang open and I could see to the inner man. He may have been The Dish or a knight in shining armour but the dish was empty under the cover and the suit of armour hollow. What had I done? Would I ever find Mr Right? Was I on the shelf at 23? Panic set in for a few days then, quite suddenly, an irrational calm descended with the certain knowledge that I would be married by the time I was 25. To whom was less clear.

Living out one's romantic turmoil under the parental roof is not ideal. My mother, in particular, tried to push me to break the engagement, which actually made it more difficult, as I had to be sure I was doing it for the right reasons, not just to please her. She initially favoured The Dish, while my father took instantly to Graham. They watched the unfolding saga somewhat mystified. In all, it took four Parklangley productions to travel from first beginnings to happy ending. Soon after the abortive proposal The Dish ran off with a Spoon, becoming engaged to her instead. Subsequently I bumped into Graham at the local drama festival where he had written and directed his own one act play. Afterwards we talked over a coffee and I realised what I might have thrown away.

One morning in February I answered the door to the postman, knocking like the hand of fate with an unstamped letter in his hand addressed to me. Indignant at being asked to pay some hefty sum the equivalent of 50p I nearly refused to take it, but curiosity prevailed. It was from Graham, asking me to meet him under the clock on Charing Cross Station on 15th March, offering me dinner in a *bistro exotique* to celebrate his birthday. He asked me not to reply but just to keep, or not keep, the tryst, 'as the Good Lord determines.' Keep it I did.

A little wary this time, and who could blame him, Graham suggested a month's pause while we both looked into our own hearts, not communicating with each other at all. At the end of that month we would meet and see how we felt, although I think we both already knew. The Pause ended in a restaurant called Salamis, 'hard by the Fulham Road'*. I was to play Sheila Birling (the fiancée) in *An Inspector Calls*, from the Wednesday to the Saturday of the following week, a production in which Graham was not involved, but I floated through the performances on a pink bubble of happiness. Graham's hoped-for proposal came on a lumpy sofa in his Kensington apartment on the Sunday after the play had finished. This time the response was not only a thrilled, 'Yes please', but a push from me to make our marriage sooner rather than later.

My parents and sister had gone away to Cornwall for two weeks just before the play opened and, anyway, I had recently been playing my love life much closer to my chest. However, when I rang to say that I had some good news for them when they came home, my father had apparently said,'I think Mary's going to marry Graham,' to which my mother replied 'Oh, don't be so silly, John!' Thus, when I made the announcement a few days later, while I was touched to see my father turn pink and puff up with pleasure – an almost unheard of occurrence – I was not sure whether this was due entirely to his delight at my forthcoming marriage to the man he had always favoured, or merely the exultation of having been, for once, proved right. Probably a little of both.

Back at Parklangley Players there was astonishment, disbelief and some rejoicing. There was disappointment too, as there was at least one female member who would have gladly swept Graham to her, while my leading man and stage fiancé from *The Inspector* plucked up courage to ask me out just in time to be told that I was engaged to Graham. I am sure many people, including Graham's father, wrote me off as a heartless, feckless hussy and felt very sorry for my future husband. But Graham's brother had apparently said to him of me, 'Marry that!' My future mother-in-law wrote me a heart-warming letter welcoming me unreservedly into the family, thrilled to see her Graham happy at last, while my own mother soon recovered from the disappearance of the Dish, recognising that in Graham she would have a more than satisfactory son-in-law.

We were married in March 1967, ten days before my 25th birthday and not a day too soon for poor Minou. Shandy had indeed accepted Prince. Graham had kindly chauffeured me to pick him up once more from Deptford, and the dogs had been introduced on the neutral territory of the train-chasing park. They liked each other straightaway and we simply walked them back to Ashmere Avenue side by side. It could not have been easier. We later came to see this encounter as amazing, for our lad from Deptford could be quite aggressive to other male dogs, especially if they were on a lead. It must have been written in the stars, for everyone (except Minou) fell in love with him. My father renamed our erstwhile Prince *Tolly* after a favourite brand of ale, and would take off proudly for the local pub with a merry cry of 'Mush!' as his two-dog team dragged him enthusiastically out through the door and down the road for a swift pint.

But for Minou it was misery. Not that Tolly chased her but he was an alien animal on her territory. She missed her beloved Toby Bun who had left us a few months before, having lived his life to the full. Minou would now hardly go out, skulking in Sheila's bedroom or burrowing into the far reaches of the airing cupboard, places where she felt relatively, but only relatively, safe. We all felt sorry for her but, fortunately, the end of the disruption was in sight, for I was about to have a home of my own and so was Tolly. Two weeks after the wedding in March 1967 Graham and I were back from honeymoon on the Scillies to collect our ready-made dog, taking him to help us start our married life in a small Essex village in a lath and plaster cottage called Glenmore.

Tolly

Chapter 13

Some Years Revisited

1967 – 2002

This period of time is detailed in the earlier books . . .

A Cat in My Lap **and** ***Dear Dear Mary.***

Living at home with parents as a young adult has its snags and it is exciting suddenly to be joint producer/director of your own home movie show, with all the responsibilities that go with it. However, we were getting married before the days of the universal credit card and the idea of hire-purchase had been instilled into us as anathema by our respective families. Thus, we were happy to start married life with much that was second-hand, including the marital bed with the dip in the middle and an evil-minded spin-dryer which rattled in enraged pirouettes round the kitchen, spewing its spun water over the floor, over me, over everywhere except into its designated bucket.

People were generous to us and many asked to see our wedding list, which had been compiled by the bride, as was the custom, to avoid the hazard of receiving 11 well-meaning toasters but no kettle. I recently came across this historic document (minus any mention of a toaster as we had thought them too unreliable) but complete with the price of each requested item. I was reminded that Graham and I had worked on the principle that a good pair of kitchen scissors was as essential to married bliss as the hum of a hoover, so we had given prospective donors plenty of opportunity to suit their pockets, while receiving equal plaudits. The said hoover at £35 sounds very expensive for those days, but somewhere between that and the kitchen scissors at a few shillings, came a set of eight melamine table mats at £5-11s-6d. These have become old friends and are still as good as new, thanks to advice given to me by my father, who would have been the world's worst housewife yet occasionally came up with a gem like this one, no doubt picked up from his childhood nanny, 'Never stack mats as you clear them from the table, the backs will get ruined over time. Always wipe their fronts clean and then put them front to front and back to back'. It sounds very fussy, but this advice has kept the green felted backing on my mats pristine after more than 40 years of use. These same mats caused amusement in the distant days of our dinner parties, for each has a different,

beautifully illustrated bird on it, one or two of which must be foreign as they are very brightly-coloured and thus could be accepted as being 'marlins'. But then puzzled guests, who could have sworn they were looking at a blue tit or a bullfinch, found that they too had a marlin beneath their dinner plate. It took a while for the penny to drop that the name against the bird belonged not to that feathered friend but to the artist, a Mr A Marlin.

Sam

Our chosen village of White Roding was a friendly one and, since we were working on the cottage at weekends for a few months before the wedding, we knew several people even before we moved in. Arriving as newly-weds with a dog, the essential cat had already been booked to join us soon afterwards, from a house just down the road. This was Sam, a black fluffy kitten who was to be the first in our pageant of cats – a pageant always underscored with the dogs that came into our lives. In a sense Sam was our first baby and he was certainly Graham's first experience of a cat in the family. Moreover, if I have to admit to having a favourite in terms of feline appearance, then Sam and cats of his kind fill that niche, for he had the half Persian coat of the long-haired moggy, a coat that was still easy to care for but of an irresistibly soft texture. He was black, with a slight over-colour of brown but, despite the feel of his coat Sam was not the 'softie' I had known in Piedy. He was much more typically 'cat' in character, coming to call only when he felt like it, standoffish for a while on our return if we had dared to leave him for a few days, yet devoted in his way, and especially bonded to me after I had nursed him back to health after a nasty accident.

Being a pet owner or, in modern parlance, an animal companion's companion, carries with it many joys but also the sadness of partings and, of course, we have had our share. Our nine years in Essex saw the arrival of our two sons, Harry and Hugo, but sadly, after about five years, the loss of Tolly to kidney failure. He was replaced with another black-and-tan rescued mix-up, but this time smooth-coated, female and only four to five months old.

Timandra (Timma) grew up with the children, and though it was sad to lose Tolly, there were positives in having a young spirit about the place who could do her growing up alongside the boys, for by this time Harry was about four and Hugo a few months old. Although Tolly had been perfectly trustworthy with the children he had not wanted to romp and play with them in the way that comes naturally to a puppy and, although Timma had the sharp teeth reflecting her young age, there was never any need for the referee to blow the whistle during any of the games they played together. And the boys grew up with a love of dogs as part of their being. Sam, on the other hand, was never very interested in the children and they, in turn, while having nothing against cats, grew up to be less drawn to them.

We had bought Glenmore in the summer of 1966, arriving as a married couple in spring 1967. It was November 1975, with the team of Harry, Hugo, Sam and Timma in place, that Graham and I moved north to Cheshire. It was also the beginning of Graham's long association with the Co-op, working at its head office in Manchester. We settled about 20 miles away in Macclesfield, in the stone-built cottage that was Throstles' Nest.

Sam, who was delighted with his new surroundings, tragically succumbed, like Tolly, to nephritis less than a year after the move. It was a hard blow, but it is sometimes said that creativity grows from trauma and, with the loss of Sam, came the discovery that I enjoyed writing and that, with practice, I could become better at it. Mine would never be great poetry but sometimes passable light verse – a verse that would lead me back to performing for, on the strength of it, I joined a local poetry group called *Tarantula*. With them I read, not only my own work but ventured into parlour poetry, then eventually into Shakespeare and the metaphysical poets. There was the opportunity here for costume, a few props and the chance to work alongside skilled musicians, performing for audiences at Buxton Festival and in two of the historic houses of the area with their wealth of old timbers and wavy floors.

Timma

Moses and Aaron

Sam had been so special to us, being our first cat, that he was a hard act to follow. So it seemed fitting, as a mark of respect, that we look for some special quality in his replacement. The plan, therefore, was to have a Colourpoint kitten accompanied by some little moggy in need of a good home. However, events conspired to turn this plan into two Colourpoints, whom we called Moses and Aaron.

Colourpoints are known for their soft affectionate dispositions, their round, blue eyes and full Persian coats. Nonetheless, our two had hugely differing personalities. Moses grew to be as independent as befits the dignity of any cat and to patrol all the neighbours' gardens. Aaron, with his slightly weepy eye and mournful crying to be picked up and endlessly cuddled, was a wimp, hardly a proper cat at all but oh how we loved him, and how Moses and Aaron loved each other. Two was indeed company, good company, but, after a couple of years we were to grow to a crowd, for one cold November morning outside the boys' school I found a small, grubby, black-and-white cat desperately trying to break and enter the warmth of the school cloakroom.

Timma, who was with me, was both interested in, and accepting of, the small furry bundle tucked into the warmth of my jacket. Moses, after one astonished yowl on sighting the intruder, made no further protest at assimilating Nelle and her little pink nose into the household, and Aaron, as you might expect, was a pussycat about it. The little cat's full name was to be Villanelle as her arrival coincided with my first completed attempt at this strict poetic form (a poem with repeating lines) which she helped me to polish, purring on my knee while I tried to recapture an aspect of that year's summer holiday, spent on Menorca in the beautiful, old stone farmhouse of friends, bright with bougainvillaea, under blue skies decorated with circling buzzards . . .

Menorcan Hawk

Artist on the sky's trapeze
Graceful in a curving sway
Buzzard on the heat hot breeze

Circling with a restless ease
Feathered fingers shadowed splay
Artist on the sky's trapeze.

Scattered groups of twos and threes
Purpose in the air display
Buzzard on the heat hot breeze.

Piercing watch of rocks and trees
Over grass worn brown and grey
Artist on the sky's trapeze.

Registered, a moment's freeze
Golden poise above the prey
Buzzard on the heat hot breeze.

Merciless spike talons seize
Stunning through the blue of day
Artist on the sky's trapeze
Buzzard on the heat hot breeze.

The winter of 1980-81 was one of the coldest we had ever known, starting with snow in early December which was to stay till well after Christmas. And it was during this mini Ice Age that my parents moved up to Macclesfield from Mersea Island, where they had been living after leaving Beckenham when my father retired. He was now not very well and it seemed a good idea to most of us that they should move from Essex to be nearby, thus enabling us to offer support. So my parents came to live a seven minute walk away from us, and my father, having resisted the move almost to the point of self-induced collapse, took to his new surroundings with the enthusiasm of someone who has seen his own inspired plan come to fruition, whereas my poor mother, who had valiantly held her ground throughout the difficulties of the hard won campaign, never felt totally at home in the North West. She pined for the sea and open skies of East Anglia.

It was not a perfect solution but, on balance, was probably the right one. Certainly it was a relief to me to have my parents close by. Harris, their character of a tortie cat was thrilled with her new home, while Cindy, their 14-year-old gentle collie-mix dog, who had come close to being put to sleep that last summer in Mersea, took on a new lease of life, responding gratefully to the improved veterinary care she found in Macclesfield, and revelling in the companionship she found with Timma.

1983 was what the Queen would have called our *annus horribilis*. There were so many negative happenings in and around our little lane that we began to feel spooked. The worst of these for me was the death of my dear, soppy, trusting Aaron. Hazel, my close friend and near neighbour, found his body on her doorstep when she returned from shopping one day in June, and we can only think that he had somehow managed to get run over outside her house, but any detail remains a mystery.

As is often the way, when you want a kitten you cannot find one, and there were no Colourpoints available to comfort the distressed Moses. Thus it was left to fate to solve the problem, which she did in December 1983 when I found a cat, run over and lying unconscious in the road, while I was driving round to visit my parents. After extensive treatment and a long stay at the vet's, this semi-flattened moggy came to live with us on New Year's Eve 1983. His name chose itself, for Graham and I were having one of our bursts of trying to learn German, thus we also knew December 31st as *Silvester*. It felt as if this cat had been sent by some kindly force to break the mould of the previous year, and to bring us happier times.

Silvester was indeed a healing influence. He was affectionate with everyone, cheerful through any adversity, had an impish sense of humour and was an instant success with Moses. They were best friends within days of their introduction, thus making an established team of three again, Moses, Silvester, and Nelle who had certainly missed Aaron too. She had never had the same bond with him but, a few days after his death she was taken very ill and vomited fit to bring her heart up. Where? On Aaron's grave.

In a garden our size this was surely no mere coincidence. So Nelle needed comfort too and she took well to Silvester, even if he did tease her sometimes. But then everyone took to Silvester for he was such a likeable chap.

We were back to three not feeling a crowd, unaware, until 1985, that the optimum cat number is four. Sadly, a close friend of mine died very suddenly, leaving Daisy May in need of a home – Daisy the diva. Pure white, green-eyed, slenderly elegant and incurably vain, she had a feisty will of her own but, once recovered from the indignity of being rehomed, she settled down well enough with the other three cats, liking Silvester even though she thought he did not take her quite seriously enough. Nelle (pronounced Nellie) was glad to have a female companion and they built a cosy, all-girls-together relationship in which the 'boys' were sometimes allowed to share.

Moses, Silvester, Daisy May, Nelle

Meanwhile, Timma had her own close female companionship with my parents' dog Cindy. Two elderly ladies ageing gracefully together and, in the autumn of 1986, both slipping gently from us . . .

Going Gentle*

Autumn is the soft goodbye.

Slowly the trees undress

let fall a shawl of gold

to warm the earth

and make a promise

of spring flowers.

Rosie entered our lives in January 1987 at the age of seven weeks, a Labrador/collie cross, a mix for which I coined the term *Labradollie* long before the name *Labradoodle* was invented. She truly was a bit of a 'doll', a honey of a dog. A golden bundle of affection and fun she was never a scrap of trouble. That is always my first thought when I remember Rosie for we all loved her so much, but it is not quite true. She did have a few faults, the worst of which developed when she was about six-years-old. A quarter of a mile away a field was being developed and Bob the Builder would leave delicious remnants of his sandwiches behind. Somehow Rosie made this discovery and started running off for a sly feast if she could. This would not have been so bad, for at least we knew where she was, but the habit grew and developed well beyond Bob the Builder. Sometimes she would be gone for several hours, leaving me awake half the night worrying about her and muttering, 'I'll kill her when she comes home.' Of course I was always much too relieved to see her even to scold her when she did come back, but nonetheless she knew she had done wrong and, more than once, woke my parents at 3am to be let in there, rightly gauging that my mother would open the door with hardly a raised eyebrow, whereas at home questions would be asked.

Out on a walk Rosie never left us, constantly demanding the throwing of a stick for her to retrieve. These sticks were chosen carefully as we had heard too many horror stories of dogs impaling themselves on sharp ones. Rosie's great escapes always happened from home and they became something of a family joke, known as 'buggering off'. But I was always anxious when they occurred and sometimes they caused more than a minor irritation, like the time she made us three hours late setting off on holiday.

Rosie

When Rosie was two or three years old she acquired a bosom pal of her own with the arrival of Bruno from Windyway, our local animal sanctuary. My parents had always had dogs that lived well into old age but Cindy's immediate successor had not been so lucky. She was a busy little Jack Russell. Her eager face had appeared at the door in the arms of a friendly acquaintance who said, 'I have a problem. I wonder if you and Dandy could help each other out.' Dandy, found abandoned, needed a home. My parents needed a dog. It was a good fit. Small in size, big in personality, she loved not only my mother, but became devoted to my father, lying across the back of his massive armchair, draping her head over one of his shoulders, her hind feet over the other, in a manner reminiscent of those ghastly fox furs.

Dandy was a lively, bossy little dog who kept the puppy that was Rosie in her place. We were all fond of her and I was especially grateful for all the pleasure she gave to my father, for there was no doubt that he was her special person. Dandy gave two years of her devotion before being struck down with a rampant cancer. It was heartbreaking, especially for my father who had found such a loyal little friend. We were all shellshocked and, though usually we would have had much more of a pause, in these circumstances I encouraged my parents to visit Windyway a few days later to see if they could find a likely new companion.

My mother had decided that she wanted a male dog this time, to try to ensure a good relationship with Rosie, whom Dandy had rather bossed and dominated. Nonetheless I have a few guilt pangs about that visit to the animal sanctuary as the dog we came away with was probably not my father's first choice. Unlike all the other contenders who came barking and eager to the wire, Bruno was sitting, shaking, at the back of the run with a desperate pleading in his eyes for someone, please, to rescue him. He was larger than might have been sensible for elderly owners, but he had a dark, fluffy coat and something of the *Labradollie* (or *Collabralad?*) about him, though the only thing certain about his ancestry was that it was uncertain. We were able to take him for a little walk and he hardly pulled at all, while his pleasure at being taken from that scary pen was obvious. My parents now had a ginger-and-white cat called Barnaby so it was important to test Bruno's reaction to cats. This was easy enough since there are always numerous cats at Windyway, some of them wandering freely through the courtyard and grounds, since this has become their permanent home. It was clear that Bruno was no cat killer for he appeared more or less indifferent to them. So it was decided, Bruno came back with us in the car, where he shook and wittered and whined throughout the short journey, and then was travel sick. A few doubts did cross my mind but, nonetheless, there was something about this dog which gave me the feeling that he would prove to have depths of gold.

This was all very well but Bruno was going to my parents, not to me, so it was a risk. Certainly my sister thought so when she first met Bruno. He was much bigger than she had imagined, and was excitable and noisy in his initial welcome of visitors. Nor was his first night overly successful. Wisely, my parents had not shut their new companion in the kitchen but had put an old baby-gate across the stairs to contain him downstairs, and he did settle without too much whimpering. However, the hall carpet was of a darkish floral design, a perfect camouflage for the deposit Bruno left on it – a landmine awaiting my mother's unwary slippers. Fortunately she forgave him and, from then on, his star was in the ascendant.

At Windyway they had told us as much as they could about Bruno's history. He had spent most of his life in a flat in Manchester, adored by his owner who, nonetheless, was at work all day, so that the dog would go frantic with joy on her return. She, in her turn, would anticipate his welcoming face at her window. Then she met someone she loved more, who became her partner and did not like dogs, so that it came down to 'Love me, part with your dog'. She was very upset, but not upset enough to tell this troublesome man where he could go. Feeling very sad, Bruno's owner took him to Windyway where he was quickly rehomed to a man who lived down in Dorset. A week later the poor dog was returned, further traumatised. Dorset Man said Bruno had been chewing the carpets. It transpired that this temporary owner had made little or no attempt to settle the dog in his new surroundings. He had got him home on the Sunday and gone off to work on the Monday morning, leaving him alone in a strange setting. He then expressed surprise that the dog had done damage during the day and possibly had punished him. Few marks then for Dorset Man but at least he had the grace to drive the considerable distance back, returning Bruno to Windyway and another opportunity to find a satisfactory home, which he certainly succeeded in doing once we spotted him.

Bruno was now in surroundings where he was rarely, if ever, left alone, and Graham and I were on hand to make sure he got several good long walks a week. He soon settled and proved to be the most loyal and loveable dog, devoted to my mother, though admittedly never quite bonding with my father as Dandy had done. He never left land mines again and certainly never chewed up anything except doggy treats. One of his remarkable traits was that, for an excitable, lively chap who could easily have pulled my mother off her feet, he always walked gently beside her, neither did he ever grow impatient with my father's slow meanderings round the block. Moreover, he would wait politely during long pauses while my father chatted to people he met on the street or passed in their gardens. On the other hand, when Graham or I took him out with Rosie he would rush about the fields and hills as fast as she did, and they instantly became best friends. My mother was strong and fit enough then to accompany us for some of these walks, venturing into the beauties of the Goyt Valley or along the paths of Macclesfield Forest. (For the record, Graham and I usually called my mother 'Margie' as a term of endearment. It had originated with my cousin Lyn, who, as a little girl, had been staying with us and coined the name 'Auntie Margie'. It stuck.)

As my mother grew older and her hearing deteriorated Bruno was to show himself a self-trained Hearing Dog, for he would bark, not only if the doorbell rang, but also in response to the phone ringing in the hall. To my knowledge Bruno never showed aggression towards anybody as, thankfully, Margie was never threatened by anyone to put his defence of her to the test. But his deep bark, bigger than his actual size, was enough to warn people that there was a large dog about, and he became both her helpmeet and protector – a far cry from the shivering waif we had first spotted at Windyway.

During the late seventies to mid-eighties we grew used to having four cats. It was a good number, so that when we lost our dear little Nelle to illness in 1989 it seemed natural to try to fill the gap, but we waited a while to do this. The new family member was a splendid half Abyssinian, intended by me to be called Taj. However, on his arrival my plan was instantly scuppered by a teenage Hugo who announced that the kitten's name was Bernard and he proceeded to bond with the new arrival in a way that he had never done with any of our previous cats. Somewhat nervous as a youngster Bernard grew to become a macho cat and king of the local terrain. Heaven help us if he had not been neutered.

He grew to be a big cat and a power pack of muscle, lavish with his affection, which could be rather overfacing, leaving scratch marks and love bites all over one's arms. He, like Silvester, would tease Daisy May, which she did not think at all funny, and she would swear at him, in a somewhat unladylike fashion, to put him in his place. He was not aggressive or spiteful, just a young lad who did not know his own strength. He became a good friend to both Silvester and to Moses, whom he respected as senior cat.

Bernard

The number remained at four until Moses gracefully bowed out aged 17. We did not replace him as, by this time, there was a problem with Silvester spraying and we thought it might exacerbate it to introduce another cat. Spraying is of course a nuisance and we never really sussed out why he went through a phase of showing this anti-social behaviour since it is, supposedly, related to stress and Silvester appeared totally at home with everything and everybody – the most relaxed cat you could ever have met. However he was, after all, a cat and that implies territorial concerns. Thus for a few years we were down to three, Silvester and his best friend Bernard, plus diva Daisy May, who was admired, and gradually became less teased, by the 'boys'. She was, nonetheless, a little apart, mostly because of her sense of her own importance, though we think she may have missed the female companionship of Nelle. However, she was very affectionate with us, loved any visiting baby, and had an easy-going relationship with Rosie. We never knew Daisy May's exact age, only that she had been rescued by my friend as a young cat. Her slender, white form thickened as she grew older but she was still a beautiful cat and we had never thought of her as growing old. Therefore, her illness came as a shock although she must have been around 14 when we lost her. It grieved me particularly that I was not with her at the end, for she died at the vet's, only hours after we had been told she was much better and could come home next day.

I told all my cat-minded friends the sad news and, a few days later, one of them, the illustrator Jo Berriman, rang to see if we could help an older friend of hers by offering a home to her cat Amber, who was about four at the time. 'Amber's Mary' was fast losing her sight and was growing generally frail. She needed to go into sheltered accommodation but would not consider it until her beloved Amber had been safely rehomed. It was much sooner than we would usually have taken on a new cat but we did not feel we could say 'no'. It was upsetting to see Mary heartbroken at parting with her friend, and poor Amber found it tough being in a strange place that had two well-established bully boys, as she saw them. So we not only phoned, but wrote letters home, as if from Amber to her 'Dear Mary'. With eccentric feline spelling and huge print Mary's failing eyesight could, just about, cope. It was these letters which slowly blossomed, growing into the book that is *Dear Dear Mary*. It tells the story of how Amber eventually found her feet with us and learned to live with 'Lion' as she called Bernard, though she never really liked him. She was a sweet-natured, gentle little cat, somehow motherly, even though she never had kittens.

Amber grew very fond of Silvester and was most concerned about him when, some years later, his health began to fail. Dramatically, he had a stroke and went blind, though continued to be cheerful through all adversity. When he had first come to us Silvester had had trouble finding his lost purr, needing to practise hard, but once recovered it was seldom out of action. To the end he was one long chirrup and rumble of contentment.

When at last we were down to only two cats, Bernard and Amber, it seemed an opportunity to begin the new millennium by reverting to our optimum cat number of four. The kittens from Crewe arrived in February 2000. Mille and Lenni were our millennium kittens. Long-haired moggies both, this brother and sister had to be two

Amber caring for Silvester

of the most enchanting kittens ever seen. Mille was black, reminding us very much of Sam, while Lenni was a delicious marmalade and white.

Bernard and Amber were somewhat miffed at first. Indeed their shared huffiness about these two little invaders helped to bring them closer together, in a pact of shared disapproval. It was hard, however, even for two huffy, older cats, to resist such little charmers for long. But the improvement in relations between 'Lion' and Amber continued, even when Mille and Lenni had become fully integrated members of the household. However, the real difference to Amber's confidence and lifestyle came with our purchase of a cottage in the Lake District.

Mille and Lenni

Greengarth – as advertised

Chapter 14

Hunting the Hide-out

Graham had joined the Co-op in 1975 to take up the secretaryship of what was then known as the Co-operative Wholesale Society (CWS) at its head office in New Century House, Manchester. The Co-op is a complex animal, and he was to have many a hairy encounter with it as he built his career. However, he rose to be not only the President of the ICA (International Co-operative Alliance) but also the Chief Executive of the CWS itself from 1996 to 2002, where we found it could also be rough at the top.

It was when Graham was about to become Chief Executive that we thought about having a holiday home, either by the sea or in beautiful countryside. Since we wanted to be able to go for weekends it could not be too distant, so the only likely coastline seemed to be that of North Wales but, much as we admire and enjoy its scenery, we did not fancy being regarded as the invading English, so decided against it in favour of the Eden Valley in Cumbria. This came recommended from friends as being less crowded and less expensive than the Lake District. It was also rumoured to have better weather. So off we set for our week's cottage-hunting, armed with a dozen possibilities gleaned from the local papers – eleven of them to the east of the M6 and just one to the west, one which had somehow crept under my wire, if not under Graham's.

Rosie was with us of course and Graham had the unwelcome companionship of a double hernia for which he was awaiting surgery. It was early in March with some late snow still on the ground, so it was not the most propitious of expeditions. Fortunately, the little hotel in Temple Sowerby was warm and welcoming and, though they did not have room service, they made an exception for a cream tea in our room every afternoon, so that Graham could rest up in luxury after a hard day on the country cottage trail. The staff were besotted with Rosie and it may have been the appeal of her brown eyes that won us our room-based scones. She was certainly not averse to hoovering up crumbs.

Many of the potential idylls on our list were already holiday homes with the owners absent. Being empty, viewing these places was consequently more difficult, since it was not always easy to persuade agents that, if they wanted to sell a property, it might be a good idea to provide someone to show us over it. The pace of life is slower in Cumbria and these pushy people from Cheshire were surely being unreasonable to expect to get appointments, let alone find a property, within a week. One or two places we were able to rule out ourselves at an early stage by checking their positions and, as usual with house-hunting, there were several disappointments along the way We did, however, have the positive experience of making friends with an endearing couple who had worked so hard on their Old School House – the very first on our list of 'possibles' to be viewed properly. Although it was not what we wanted the craftsmanship on it was superb and, since Brian was a working joiner, we kept his name and number by us, and were more than glad to use his expertise in later months.

By Wednesday evening we had found only one house which we would even have half considered – a semi-detached stone-built cottage high on Stainton Moor. It was attractive and in good order, with a pleasant, sensibly sized garden. It was also well within budget but the location seemed too wild and bleak. Heathcliffe and Cathy would have been instantly at home there, and later we discovered that it lay not far above that stretch of the A66 which is often closed to high-sided vehicles in strong winds.

At midday on the Thursday we ate a rather dispirited lunch in a pub just north of Penrith, having that morning rejected, with considerable animus, the penultimate possibility on our list. With little hope in our hearts, that afternoon we set off for the final contender of the week which, on paper, had a great deal against it. First, it was a bungalow, which Graham has always said he dislikes. Secondly, it was in the Lake District which we had ruled out. And thirdly, it was on the outer edge of our budget and would probably need a great deal of money spending on it. So why were we even going to look at it? I suppose it had to be that old irrational stand-by, intuition. I had been unreasonably attracted by a tiny and very poor photograph in the paper. Two sad, square eyes had peered at me from under a heavy fringe of tangled greenery which made me think of Sleeping Beauty's Castle (or Cottage if she had been a peasant) and, as I said in persuasive tones to Graham when trying to convince him it might be worth a peep, 'It is in the northern Lakes and they are much quieter.'

We therefore embarked on our daring drive over the border into Lakeland on this wet and windy March day, to seek out our last-hope dwelling. The directions were not hard to follow and we felt a shaft of optimism as we turned off the scenic main road through the village, up the little track, then drove 100 yards or so up to a closed five-barred gate which opened onto the fell belonging to the National Trust. Greengarth lurked 30 yards beyond the gate, forlorn under mighty conifers, rampaging clematis and general overgrowth. The windows were hideous and, once inside, the decor was vintage 1973. It had probably been the last word in country chic then but, to the modern eye now looked tired, neglected and, frankly, naff. We stood in the rather ropey, pine kitchen while the agent searched for something positive to say. Trying not to give the game away, and anyway not sure what Graham was thinking, I said, 'Well it would need an awful lot spending on it.' 'I know,' she sighed, 'I suppose that's why it's been on the market for six months.' Meanwhile, the little house was crying out to me with the strength of all its walls, 'Please, please, somebody love me and make me as beautiful as I deserve to be.'

We walked all round the outside of the building and were enchanted by its situation, for it sat lengthways to its site with its small garden surrounding it, the front door sitting on the long side of the bungalow facing the high stone wall of our neighbours' gardens. To the rear was a pretty little patch of lawn only 15ft deep, which met the hedge-masked wire fence. This separated us gracefully from the piece of land which extended a neighbour's garden into a copse behind our own. The copse then ran down to the stream, which tumbled its music past. On the other long face of the property, which faced roughly west, the garden was only eight feet wide or so, but gave onto a

Greengarth – transformed

lower, dry-stone wall with glorious views straight up the fell. Our only neighbours here would be sheep.

Although the sorrowing eyes of the bungalow peered out into a neglected frontage, which would have to be cleared, the potential charm of its courtyard was obvious even at this stage, for it was sheltered on one side by the pretty little stone barn belonging to neighbours, and on the other by our own barn, an interesting shape despite its flaky, dark green paint and leaking corrugated iron roof. It was certainly rustic and Graham had early designs on it. My own designs were confined to the immediate living space and, long before the deal was signed, my head was whizzing with ideas, the main import being to transform this pitiably sad, boring and neglected square box of a bungalow into a cottage that would be cheery, chunky and cosy. The surveyor's report was surprisingly reassuring, for it seemed that Greengarth had been solidly built, but the plans I had in my head would need people we could trust, preferably sympathetic to some of my more way-out ideas. I had it in mind that Scottish and Irish crofters lived in one storey houses that no one ever referred to as 'bungalows' but as 'cottages', so why should we not follow that pattern with our little place?

Whilst normally supporting the idea of using local people for any work done on our property, at this early stage we did not know any local builders, let alone anyone I was confident would want to work with my pernickety thinking. We were fortunate in having Phil, a good friend and family member, who was an architect skilled at handling planners and, after one false start, we succeeded in gaining permission to add a porch to the building. This would enable the front door to be situated actually at the front of the cottage and, internally would give us some valuable extra space. There was not much else for the planners to worry about. They did not baulk at the idea of French doors looking up the fell, or carp at the new-style windows. How could they, when the old ones were so unsightly? Our Bolton builders were the five star team who had achieved so much for us at Throstles' Nest. They were willing to camp out, in some chaos, two or three nights per week as work progressed. Recycled beams from old mills in Derbyshire were brought up from Buxton and installed to give an impression of age, and the horrible MDF flooring became either ceramic tiles, slate, or recycled, honey coloured planking from the same source as the beams. There had to be a new kitchen, of course, and the re-siting of its doorway helped to create a more amenable work space.

Lighting needed to be special. I find the current fashion for sprinkling the ceiling with viciously dazzling down-lighters, unattractive and boring. They can also be tricky when it comes to bulb changing, and we wanted everything to be as easy as possible for any friends or relatives using the cottage in the future. I like old light fittings, and I had a favourite shop in Camden (alas no more) which had a tempting selection, much of it coming from France. I have conducted many a raid into Homeline over the years as both Throstles' Nest and now Greengarth can bear witness.

In the end the only room which did not have a complete make-over was the bathroom. After much deliberation I decided that the avocado suite was something of a period piece and that we could work round it. We rid ourselves of the beige, genuine-tile-effect-wallpaper, replacing it with cream ceramic tiles interspersed with some hand-painted with daffodils. The new siting of the front door did create a minor difficulty, as anyone standing outside it would have an interestingly direct view into the bathroom! I am no fan of either net curtains or frosted glass but where there is a will there is a specialist glass maker who can create a window that is both beautiful and opaque in all the right places. Our inspired soft furnishings' designer also suggested using shower curtain material at the window, so that night-time privacy had no conflict with dowsing the curtains when showering.

Greengarth's windows were the most obvious change to any passer-by. No longer did those sad 1973 eyes peer out anxiously to the light, but little sparkling panes were set in chunky pine.

It was this transformed cottage which became Amber's haven, her 'No Other Cat House' which she adored, where she built up her confidence so that she could cope so much better with Bernard, feeling settled at last in her life with us at Throstles' Nest.

Chapter 15

Career Paths

Our style of marriage, now of more than 40 years standing, would seem old-fashioned to younger people. I enjoyed being at home; it never occurred to me that I should go out to work when I had the important job of caring for the children. Though admittedly, we were both amused but also shocked, when Harry, at the age of five, while fumbling for the word for 'wife' stuttered out, 'Oh, oh . . . you know what I mean . . . a father's servant.' Out of the mouths of babes? Perhaps. But, as today we see more and more marriages fail, there are surely lessons to be learned about tolerance, not expecting perfection from our partners, and not giving up as soon as the going gets a little rough.

In 1967, when we were newlyweds, marriage was a much more stable state of being than it is now, but statistics seemed to show then that many couples found the first year of marriage difficult, with a high proportion of marital breakdown occurring in the first twelve months. The implication was, that if you came through that early trial by partnership you stood a good chance of a permanent, successful relationship. We never found that first year, or marriage in general, a difficult experience, but then we were both prepared to make allowances, and the underlying feelings were strong on friendship, not mere passion. It was just as well, for we have had our moments:

Sam, our first marital cat, came to us as a small kitten and, as sometimes happens with kittens when they have a change of scene, he suffered an upset stomach after the move. I came down one morning to find the kitchen bespattered with little heaps of accidents. As a new bride my first reaction was to clean up the mess before my loving husband came downstairs for his all important toast. With a highly disinfected kitchen floor I had soon made a good job of restoring cleanliness but, alas, failed to make the toast in time to meet the morning's running order. 1960s toasters were trendy but not very reliable, either producing pale shadows of the desired slice or charred offerings which sat malevolently in the rack. So we had eschewed modern technology. Instead, with the devotion of the novice, I would watch and nurture those pieces of bread under the grill until they were browned to perfection. At least I had been doing so, with some success, until our crisis hit us. There was an angry outburst of, 'Where's my toast?' then a hurried, toastless departure, leaving a tearful young wife with no goodbye kiss but only the conviction that her husband did not love her any more.

However, neither of us was one to bear a grudge and, as we were both enjoying the physical side of our marriage, that evening everything was put right – till the next time. But now I knew what to do. When the accidents happened again a few days later I carefully ignored the minefields on the floor and concentrated on browning the ritual toast, so that it was sitting smugly in the rack just as Graham came down. He took one look at the scene, blanched paler than the original white slice and snapped, 'I can't eat breakfast in this filth, couldn't you have cleaned it up?' Once more he travelled toastless to work, leaving me collapsed in tears amidst my cornflakes, soggily convinced that he no longer loved me. Once again the evening saw us reconciled, the kitten's stomach settled down and so did the marriage. Thus I had no chance to test my resolve 'to get it right next time'.

At least, I didn't get that chance for several years, not until we had moved to Throstles' Nest. This time, the morning's special greeting had been made by the dog – a larger animal's deposit on a larger kitchen floor. But by now, as an experienced wife and mother, the situation did not throw me at all. With the confident brilliance of the know-it-all I simply covered up the offending islands of mishap with newspaper and got on with making the toast. How was I to know that Graham's mother had had her own ritual with newspaper? After washing the kitchen floor she would apparently lay rafts of paper, like stepping stones for people to walk on, while the floor dried. As a youngster Graham had been trained to walk on these pathways and today was no exception. He skidded deftly across the kitchen emitting blue smoke as he went. But his own volcanic eruption was well matched this time. Secure in the years of love we

had shared, and with the knowledge that a quick temper fades as quickly as it flashes across the domestic sky, I found myself remembering those two previous occasions in our marriage, comparing them with the present one, and collapsed, not in tears but in helpless giggles. Graham had hardly started to say, 'What the hell are you laughing at?' when the memories hit him too. We were both convulsed, falling into each other's arms while the dog, author of this mayhem, looked on bemused. It was another milestone which helped to cement our marriage and we celebrated by purchasing our first pop-up toaster.

Early on in our marriage we had confronted the scenario familiar to most male/female partnerships. Rather than making a direct request, thinking (female fashion) that it is so much nicer for someone to be able to offer their help, I would say, 'It's a bit chilly in here,' expecting Graham to react by offering to close the window whence the cold air was drifting. He would probably shrug, continue reading his newspaper and say, 'Well you feel the cold more than I do.' I would then ask if he minded if I shut the window, and he would respond, 'No, of course not, I'd have done it myself if you'd asked me.' He could not understand why I could not be direct and say outright what I wanted. Eventually I got the hang of it, for Graham was amenable to being helpful, once asked, the only snag being that his gesture would be accompanied by, 'All right bossy boots.' Somewhere over the years we have effected a compromise and learned to laugh when Venus and Mars collide.

I confess that I am yesterday's woman in terms of putting my own career well behind that of supporting my husband in his but, as feminism took a firmer root in society, many women like me began to feel that you could not call yourself a proper person unless you had a job of some kind outside the home. Therefore, I felt much more at ease as the years went by when asked the inevitable, 'What do you do?' to be able to quote my various part-time activities, even though Graham's career took him globe-trotting in his international co-operative hat, while I could only boast work as far afield as inner Manchester, Runcorn and Bury.

I helped to run two Darby and Joan* clubs in Macclesfield, then from the springboard of experience with the poetry group, *Tarantula*, was able to add some paid work when I started going into schools, reading my poems to the children and encouraging them with their own writing. This came about through Jackie, a head teacher who had joined *Tarantula*. She invited us into her school in Gorton, Manchester, and it was in Jackie's office that I was introduced to Malcolm Brown, who had a senior position in Physical Education and had a special interest in dance. He was concerned that many teachers found the skill hard to teach and he wanted to produce a book to help them. He had also found that, while words were good to move to, it was unnerving to use sacrosanct gems of the English language for this purpose. His idea was to have a book in a simple A4 format, with the poem on the left-hand page and his notes for the teacher on the right. Photocopying individual poems would be actively encouraged. He therefore asked me if I would be willing to try to write some poems suitable for children's dance lessons – poems that teachers could chop about as they wished, maybe only using a chorus here, or repeating a favourite verse there, changing the order to suit a particular class – and so on. I took it as a great compliment that Malcolm thought I might be able to help in this way, even if it did imply that my poems would never become jewels in the English language. It was a challenge to which I rose with enthusiasm and I soon managed to write a few pieces which Malcolm felt were on the right lines, so we were able to start road-testing them with children in schools, with rewarding results.

Of course Malcolm is a gifted dance teacher, which did not come amiss. He also had an educational publisher, not merely up, but on the edge of his sleeve, one who was anxious to take the finished book *Feet First – Poems for Dance*, thus making me a properly published author. That was exciting, the more so when the publisher requested a sequel which we called *Footsteps – More Poems for Dance*. Both books went into reprint and I still get small royalty cheques from them. It thrills me to know that, not only are the books still selling, but that teachers in schools in Holland, Germany, Canada and other countries are paying to photocopy and use the poems for their dance classes. There is a particular poem from the books which seems to work well for adults, though admittedly I have never seen them dancing to it. I think it appeals because I can say exactly how it came to be written. One July day, climbing the steep steps we call The Beanstalk, near the reservoirs above our house, I became aware of tiny froglets all over the ground and, as I found myself stepping ever more gingerly to avoid trampling them, the first line came into my head . . .

Small Things

Take care of the small things
That scurry below,
Tread softly through grasses
Wherever you go.
Take care there are small things
That move without sound,
That creep under leaves
And move close to the ground.

To them you're a giant,
Step sideways, step slow,
Step roundabout, backwards,
Step high on tiptoe.
But sometimes tread loudly,
Your feet like a drum,
A heavy beat warning ...
It's me, here I come!

Take care there are small things
That move without sound,
That creep under leaves
And move close to the ground.
Take care of the small things
That scurry below,
Tread softly through grasses
Wherever you go.

It was at a meeting for NAWE* (Northern Writers in Education) that I met the established author Alison Leonard, who was looking for someone to support her in the newly founded group for disabled writers at Daresbury Hall in Cheshire, a residential home run by the organisation now known as Scope. Calling themselves *Disabled Not Daft* these writers were people severely affected by cerebral palsy, some of them having no speech at all, or speech that was very difficult to understand, but all with stories they wanted to tell. Alison was well aware that not everyone would find this milieu an easy one in which to work, and told a hilarious story against herself about the pilot meeting. Leaning forward intently to try to understand what one member of the group was saying to her, she had inadvertently touched a switch or handle on the electric wheelchair, sending it into a waltzing spin which no one seemed able to stop for long drawn out seconds – I suspect partly because they were laughing so much. Alison also confessed to having been unable to work the vital computer that evening, and to being on a steep learning curve generally where the technology was concerned. I suspected that this would also be my north face of the Eiger. At the time I did not even know how to switch a computer on. Nonetheless, the idea of working with disabled writers attracted me and I volunteered my Wednesday mornings for the autumn of 1987.

Everyone was very welcoming and I found an instant rapport with the enthusiastic members of the group. I had to learn not to mind feeling silly when I could not understand something that had been said to me, having to ask for it to be repeated maybe three or four times. The danger is that, in not wanting to appear foolish, and not wanting the speaker to get exhausted, you pretend to have understood something a severely disabled person has said. You have to learn to accept that he or she usually does not mind repeating something several times. Overall, I felt instantly at home with the people I was working with but the computers were an alien force and, although there was extraordinarily patient expert back up, I recognised that, if I were to be of real use, I must tackle my computer illiteracy seriously. So, in the New Year, I took myself off to conquer the basics. Armed with this new knowledge I felt competent to fill in for Alison when she was away and slowly became more and more involved with the group on a paid basis, for these were the days of a sympathetic local authority which could provide funding for such worthwhile activities.

Soon after Daresbury Hall closed to enable all the residents to move out into purpose-built bungalows in the community, I took over the editing of the magazine *Disabled Not Daft* and, eventually, when Alison felt she had to concentrate more on her own writing, I ran the group singlehanded, which involved tutoring in people's homes. My Mondays spent tutoring could often be long days. I would never have left Rosie on her own for all those hours and, although my mum would willingly have had her, Rosie was very much a home bird – or *home dog* perhaps! So my mother would report, marginally hurt, that, despite all her own best efforts, Rosie never quite settled and would lie resolutely in the hallway trying to peer through the frosted glass of the front door, willing my return. So Rosie often came with me, always good company in the car, travelling like a duchess on the front passenger seat, the warm softness of her gentle head a welcome friend, even if the price was clouds of golden fur festooning the seat, and much of me.

The group members had often asked about my dog during the Daresbury days so, when I began going to their own homes, they were all keen that Rosie should come too. At first she was a little nervous of the wheelchairs but she grew used to them and would doze companionably beside us while we worked. She was very popular, not only with the writers but also with the other residents in each bungalow, so it came as a shock, on returning after the summer's break, to hear that there was a new health and safety directive from head office preventing visitors from bringing any animal into the bungalows. I am not a naturally combative person but this draconian ruling offended my sensibilities, not only on Rosie's behalf but, more importantly, on behalf of the disabled people. Wasn't the point of them being in these bungalows that it was supposed to be their own homes, where they made the decisions about menus, how they spent their day and whom they wished to invite to visit them? I also knew that research was showing how beneficial the presence of an animal could be to vulnerable people. I therefore took the line with the staff (who were themselves uncomfortable about having to confront the issue with me) that if any one of the residents in the bungalows we visited was unhappy about Rosie accompanying me then, of course, she would no longer come, but otherwise I had no intention of leaving her behind. I duly made all the necessary consultations and the reaction was the same everywhere – everyone loved Rosie with her gentle ways, and some people probably looked forward to seeing her more than seeing me. Thus, through all the years I was working with the disabled writers Rosie continued to be my support tutor.

Chapter 16

Goings and Comings

It was satisfying to find that my childhood passion for drama was finding a comfortable outlet in reading and performing poetry and that my social work training was proving invaluable in my work with the disabled writers. Wheels had turned full circle, and wheels within those wheels helped me to find links to other people. Alison and I had met in this way and through her valued friendship I met Jen Darling who took over the layout and printing of the magazine *Disabled Not Daft*, making it look so much more professional. Over the years she too became a good friend and was also to become the publisher of my cat books. Not a bad find. Similarly, the singer who performed with us for the costumed performance of Elizabethan poetry introduced me to her neighbour, a professional illustrator called Jo Berriman. It was Josie who made the essential difference to my cat books with her drawings, which were not just well executed, but somehow managed to get inside the character of each cat.

Meanwhile, the cycle of death and birth continued to turn. My parents' cat Harris had long ago been replaced by Barnaby, a cat not unlike Piedy in appearance though without his extra special nature. A lovely chap nonetheless, he lived about sixteen years, during which time my father had died. My mother's animals were even more important to her now and she could not bear to be without a cat so, after she lost Barnaby, we took ourselves up to Windyway to try to find her a new friend. Sadly in one way, there were plenty to choose from and my mother – or Margie as we still called her – was able to settle on a pretty little tortie who had been confined to Windyway for several months and was certainly well deserving of a good home. It was early December so we were beginning to think about Christmas. From here Margie moved by association to snow and from there to *Dr Zhivago* and the lilting strains of *Lara's Theme*. So Lara entered our lives, beautiful but neurotic little Lara. Was ever a cat more nervous or suspicious of her human well-wishers? She must have spent at least the first month hardly emerging from under my mother's bed except to eat, or to use her tray.

One evening, however, as Margie sat watching the television, a pair of huge, green, round eyes owled their way round the edge of the sitting-room door, followed by the tensely, slowly moving body of the cat, creeping forward on paws so soft that Bruno was unaware of her presence. Considering her extreme nervousness Lara coped very well with Bruno, not the quietest lad on the block but all good nature. Lara seemed to sense this and, though cat and dog vied for my mother's affections, never being close friends, they tolerated each other well. We talk about one-man dogs but Lara was a one-woman cat. She adored my mother, sleeping snuggled up to her on the bed at night. But she had little time for anyone else and is the only cat I have ever known to dislike me. I think it was because I was associated with all the disrupting factors in her life, like going to the vet or having *Frontline* applied to prevent fleas. Anyway, I was largely *persona non grata*, as was my mother's Mary, because she wielded the hoover, Graham because he had a deep male voice, and so on. Given that Lara was always going to be one to find life hard, she eventually settled down to maximise the happiness of her new surroundings, using the cat flap, going out a great deal (especially if a visitor walked in the front door) and becoming a lithe and skilled hunter. I was astonished, and somewhat horrified on one occasion, to see her leap high in the air up to the bird table and snatch a bird from it. She was certainly a true cat and the table had to be fitted with repelling wire mesh round its edge.

So Lara settled in and Bruno continued to be a loving and loyal companion to my mum, acting naturally as a Hearing Dog when her own hearing began to fail. He would tell her not only of the doorbell but also of the telephone ringing in the hall. He had always been a very healthy dog but, in 1998, when he was about 12, it became clear that something was badly wrong and he went downhill very fast. I shall always remember our last little walk together. I tried to take him a short distance up the road on his lead and he was eager to go but, after a mere 50 yards he stopped and looked up at me with pleading eyes to go back. We had excellent veterinary care but cancer is cancer. Our vet took Bruno in to examine him under anaesthetic and my mother and I waited, both chewing our hankies with anxiety till the phone call came. It was as bad as we had feared and the vet advised that it would be kinder not to bring him round but to let him slip away. We all felt dreadful. I was as upset as if Bruno had been our own dog, for both Graham and I loved him very much, and it was a cruel cut for poor Margie, who might have hoped for another three or four years with her beloved companion. She was beginning to be quite frail herself so it didn't seem very sensible for her to have another dog, but she was adamant that she couldn't cope without one, deciding she would take in some little old dog that would be hard for any sanctuary to rehome.

Consequently, a couple of weeks later we were at Windyway looking for a likely candidate. The Dawber family, who live on site and are in charge of all the day-to-day care of the animals, are always helpful, and Wendy Dawber was doing her best to think who might suit my mum. Realistically, finding a new dog for a frail old lady was not going to be easy. There would have been one small peke/pug cross but she had just been spoken for. Every other dog Wendy thought would be too lively. For a few minutes Wendy was stumped, then doubtfully she suggested to a staff member, 'little Shandy'? The small dog was about the size of a sheltie. She was a pretty, pale gold colour, with a wavy coat and a feathery tail. She was not exactly unsteady on her four legs but looked as if she soon could be. She was said to be 13 but could well have been older, and she had a slightly bewildered look about her. She had come to *Windyway* because her previous owner, an elderly man, had died. She had been greatly loved and had been his main companion after the death of his wife. The family, though concerned for Shandy, felt they could not take her in since they were out at work all day. It must have been heartbreaking for them to have to take the dog to Windyway, where she had been living for the last month or two.

For Margie it was love at first sight. I felt dubious, not because Shandy was not a sweet little thing, she was, but I could foresee that my mother might lose her as she had lost Bruno and it would mean more heartache for her. I therefore suggested we went and had some lunch and talked it through, which we did, but Margie would not be moved. She was determined to give a lovely home to 'that poor little dog' so, next day, we duly went back to collect her. The only aspect Margie was not happy about was the name. There had already been a much loved Shandy in the family so she decided to call the dog after Wendy at Windyway. Thus the Wendy Dog came into our lives, her new name somehow really suiting her. She was a huge contrast to her lively, boisterous predecessor, though she was a bit of a yapper, so was no quieter. Fortunately in a way, she was fairly deaf, so did not react to every sound, though of course she was no help to my mother – their hearing being equally unreliable. I would try to walk Wendy with Rosie but she did not want to go far and was happier just to toddle out with my mum, who was thrilled to show her off to her neighbours and doggie-walking acquaintances.

Through Windyway we were able to contact the daughter of Wendy's former owner and she came over with her husband to visit the erstwhile Shandy in her new home. They were caring people and were hugely relieved to see their parents' best friend contented on Margie's sofa.

Wendy

The next year brought a rather different character onto the family scene. Our younger son Hugo and his fiancée Jo decided to add a dog to their two-cat family of Pudding and Pie. This was not just any dog but a Great Dane called Cowley. I suppose he was what you could call a Danish Blue – very handsome, his head a proud grey and the rest of his body a mixture of lighter grey with deeper patches or speckles. He was six months old, a great gangling youth who had a few hang-ups from his upbringing so far. He was initially frightened of the stairs, never grew up enough to enjoy being out in the garden on his own, and was prone to nip people's bottoms. Fortunately it was only a nibble, nothing worse, but Cowley was more than we felt we could cope with. Neither Graham nor I would ever have offered to walk him, for example, although we loved him dearly and had no problem with him visiting us here, except perhaps his first Christmas, when glory was not what he covered himself in.

Jo and Hugo had thought it best that Cowley did not come to us till the evening, when the meal and the chaos of present-giving were safely over. Hugo duly went back to their home to collect him about five o'clock, only to find that 'the big girl's blouse' had somehow got himself trapped in the bathroom, frantically rucking up the carpet behind the door so that it was impossible to open it from the landing. Reinforcements were summoned from Throstles' Nest and the big silly rescued, but unfortunately in his struggle to extricate himself the dog had scrabbled up and eaten large quantities of carpet, which had a black rubbery backing. I discovered this with enormous delight when he regurgitated it in three rather neat, black heaps on my new and very expensive Aubusson rug. Cowley was to have other adventures and was altogether too much for Great Aunt Rosie. She neither approved of, nor enjoyed, his visits and would usually retire, more than a little disgruntled, to the peace and quiet of our bedroom until the house was once more a Cowley free zone.

A year or two after Cowley's arrival on the scene I went into Manchester for a theatre visit with my dear friend Lynn and her twin boys, then aged eleven. A year earlier Lynn had been brutally widowed, when her husband was killed on his motorbike in an accident which was no fault of his own. She was left with very little money and five children, three daughters aged 18, 13 and 12, then 10-year-old twins, Tom and Jack. I had been trying to give what support I could, one small contribution being to take members of the family on suitable theatre outings. On this occasion it was a trip during the Easter holidays to the studio at the Royal Exchange, for a play called *Wild Girl, Wild Boy* by David Almond who wrote *Skellig*, which the boys had read at school and enjoyed. The show was billed as suitable for children of eight and upwards. I had wondered if it might be too young for them but decided to risk it.

We had arranged to leave the car at the Co-op head office in its specially designated garage space and, as we drew in to park, were all riveted by the sight of a puppy, or young dog, being held on a lead by a woman commissionaire. This little honey was a lively, total mix-up, but obviously had some kind of hound in his breeding. Of course we all went over to make a fuss of him, thinking that he belonged to the commissionaire. However she told us that, unfortunately, this was far from the case as he had been found running around lost and the dog warden had been sent for, to take this little chap of 157 varieties to Manchester Dogs' Home. For our part we had a show to go to and the matter seemed in hand, but none of us could get the animal out of our minds as we walked to the theatre.

The play started well, with an actress playing the part of a little girl of eight or nine who struggles to read and write (something the boys could identify with) but who lives a happy family life with her parents. Then, four minutes into the story, the dad died.

I could have fallen through the floor and Lynn was in tears beside me. It was actually a very good play dealing with important issues but it certainly did not augur to be the cheerful treat I had had in mind. However, partly because we were all more than a little frozen to the spot, we stayed with the play and, in dealing with the terrible bereavement she has suffered, the child returns to the allotment where she and her father had spent so much time, allowing many wild plants to grow and where he had shown his daughter the theory of how to catch a fairy. This had never worked for them in his lifetime, but now the girl tries again, catching a seed from the air, planting it in a pot, spitting on it and saying some magic words while blinking her eyes 99 times. Sure enough the 'Wild Boy' appears, to become her friend. She decides to call him Skoosh.

Over lunch, as we discussed the play, we were all still thinking about the little dog we had seen earlier, and Lynn said, 'Wouldn't Skoosh be a lovely name for a dog?' Of course, by the time we returned to pick up the car the dog had gone to the Dogs' Home, and we tried to tell ourselves that he was so gorgeous his owners would surely be joyously reclaiming him any minute. However, I could not quite get him out of my mind and, when seeing Lynn the next week (for an ice show with the girls) found that she was having the same trouble. On the Wednesday, a week since we had seen him, I could stand it no longer and, failing to raise a live person to talk to on the telephone, I gave up on the recorded messages and set off on safari to track down the Manchester Dogs' Home. Long before the days of Sat Nav, this was achieved with some difficulty,as it seemed to be secreted away round some perplexing corners in order to prevent too many people finding it. However, once there I was able to establish that the dog had not been claimed and therefore would be coming up for rehoming next day.

After much persuasion (because today he was not yet scheduled to be available for said rehoming) I managed to visit him in his pen. He was, of course, wildly excited to have a visitor and I was more determined than ever to see if we could rescue him, despite the fact that it would not have been kind to our elderly Rosie for us to take him in. I therefore talked to Lynn and she discussed it with her own family. We then evolved a plan whereby the dog would live with them but I would pay all his bills. On the strength of this, the next day Lynn, Tom, Jack and I set off for the Dogs' Home, only to discover that it was unwilling to release the animal because he had developed kennel cough and the vet had not yet seen him. We had to creep away and try to find something to eat and drink to pass the time. This did not prove easy either and Macdonald's was the best we could manage. Lynn and I both being vegetarian we sat uneasily with a cup of tea and an apple based pastry until it seemed safe to return to rescue our captive. We didn't have to spend time discussing the dog's name as it had chosen itself the day we first saw him. The vet at the Dogs' Home was reluctant to let Skoosh go because of the cough, but we managed to convince him that we had travelled a long way, could not keep doing it and we had a perfectly good vet in Macclesfield where, we promised, we would take Skoosh for immediate treatment. Finally, feeling as if we had succeeded in springing a prisoner from Strangeways, we escaped with our prize, who was as good as gold on the hour long ride to his new home, despite having what proved to be an excitable nature.

Skoosh settled in very well, bringing a new focus to the family and was especially important to the twins, who felt that he was meant to be for them, and had indeed arrived by magic, like the Wild Boy in the play. He was a bit of a wild boy himself, though passionate in his affection for everyone and loyally devoted to Little Jenny, the baby born to Lynn's oldest daughter a few weeks before.

We had the garden dog-proofed so that Skoosh could play safely there with the boys. He did not like being left alone, probably in the light of his earlier history, as he associated it with being abandoned and, though there was usually someone around so that he was not by himself for long, if he did have to be alone for an hour or three, he did some chewing, and not just of the bones and toys provided, so plenty of exercise was a priority. This was where some more mutual therapy came into play as, in late 1999, our elder son Harry had come back to live at home while going through a difficult patch. He was not well enough to work but it was important for him to have something worthwhile to do and, within a short time, he had three devoted doggy clients to walk, one of whom of course was Skoosh, the second being Cowley, both dogs adoring their 'Uncle Harry', each thinking he was theirs. The only problem arose when Hugo was walking Cowley himself in the park one day and the mighty Dane spotted his special friend out with a rival canine, namely Skoosh, who, understandably, thought Cowley had got it all wrong because he knew for sure that Harry was his. The green eye of jealousy flashed and the fur flew a bit, though fortunately no one was hurt, as Hugo managed to drag Cowley off to a safe distance before harm ensued.

It was as well that neither Cowley nor Skoosh found out that their favourite uncle was not just two timing, but three timing them, for he had also added a young, lively and very beautiful Alsatian called Misha to his list of conquests. Misha belonged to a small, elderly lady called Milly, a great animal lover with numerous cats. In the past Milly and her husband had enjoyed having Alsatians and, after being widowed, Milly got Misha as protection, rather forgetting that Alsatian puppies take a lot of handling and that, in the intervening years, she herself had grown frailer. Misha was more than a little on the wild side, desperately needing to be properly exercised, which Harry undertook on some land close to where Milly lived. He had a busy time as, besides walking Skoosh and Cowley once a day, he took Misha out twice, even at weekends. It was good for all parties. The dogs got their exercise, Harry was out in the fresh air and the friendship of a dog comes without any strings of critical judgement attached. Dogs don't care what you earn or whether you have a successful career, will not be impressed if you are a celebrity, nor deprecate a bin man or a seller of the *Big Issue*. They don't ask questions you don't want to answer, nor do they give well-meaning but unwanted advice. They are just there beside you with their comforting warmth and unquestioning devotion, helping many of us through trauma and crises in our lives. Besides the ever faithful Rosie, Harry now had three other dogs to help in his life . . .

No Fairweather . . .

Here's a friend
rides with your highest rainbow
or through your dark of storm

treating cloud or sunshine both the same
indifferent to the richer or the poorer
beside you – sickness or in health

with no vows taken
but for better or for worse
this is for life.

Skoosh

Cowley

Misha

Chapter 17

Rollercoaster

'We are a grandmother.' I don't thank Mrs Thatcher for much, and she certainly didn't give me many laughs, but the giggle raised by her reaction to the birth of her first grandchild is one to remember. More touchingly, her queenly gaffe could have been revealing a softer side to her nature, she being sufficiently thrilled as a woman to throw caution to the wind as a politician.

I have to admit to feeling faintly disappointed when Jo and Hugo had said, back in 1999, that they had something special to tell us and the news had proved to be their engagement, for I had been hoping to hear that they were going to have a baby. But they were old-fashioned enough to do things in the right order. They married in September 2000, the reception being held in a marquee in our garden here, following a ceremony in the beautiful setting of Gawsworth Hall. Less than a year later we were overjoyed to hear that we were indeed going to be grandparents in the spring of 2002, which promised to be an exciting year, commencing with the Queen's New Year's Honours List, in which Graham was awarded a knighthood. I insisted that he ring my mother (Margie) himself, from Greengarth, where we were staying as usual for the New Year, and he still treasures her delighted, 'Yippee!'

I had retired from my work with the disabled writers at the end of 2001, having given more than a year's notice, and arrangements had been made with Halton Arts for the continuation of the group. I would keep in touch with the members informally and run the occasional workshop as a visiting tutor. I liked all these people too much to have done otherwise. Graham's own retirement was planned for September and, meanwhile, my 60th birthday was approaching in March, with several 'jollies' planned. Then a bombshell hit us. Hugo rang one morning in early February to say that Ann, Jo's mother, had died. It was a great shock to everyone and so dreadful for Jo, especially being pregnant. Ann (of whom we were all very fond) had previously been ill with cancer but had seemed so much better in recent months. True, she had begun having some problems again but there had been nothing to prepare us for her sudden death.

Jo was very brave. Nobly, she came to my birthday celebrations which were spread out from early March. With my own experience of giving birth several weeks early to both our sons, I am always twitchy for mothers-to-be once they get to seven months, hence the first 'jolly' (a weekend for all the family's young people in a luscious hotel in North Wales) had long been booked so that Jo would not be too near her time. It must have been very hard for her, less than a month after losing her mother, having to try to be cheerful so as not to spoil the party for the rest of us. Cowley came too, as we were in cottages in the grounds of Bodysgallen Hall, and his huge, lumbering presence was an amusing comfort to everyone. Rosie did not join us as, by now, her bowel control was becoming unreliable and she was apt to drop neat, but unpredictable 'parcels' about the place – not a problem at home but it did not bode well for a posh hotel. Thus Rosie stayed with Margie and her full-time carer. Sadly, Wendy had left us the previous October so my mother was always delighted to have Rosie to stay. The weekend was a great success, as was the lunch held mid-March, in the Savoy, for southern based family and friends. From London we travelled by Eurostar for a few days in Paris and the month was rounded off with an 'at home' for local friends on 27th March, my actual birthday. At the end of it all I felt very fortunate and greatly spoilt. I had hated being 50 and had hidden that birthday under the cover of our Silver Wedding (also in March) but 60 was somehow different. I felt quite proud, self-satisfied even, to have achieved 60 unscathed; it seemed there was some cause for celebration.

In April we were at Greengarth again for the good news of Phoebe's arrival. Although we would have been thrilled if the baby had been a boy, Graham and I had had a secret wish that it would be a girl for, having only had boys ourselves, we had always had a yen for a daughter, so this beautiful little granddaughter was doubly welcome. We were all ecstatic about the new arrival but wondered how Cowley would react, for we knew he could be prone to jealousy. Would he resent the arrival of this sudden little stranger? We need not have worried. It is perhaps worth asking oneself whether animals can sense a baby in the womb, a small being that is a part of the person they already love and, once born, having a smell that is half familiar. Whatever the case may be, Cowley became Phoebe's devoted slave. As she got to the crawling, then the toddling stage, she could roll on him and cuddle him without the slightest moment of adult anxiety, though it has to be said that she was always the gentlest, kindest little girl, and would never have pulled his ears, poked a finger in his eye or done anything to hurt him. Phoebe spent her very early formative years in the comforting cuddle zone of Cowley's strength and devotion. With 'Cow Cow' as a best friend there was no terror that dogs in general could hold for her. We were glad about this as it is distressing that so many children react with panic when they sight a dog, let alone if one approaches, however friendly the overture.

With the joy of our granddaughter's safe arrival in April we then looked forward to May, when, over its second Bank Holiday weekend, Graham would be President of the Co-operative Congress in Belfast, wearing a silver medal. Hard for this event to be outshone, but we flew into London on the Monday, taking up residence in Brown's Hotel, ready for our trip to the palace for the Investiture and the receipt of even grander insignia, this time from a royal hand. We called it our Two Gong Weekend, and I had given myself the treat of some designer clothes. Seats for an Investiture are strictly limited to three guests. Our sons, Harry and Hugo, arrived from Manchester in Graham's chauffeur driven car and, on the Tuesday morning, we were all driven up The Mall for the appointment with Prince Charles. The Queen herself was experiencing a problem we all have - needing to be in two places at once. It was an especially busy time for her with the Golden Jubilee so close.

London was looking glorious in readiness for the Jubilee celebrations which were to follow at the weekend, and the interior of Buckingham Palace is impressive. We had thought it might look a little faded but it gleamed with gilt, beautifully polished floors and rich carpeting, not to mention all the wonderful pictures. Moreover, the palace certainly knows how to handle events; every detail thought through, every moment timed to the last second. Nervous recipients were calmed and gently instructed in their part in the proceedings, the proud relations soothed with suitable music from a live orchestra while they waited for the ceremony to begin. None of us would have missed that day and the official photographs are fond souvenirs.

We were driven home from London in time to get ourselves organised for the Queen's Jubilee weekend. Street parties would be held all over the country and the equivalent was to be held in our garden on Monday 5th June. There are eight households on our little lane and we are lucky with all our neighbours. Counting Margie, and offspring at their various ages (including Harry, Hugo, Jo and baby Phoebe) there were nearly 30 of us. Everyone was bringing goodies to contribute to the party so there was not a huge amount for Graham and I to do. We were looking forward to fun and sun, but the dawn came upon us with rain in the air, as only an English summer day can bestow when it really matters. Coronation Day back in 1953 was much the same. The weather's damp squib threw a rather different complexion on the arrangements for our party; we would have to base much of it indoors, which was manageable but far from ideal. However, everything seemed to be going with a swing until late afternoon when Rosie dropped one of her unfortunate 'parcels' and I rushed to clear it up. Hugo had offered to fulfil this role but, being a multi-tasking woman and ridiculously over conscientious, I had insisted on whirling to the clean-up myself. I mean, why wouldn't I with a house full of guests, none of whom I wanted to witness Rosie's little weakness? The 'parcel' was soon dispatched, the floor wiped, the disinfected sponge squeezed out and I hurried to return to my guests. Hurried just that fraction too fast, caught the side of my left foot on the mop bucket and tripped forward – such a little trip, not enough to throw me against the wall ahead; instead, I fell sideways through the open doorway onto the stone-flagged floor of the porch, my leg, curved ominously under me, developing an instant reverberating ache. For heaven's sake, I was hosting a party, so I quickly picked myself up off the floor and stood to get my breath back, leaning against the worktop in the utility room, which was where Hugo found me a moment or two later, looking, no doubt, like a wobbly ghost. Kindly hands helped me to a sofa, brandy was poured down me and the party carried on, with a rather less active hostess, but it did not seem to spoil the fun and, when everyone had gone, I limped about trying to help Graham put the place to rights, which I think we managed to do quite well - though I was feeling far from well myself. Never mind, I would surely be much better in the morning.

I was not better in the morning but, nothing daunted, we made an appointment with my trusted physio who had been treating me for back trouble for many years and had, eventually, made me pain free, so long as I was careful. He thought the fall had badly shaken my back, sending referred pain down into my groin, but he was hopeful that, with intensive treatment, I might still be able to go to Highgrove later in the week. It was a special visit to which Graham had been invited in his Co-operative Chief Executive hat, and he had had to work hard and persuasively on the royal gardeners for me to be allowed to join the party. I did not want to miss it. My physio did not want me to miss it, but miss it I did. I also missed seeing the Queen's birthday carnival parades in colour, as I had to watch from bed on our antique black-and-white tiny television. Despite the treatment and some self-delusion I was not improving. I was hobbling around using a stick and feeling more like 106 than 60. I thought it was the best possible cure for any earlier attack of smugness, but I was wrong, for there was far more to come.

On the Saturday morning I went down to the kitchen (leaving Graham asleep in bed) to potter about on my stick, doing a little tidying up and feeding the animals. The milkman came and I had a chat with him through the kitchen window while he placed the bottles safely on the inner sill, where it would be easy for me to take them in, one at a time, ferrying them at least as far as the worktop. He was to be my last sight of land before being washed into an ocean of pain, for the next moment I made the tiny but unwise movement of trying to steady myself by putting my left hand across onto the handle of the stick held in my right hand. In that moment 'there she blows!' It was enough to send harpoons of pain through me which, on a scale of 1 to 10, were at about 25, and I was rooted to the spot feeling sick, swaying, my tummy going to water, and chanting the mantra, 'I must not fall over, I must not fall over . . .' Along with this was a prayer that Graham would somehow wake up, miss me and come looking for me, as I did not have the strength to cry out and, anyway, any pathetic squeak I did manage would never have reached him through the long length of our house. So I swayed there for endless minutes (probably about three) until, mercifully, my prayers were answered and Graham appeared. There then followed an undignified but desperately necessary visit to the downstairs cloakroom, whence I then had to be rescued by Harry. Fortunately, he was still living with us and was asleep upstairs until he was roused to act as cavalry by his perturbed father, whose wife was stuck in an unmentionable place in intolerable pain. With the clutch of a limpet I clung to Harry's neck and was raised from ignominy, then somehow manoeuvred into the sitting room, to perch on a mountain of cushions piled onto the sofa, for I was certainly not going to try sitting down low again and to lie down would have been mission more than impossible. From my temporary haven we reviewed the options and, with the huge presence of three minds, decided to dial 999.

Oh, the relief of the cool professionals in a crisis, which is, of course, to them just a routine part of their working day. The ambulance crew arrived so quickly we thought they must have been parked by Swan's Pool having a coffee break when our call came through. We soon discovered that the way Harry had lifted me was wrong as he could have injured himself. My overwhelming urge was to cling to the ambulance staff too as they lifted me into the special chair to transport me, but I was told to cross my arms and clutch each of my own shoulders against the pain. I don't think I was good at this, but they managed, and it was not long before I was at the hospital, x-rayed, and hearing the surgeon say I had broken my hip and would need a full replacement. I suppose the agony I was in had made me unusually stupid, as I was astonished to hear that I was to have an operation. What on earth had I thought they were going to do – patch me up with double-sided sticky tape?

The NHS comes in for much criticism but I have nothing but praise for my treatment over the next few days and, if ever I had to respond to a question as to where in my life I had been most glad to be, the answer would be, in that hospital bed that Saturday afternoon on the ward, with competent people to look after me and medication to ease the pain. The surgeon operated next day, although it was a Sunday, and I went home eight days later to begin a full recovery. Graham had a hugely demanding job, which often took him away from home in the week, and there was no way this high trauma patient was in a fit state to fumble around alone, even with Harry's help. However, we were lucky. My mother had been needing full-time care help for some months and we had been using an agency called *Country Cousins* which provided someone to live in with the client, run the home, cook, shop and give personal care. Usually a *Country Cousin* stays two weeks, then is replaced by someone else. Inevitably, some of them were more successful than others, and Leo was one we all loved dearly. Graham rang her and she was free to come to us for a month, which was perfect. Harry was there to give Leo lifts to get heavy shopping and, later on, to chauffeur me, for it was to be a while before I was well enough to get back into the driving seat of a car.

Back in 2001 it had been decided that, with Graham's impending retirement in September of 2002, it would be better for all parties if Harry had his own home. Consequently, he and I had started house-hunting in January 2002 and, by the end of February, negotiations were in hand for a pretty little terraced cottage in Bollington, which had a small but secluded garden and its own parking space. It was ideal. The sale went through in early June and, under normal circumstances, we might have been encouraging Harry to move house sooner rather than later. However, he could well have found the sudden change traumatic and, as things worked out, it was far from anyone's mind to encourage him to go immediately. He was needed at Throstles' Nest.

The cats were thrilled to have Mum confined to bed so much. They took it in turns to visit me and purr alongside. Since they were keen on Auntie Leo too they probably thought the whole episode was designed for their enjoyment. I grew stronger, and the wonderful Bev (another physio in the practice) worked her magic to get my leg moving so that eventually I could walk with no limp. This took some months but, at an early stage Bev was encouraging me to go for walks, this being the best form of exercise for bedding in a new hip. Thus I would set off on my two elbow crutches, Leo at my side, adventuring a mere 300 yards up to Swan's Pool, then back again. Dear old Rosie would poddle along behind us, grinning, her tail wagging, and in her wake would come Mille, Lenni and Amber, so that we formed an intimate little procession. Mille and Lenni would not come beyond the end of our lane but Amber (nervous little Amber) would continue along the longer lane up to the pool, scuttering into the hedge and neighbour's garden if she perceived any threat on the horizon. On returning to the corner of our lane, the other two cats would be waiting, and we would then all process back home. It was touching the way they liked to keep an eye on me. Bernard, of course, being our macho cat, would not have done anything so soft, preferring to give me a sharply welcoming hook of his paw from the kitchen worktop as I came back into the kitchen.

Six weeks after the operation, came my checkup with the hospital, where I was pronounced a great success. I had some reservations about this myself as a stiff knee was still making me limp badly, but doctors seem to have a capacity to think in boxes. My hip was fine, so that made me a tick on their records. My GP had warned me that some people, with the kind of post-operative stiffness I was experiencing, were left with it as a permanent fixture. But not if Bev and I had anything to do with it; extensive physio over several months gradually brought my knee back into good working order. Moreover, the enforced rest seemed to have done my dodgy back a great deal of good.

However, a return to full fitness was still distant when, after the hospital checkup, Graham, Rosie and I set off for a week in our cottage in the Lakes. It was much harder work for Graham than usual as my capacity to plan, shop and pack was at about a third of normal. So far as I remember we enjoyed our time there, though the memory is very blurred, indeed almost entirely obliterated by what happened on our immediate return. It was Friday evening when I rang my mother to say we were back. She seemed fine and content to wait and see me the next day, understanding that I was tired after travelling home. On the Saturday morning came a call from the then resident *Country Cousin* to say that my mother had had a fall and was being taken to A and E. Understandably Margie wanted me to be with her, so Graham took me and my crutch to hold her hand and lay siege to the doctors and nurses, while an x-ray and other numerous tests were undertaken. There were no broken bones but the likelihood of a urinary infection could have caused a lack of balance, provoking her fall.

Margie was distressed at having to stay in hospital overnight but a new and, as it turned out, a much more committed *Country Cousin* was due to arrive on the Monday, so our assumption was that my mother would be able to come home in a day or two, and be looked after there. I was still among the walking wounded myself so, frustratingly, of nil nursing use to my mother. As it happened, care on her home front was never needed again, as Margie did not recover. Slowly she faded, despite good, kind, hospital care. Several years of suffering mini-strokes or TIA (Transient Ischaemic Attacks) had gradually been weakening her and this final trauma was to prove too much. It was a sad, lengthy corridor I limped down each day for three weeks, with Harry a willing and caring chauffeur. It was a depressing time, with the realisation striking its chill as the days went by that I was travelling the long corridor of loss. My beloved mother was going to die and it made me feel ever more vulnerable. How many of us, far into our adulthood, when feeling hurt or in despair just want our mum again? Of course, for sometime now our roles had been reversed, with me trying to look after and comfort her, but nonetheless she had always given me her love and support as best she could, until these last days of her life. Even now, sensing her situation, Margie had thoughtfully told Harry he must take and use anything from her home which would be useful to him in his little cottage. He gulped an emotional, 'Thanks Nanna'. We were all going to miss her so much.

Never having been a religious woman, Margie suddenly asked for a copy of The Lord's Prayer so that she could hold it, and I could say it out loud to her. She would even ask one or two of the other patients to share it with her. The other extraordinary phenomenon was that, although she had been hard of hearing for some years, had never got on with a hearing aid and often found my voice difficult to pick up unless I raised it skyward, now I could sit beside her holding her hand, and my merest whisper would reach her.

As the days passed it was becoming obvious that my mother was sinking. Palliative care was all that could be offered and it was agreed that she should have somewhere less clinical to end her life. Alas, going home was not an option, but arrangements were made to move her to a local nursing home where she would have her own room and some of her own things around her. It was a Thursday afternoon when Margie arrived in that room and we took in her radio cassette player so that she could listen to some of her favourite music. We also took two of her best loved pictures. One was of boats at sunset on a Mersea Island creek, the other a portrait of Bruno, which we had commissioned Jo Berriman to paint as a comfort for Margie after she lost him. I think she was just about aware of their presence and of her pleasanter surroundings, for when I mentioned the pictures a tiny half smile flicked the corner of her mouth. I was with her till the evening, and there again by 10am next morning, ferried by the ever faithful Harry.

On that Friday, friends had promised to travel over from beyond Buxton to visit me in my 'poorly person hat', not having managed it, for very good reasons, earlier on. They were friends who had always been fond of Margie and had been extremely kind to her, so they would certainly have understood had I cancelled their visit at the last moment. My thinking was probably very scrambled at the time, but the decision to stay home to see them that day was also influenced by the phone call from my mother's GP, which came at 2pm while I was at home for lunch. Although his kind intention was to prepare me for the worst, in fact I found that call reassuring, as I had been thinking that perhaps I ought to spend the night at the nursing home. However, the doctor thought my mother would be with us for several days yet. Nonetheless, I must have been miserable company for my unfortunate and sensitive visitors, who stayed barely an hour, in order to release me to return to my mother's bedside once more.

When I walked into the room just after four o'clock it was to find that Margie had already left us. The long journey of grieving was to begin. Somehow I tottered through the organising of the funeral and, one truly bright moment shone out during the service itself, the moment when the good friend who was making the oration for my mother, said how thrilled Margie had been to become a great-grandmother to a beautiful little girl. Absolutely on cue there resounded a joyful, 'Wheeeeee!' from the small Phoebe, not yet five-months-old but already showing a talent for dramatic timing.

The funeral over, the agonising time of clearing the empty house began, for it had to go on the market sooner rather than later, for various complicated financial reasons to do with inheritance tax. Of course Graham and the family were all supportive, but in my weakened state I found this period painfully traumatic. I would walk into Margie's hall finding it hard to grasp, as I know many people do, the reality that I would not see this beloved person again, and asking the unresponsive air, 'Where has she gone?' for my heart was telling me she could not have just vanished, she must be somewhere. To have a religious conviction and faith in an afterlife must be a hallowed gift at these times. As it was I coped as best I could. Somehow I had held myself together for the evening of Graham's farewell dinner at the Co-op, which had fallen a few days before the funeral. Italians believe that if you look good you feel good, so I tried out this advice, dressing up to several nines. A few trusted people were primed to know the situation, yet asked to make sure no one came to me with sympathy, as that would have destroyed the dam of my determined smile and released unwelcome floodwater.

There was no shortage of the latter each time I found the sad imprint of Lara's loyalty on Margie's pillow. I never saw her, for she must have evaporated through the cat flap every time she heard my key in the lock. The kind neighbour next door was feeding her but I knew how miserable she must be and, if I was questioning my mother's whereabouts what must Lara be making of Margie's disappearance? She had been in the house on her own for several weeks already and it was impossible to know how to comfort the little cat. I knew she would be unhappy trying to settle into our household. Apart from the fact that she did not like me I was sure she would not enjoy living among four other cats in a much busier environment. Somehow she had to be rehomed, somewhere quiet and understanding but, as we all know, finding homes for older cats is never easy, even when they are placid and easy-going. I began putting out feelers but, in the meantime felt that the kindest thing was to leave Lara in her familiar surroundings, with May from next door calling in on her. At least Lara did not run away from May, who even considered offering the little cat a home, but we knew that it would be too close to her old setting.

The problem of Lara's distress added to my own and, by the time it came to following our mother's wishes for her ashes to have their final resting place on Mersea Island, my energies had been totally sapped, and I was more than relieved to leave all those arrangements to my sister, who organised a perfect day in late November. The sun shone on us as we stood by the designated place in Mersea's memorial meadow, its role being to stay looking natural, close by a creek, under a wide East Anglian sky. The service was brief, simple but memorable. My only contribution was to read the poem based on that portrait of Bruno, whom our mother had loved so much. As I came to the line about the geese, a skein of Brent, as if awaiting their cue, rose from a far meadow and flew the length of the creek, as if in salute to Margie's homecoming.

Come

'Come', says the dog,
'It is time for our walk.

Look, you can see
the stardust of my coat,
the shimmer of beyond.

Come, I will show you the way,
the path to the beach,
where geese skein wide skies.

And we shall walk in sunlight,
as the tide swirls in over the marshes
and the boats bob golden forever.'

In very ancient scripture the dog was revered as the guide into the next world. This illustration is France Bauduin's interpretation of Bruno's portrait by Jo Berriman. It is now on our landing at Throstles' Nest and is included here as tribute to Jo, a fine artist and a good friend.

Chapter 18

Lara, Rosie and the Lakes

As the autumn of 2002 progressed I grew physically stronger again and, slowly, with the physio's help, my limp began to fade, though it would be well into the next year before I could say I had lost it altogether, and my confidence remained knocked for much longer than that. The combination of events had taken their toll, though mercifully, although Rosie was getting older and frailer all the time, we were spared losing her on top of everything else that year. From mid-September I was driving again, switching to an automatic car giving my confidence the necessary boost, and I would take Rosie a short distance, to the park or the canal, always somewhere flat, so that she could feel the excitement of going somewhere different for a walk, rather than the all too familiar potter into the field or along the lane. Travelling, as she always had done, beside me on the front seat, where I could caress her whenever stationary, these little outings gave us both pleasure in something that felt special.

One of Graham's maxims is 'when the tree shakes, hold on tight' and eventually this paid off with Lara. I had had a strong feeling myself that if we held to the tree long enough, as Dickens' Mr Micawber would have said, 'something will turn up.' However, by mid-October my faith was wavering. I was feeling more and more sorry for poor, lonely little Lara and took the decision that, since there appeared to be no alternative, we would have to try rehoming her with us. We were about to go to Menorca for two weeks to stay with the friends who have an old farmhouse there. It felt like a watershed. If no miracle occurred while we were away, once home again we would have to try to assimilate Lara into our household. Rightly or wrongly, I thought it might be better for her to have a break from her former home first, so that coming here might not seem all bad. Having talked it over with our vet, I had therefore booked for Lara to be boarded with him for two weeks. It would also be a good opportunity for her to be thoroughly checked over and given the booster inoculation she needed.

Catching Lara was not easy and had to be planned carefully. However, even though wary, she would still appear for May, the helpful neighbour, whom I asked to lock the cat flap on this particular day once Lara was indoors, so that she could not go out again. It was then a question of my finding the cat in the house when I came round. The first time it did not work as, unbeknown to me, the door to the extensive cupboard under the eaves of the dormer bungalow had somehow come open. So Lara had dug herself deep inside, where I could not reach her and where she was revealed only by the flash of green eyes in the beam of my torch. We left it a day or two to let the poor little cat calm down, then May and I tried again. This time, with the escape-cupboard door shut Lara had resorted to her old hideaway under the bed.

This was a challenge. I had effected the manoeuvre in the past when needing to take Lara to the vet but not when I was fitted with a hip replacement. With the basket open at my side I gingerly flattened myself to the floor and reached under the bed for my victim who, true to form, rather than rushing off as I fumbled around, became nailed to the carpet with her claws. Fortunately, it was only a single bed and I could take hold of Lara relatively easily, then begin prising her from her place of safety. I had always worried she might rip her claws in panic but she had never resisted as much as one would think, and today was no exception. Slowly, I eased her towards me and we rolled into an inelegant cuddle, with me on my knees on the floor. Once caught, it was as if Lara wondered what all the fuss had been about. She snuggled up to me, purring loudly, as if being gently held and stroked had been her one desire all along.

Having delivered Lara into capable hands at the vet's I went back to the house to tidy up Lara's food bowls and so on. Margie's erstwhile home felt even more dismal now and, by the time I left to drive to my own house, I was feeling at low ebb. Halfway up the road I saw a familiar face, not someone I knew well but Maureen was an acquaintance I knew to be a kind and caring person. I got out to say 'hello' and make sure she had heard about my mother's death. As I did so a glimmer of hope came into my watery eyes for, as I told Maureen where I had just taken Lara, and how desperate I was to find her a home, she said that she and Reg had been wondering for a while whether to have a cat. Maureen and Reg lived on a quiet cul-de-sac with a garden that backs onto the canal. It would be perfect. I held my breath, and soon had a call asking me to call round and tell them a bit more about Lara. I remember Reg being horrified that we only fed her on dry biscuits from the vet, and I could see by the gleam in his eye that no cat living with him was going to be so mistreated. Reg had plans for refined dining for Lara, and Maureen said that, if they decided to take her, she would buy her a cosy, purpose-built cat bed. I made gentle, doubtful noises about Lara's possible lack of response to such five star treatment, but Reg obviously thought I must be very lacking in imagination. Well you would, wouldn't you, if you have never had a cat?

To cut the story short, by the time we came back from Menorca, Maureen and Reg had visited Lara several times at the vet's and had fallen in love with her. In confinement, she must have performed her 'I love to be cuddled' act. They were warned, of course, that Lara might behave very differently once they got her home, and of course she did, hardly emerging from under the bed for the first six weeks, except to gobble her dried biscuits. Then one evening, just like yesteryear, two owl's eyes appeared round the door and she crept into the sitting-room.

To have Lara thus rehomed was a huge relief and one of my teetering steps towards recovery from my own trauma. If there was ever evidence that animals can also suffer grief at the loss of their special human companion it had been personified in Lara, and I would have felt I had betrayed my mother's faith in me if I had failed to help her loyal little friend through the crisis. It took Reg and Maureen years, rather than months, to win Lara's trust completely. They took it on the chin that she refused fish, chicken and all other tempting treats, resolutely sticking to her dried biscuits, while the posh bed, after being studiously ignored for months, was eventually recycled to the Windyway charity shop. Slowly, slowly, Lara settled. She never enjoyed outdoors quite as much

Lara

again, but she was adored by two people with admirable patience whose only concern was to try to make her happy. One fortunate little cat.

Rosie, along with Amber, enjoyed New Year 2003 with us up at Greengarth. Any celebratory fireworks no longer troubled her as she was too deaf to hear them and she was content to go for poddles rather than walks. I was hardly up to fell walking myself yet but was ahead of what Rosie could manage. Even her favourite walk around the waterfall, Aira Force, with its special places where she loved to swim, was beyond her now, though she could still potter 200 yards down the track with us, then cross the road to where the stream splashed shallow and she could delight in retrieving a stick. Gracefully she was growing frailer, her breathing not as good as it might have been. We knew she would probably not be with us by next Christmas but she was on medication and we hoped to have several months with her yet.

It was the last weekend of that same January. Together with Rosie and Amber, early on the Friday morning, I went up to the Lakes ahead of Graham in order to meet a friend for lunch at the pub. Rosie was in good form and enjoyed her short toddle up the fell, then insisted on going down in the other direction for a brief splash around in the stream with a stick. I left to go to the pub around 12 noon, leaving Rosie tucked up contentedly on her bed. My friend Janet and I had a good lunch, and an even better chat, returning to the cottage for a cuppa. Rosie was in such a deep sleep when we came in that she did not stir, which was unusual. Deaf she may have been by then, but blind she was not, nor unaware of her surroundings, or if Mum was in or out. I decided the sleep might be doing her good so we left her to it for a while, but then I grew uneasy and gently woke her. Something had happened. She was now wheezing badly. However, she roused herself and, when I made the move to see Janet back to her car at the pub,

Rosie was determined to come too. She puffed with us down to the main road and stood patiently with me at the side of the road near the stream, to wave our guest goodbye. She did not ask to go in the water this time but, once we got back up the track near the cottage, she was determined to continue up the fell, until I decided enough was enough and turned her round to go back for a rest. This whole excursion was probably less then 500 yards but, for a dog in her condition, it was more like five miles and Rosie was not sorry to be back home again, where she kept a very close watch on me, was very restless and followed me everywhere. I began to grow anxious but kept hoping she would settle and sleep, then feel better. I had to drive into Penrith late that evening to collect Graham from the London train, so decided that, since we didn't have a vet at the time in Cumbria, it was best to wait till the morning, and then, if necessary, take her to a vet together.

By the time Graham came off that train, though Rosie was delighted to see him, her breathing was, if anything, worse. The restlessness also increased during the night and none of us got much sleep. In the morning I consulted our own vet, who could hear Rosie's breathing in the background as I was talking to him on the phone. His advice was to forget any idea of trying to get her back down the motorway to him but to take her to a local vet as quickly as possible. I had a strong feeling about what the outcome would be and it was a bitter pill for both of us. Fortunately, I had a local contact who could advise us on the best vet in these circumstances and, within another half-hour, we were at the surgery in the care of a very kind, young woman, whose diagnosis was only what we had expected; Rosie's lungs were filling with liquid, her heart was under severe strain and her breathing would only worsen; soon she would begin to suffer badly. There was no choice. We cuddled her as she left us, then clung to each other in the car park before driving back to a Greengarth which, for once, could not work its magic. Thank goodness for Amber, who welcomed us with her soft purr and gentle concern, but even she could not convince us that we should stay any longer. Sadly, we packed up, then drove home to that empty basket in the kitchen and a house the poorer for being without its dog but offering the comfort of four cats.

Losing Rosie reactivated my feelings about losing my mother, so that my grieving for the dog became enmeshed in the ongoing grieving for Margie, and probably the other way round. I would not be my usual resilient self for a long time to come, though life, of course, has to move on. Slowly I pulled myself together, but not without a few setbacks and considerable patience on the part of my reliable, understanding husband.

Many years before, I had tried 'the gym' in order to keep myself in trim but soon found the experience boring and, in my case, downright dangerous, due to my ineptitude at tackling some of the exercises, especially those that involved anything to do with weights. I came rapidly to the conclusion that keeping fit is a question of what suits each individual and the gym was not for me. Why spend time, effort and petrol driving somewhere to perform meaningless, heavy choreography, either alone, or alongside people who are too preoccupied even to say 'hello' never mind engage in any form of conversation? I had therefore reverted entirely to my former fitness programme of eating sensibly and using that relentless all-weather exercise machine called a dog. The Old Rosie version of this mechanism had suited my post-recovery state very well, since short walks were all I could manage, but by the time she left us I was needing to do more.

Our long term plan was to get a much younger, faster model for our daily work-outs, which would certainly keep us on our toes, but meanwhile I relied turn and turn about on two old friends of Rosie's, a lively brown collie called Moss, who had often romped with her in 'our' field, and Murphy who lived next-door-but-one. He was a handsome lad – as Shandy had been, a Labrador/collie cross (a *Labracol*?) but an All Black. These two dogs were a great comfort during the following months and it meant that I saw some of my erstwhile dog-walking friends again. But it was not the same as being plugged into our own four legged friend. Then we had to acclimatise ourselves to missing Rosie all over again when we returned to the Lake District. The first time we went up after losing her it was hard arriving at Greengarth, for the wave of emptiness that had greeted us on that homecoming to Throstles' Nest in January was waiting to engulf us once more. We were so grateful for Amber, who gave us all the comfort she could muster, leaping on our toes in bed to try to cheer us up.

Our contacts in the Lakes did not provide Rent-a-Dog and we missed Rosie most of all on the Magic Waterfall Walk as we had come to call it. Thought to provide one of the most beautiful of the lower level walks in the Lakes, we are lucky to have the Aira Beck on our doorstep. Rosie's favourite place to swim was a deep pool, accessed by a tiny pebbled beach, which lay 30 yards or so from the main path. Once discovered, it became her insistent ritual that we pause there on every walk, for her to delight us with her grace in the water. Even now, years later, we can never pass this enchanting place without moments spent fondling the memory of a dog much missed . . .

Rosie's Beach

A patch of shingle by a Lakeland stream.

Sunlight, golden as her coat
catches the leaves,
throws sparklers through the cloudless pool.

She takes the water
easy as a seal,
plumed tail dipping on the turn.

Trophy retrieved,
her pleasure drips upon the stones
and expectation shakes all over us.

Chapter 19

New Ventures

It was March 2003. Spring might be in the air with the hope of new beginnings but there was still a nip of frost to contend with, a shadow which fell over both Bernard and Amber. Recently, Bernard had been off-colour and the problem proved to be his kidneys. He was 14, the sort of age at which so many cats start to develop this weakness. He was put on the same medication as Amber, who had stabilised well a couple of years earlier when she had had a similar diagnosis. But now the medication was not holding her bouts of vomiting and a dramatic weight loss had set in. Looking back I cannot help wondering if the cats may have been affected by the loss of Rosie, whom they both loved. There is no way to know but their respective nose dives in health did develop soon after her death.

The prospect of more emotional disaster loomed briefly, but this time the fates were kind. Bernard did well on the tablets and specific food from the vet, the same food we were already buying for Amber. At the time, she and I were working on her book, which consisted of her letters back to her former owner, her 'Dear Mary'. These letters were in Amber's voice, describing people, places and events in her own style. Some of her terminology was becoming embedded in family parlance and to have tried to finish the book without her, would, I think, have defeated me. It was a huge relief when, almost by chance, Amber's 'Clever Vet' discovered her underlying health problem. It proved to be her heart, but only showed up because, on this particular occasion, she had agitated herself into running away from the sight of the cat basket, knowing it meant another trip to the vet's. She had hidden herself away under a neighbour's car and had had to be coaxed out. It was not like her to get in such a state but it proved to be a blessing for, in so doing, she had considerably raised her heartbeat and the problem showed up. A subsequent x-ray showed no major concerns and a change of medication, plus a little help from the blesséd St Michael, effected a minor miracle. Marks and Spencer have an expensive line in small, breast of chicken pieces, which are intended to enhance salads or other concoctions but can be highly recommended for restoring an Amber Cat's appetite. Fortuitously, I had bought some of these chicken treats and Amber happened to discover them. She began eating them for England, occasionally deigning to dip into her prescribed 'bickies' from the vet, but meanwhile starting to put on weight and to look a healthy cat again.

The millennium kittens, Mille and Lenni, were turned three years old, mature cats who could have vied for a beauty prize, each with a half Persian coat radiating fragrance when you picked either of them up. Mille, black in colour, reminded us of our beloved Sam, while Lenni was a deep gold-and-white. Both of them were gentle and sweet-natured. Mille was more shy, but loyal and affectionate with the family and, inevitably, Lenni would be on the drive to greet me whenever I got home. They enjoyed each other's company but, like the best of close relationships, they each had their own agenda too. However, cats can always surprise you and Lenni's calm gentleness could give way to wild resentment for, when it was time for the worming pill he became a different animal. Until we had Lenni I had thought the difficulty of giving pills to be a myth as I had never had problems with the task, unless you count Amber who would hide if she could be ahead of your intent but, once caught, was obliging enough, as you thought, till plipping the pill out again when she thought you weren't looking.

Mille and Lenni were on fine form. Bernard and Amber were both stable. It was safe for us to go away for a short break. Worming pills were not on the agenda and our neighbour, who would be feeding the cats, is a nurse, well able to handle Bernard's and Amber's daily medication. We were going to France, which we felt we had neglected in recent years in favour of beautiful Italy. My mother's death, with its resultant legacy, had caused us to take stock. We both loved France and had glowing memories of pine forests unfolding to dunes and huge golden beaches. We both spoke a French which, though rusty, could be readily polished up. I was aware that Margie had liked the cottage, Greengarth, but had been unable to see the Lake District with our eyes. To her the hills were looming and threatening. What she had loved were wide skies over a flat landscape and a sweeping sea. We tossed all these pieces of the jigsaw into the air and, when they came down, they fell into the same pattern for both of us.

We would look for a property in France, aiming for something with a sea view which Margie would have loved. We wanted to be able to travel by car and ferry rather than flying every time, yet neither of us fancied the huge car journeys that some of our friends with French properties undertook with such sang-froid. Anyone who has travelled through France will know that it is a very large country, in which places become twice as far away once on the road, as you had thought when looking at the map. Since my fall I had become less confident about driving on the right and could not see myself being much help to my husband in that department; a view confirmed later in the year when we were in Italy staying in an old, fortified mill near Sarnano in the Marché region.

It was our second holiday in this quietly situated, ancient building. Having enjoyed our visit there so much the first time we had been booked for a return visit in 2002, but the small matter of a broken hip intruded. So there we were, catching up with ourselves in June 2003. Over the fortnight we had two different couples coming to stay and, in between one departure and the next arrival, I attempted to go up to the local village of Gualdo to do some shopping. I had managed this short but winding journey on the previous holiday perfectly well, but that was when I was in the habit of driving a car with gears and had reasonable confidence. This time the combination of steering wheel and gears on the 'wrong side', a narrow, twisting track with deep, drainage ditches on each side, plus an encounter with a tractor which, most unreasonably, was going about its rural business, resulted in a very nasty bang to the hired car. Fortunately, the tractor was more resilient and, apart from confirming any prejudice an Italian might have had about incompetent *inglesi* drivers, little or no damage was done on that side of the prang. The Italians have a charm that is all their own and are relaxed about many of the things Anglo-Saxons might get steamed up about. I was not arrested and the car hire people were fairly sanguine on our eventual return of the car which, fortunately, was still drivable. Graham, as always in such circumstances, was reassuring, saying that I had had the dice loaded against me, though not unreasonably pointing out that I could have asked him to drive me up to the village. It served me right for 'not wanting to be a nuisance' as it upset me rather more than anyone else, taking the edge off an otherwise idyllic holiday. It also made me nervous of any future driving on the continent.

Previous to the Italian holiday in June we had gone to France in March, to launch our French, long-term adventure, via a visit to Graham's brother and his family in Broadstairs. From there we took the Dover-Calais Chunnel crossing, which dropped us into Normandy well before midday on a Saturday. We pottered down the coastal roads, at this stage having not altogether ruled out the possibility of finding a property in northern France. We were by no means sure that we could do any more this trip than identify an area in which to concentrate a future search. Both Honfleur and Harfleur are chic, with pretty harbours sporting expensive yachts, but had neither sandy beaches nor pine forests. We had not booked anywhere for that night since we had been vague about how far we would travel but, out of season and armed with our renowned *Michelin Guide* in one hand and a guide to posh bed and breakfasts in the other, there would be no problem. We rang up our first choice in the latter book and a charming gentleman said he would be delighted to offer us dinner and a bed for the night. It sounded too good to be true. It was. We drove fruitlessly up and down ever diminishing country lanes, the air growing more and more blue each time Graham had to swing the big Jag into reverse, turning it round in heavy, shunting, 12-point turns to change course. We asked directions at a farmhouse, rang our would-be host for further guidance, shunted the car round another six times in impossible turning spaces, and then, having tried, tried and tried again, gave up. Not altogether daunted, however, we moved to a different tack. We would treat ourselves to a French version of the Country House Hotel. It would be expensive but so what, didn't we deserve a bit of luxury after so much frustration? This time there was no difficulty at all about finding the place, and it looked enchanting and exactly what we needed. Gratefully, we parked and went into reception, to be greeted by La Belle Hélène.

In our experience there are broadly two types of French people, those who are warm, smiling and helpful, and those who are not. The latter type had been personified for me many years before in Corsica by a young woman dealing with car hire. At that time I was well able to drive round the deep bends of Corsica in a geared car but not in the ghastly Fiat Uno with which I had been provided at the airport. My French friend Catherine, who had come out to join me for a week prior to Graham's arrival, entirely agreed that the car was impossible and suggested we took it back to swap it for something else. Had I been on my own I am convinced the mission would have failed. Confronted as we were by the frosty stare of the girl sporting a badge proclaiming her to be 'Hélène' I would have been defeated before I started, as no amount of English charm and reasonableness in moderately good French would have melted her. To watch Catherine at work was a revelation. Gone was her usual easy-going, gentle, smiling manner. She became resolutely stony-faced and was obviously going nowhere until the matter was resolved. Under such a stalwart counter attack the opposition crumbled and we drove away in a small Peugeot which felt like a Rolls in comparison to its predecessor. Thus was born our concept of La Belle Hélène, applicable to anyone, male or female, who specialises in the fine art of '*Non*'! However, we have awarded the accolade more often to women than to men.

La Belle Hélène looked at our somewhat travel weary appearance down her refined nose as we stood on the luxury of an antique Persian rug in her decorously panelled reception area, and announced with the air of someone talking to the simple and silly, that if we had not booked '*monsieur*' there was absolutely no chance that there was any room at the inn. It was, after all, Saturday night so, of course, they were '*complet*'. Daft Anglais that we were we began to see ourselves sleeping in the car that night unless we took radical action. This meant driving on a further half-hour or so to reach the coastal town of Trouville, where we were more fortunate. This time we parked first, then explored on foot till we found a likely looking hostelry, swiftly checking it out in the *Michelin* and finding it reputable. It was also accommodating, offering a charming attic room which took me back to the one I had slept in at Catherine's childhood home, complete with the bucolic wallpaper over walls and ceiling. We found a small, suitable restaurant nearby for some supper, then fell gratefully into our comfortable bed, convinced we had turned a corner and were getting the hang of France again.

We were a little less sure about this when, next morning, after a typical, simple but delicious croissant/baguette breakfast, we were well on our journey southward when I casually asked about the bill. We then worked out that our friendly landlord had charged us per person and not for the room, as he should have done. We had paid double the going rate. Maybe La Belle Hélène had had a point; we were rather simple and silly. Could we possibly be trusted to find a French holiday home, never mind negotiate its purchase?

We explored slowly that day, enjoying a visit to Mont-St-Michel, which was relatively quiet at this time of year. We were not finding any pine forests however, and guessed that we would have to drop below Brittany to an area where Graham had good memories of a youthful camping holiday. Île d'Oléron had already been ruled out as being too far south. We spent that night in an establishment calling itself Le Grand Hotel, which was not particularly big, grand or exciting, but more or less on the beach and comfortable enough. Moreover, it had the merit of costing considerably less than half the previous night's stopover.

The next morning saw us poised for La Baule, of which we had great hopes based on Graham's recall of his camping days. We were probably unlucky to hit the town where we did, and have since got to know the place better, but on this Monday morning our initial impression was of glittering apartments with balconies bosoming out over a posh prom. We looked at each other and chorused a disappointed but firm, *'Non'*!

Onward then to Pornic, said to be a small, pretty place and, with a Bed and Breakfast recommendation that sounded second to none, billed in the guide book as being open from March. We were determined that our luck was about to change. The sun was shining and the temperature rising with our spirits as we drove into the delightful town, with its colourful harbour, bobbing boats and interesting boutiques. Unfortunately, it also seemed very crowded. Parking was nearly impossible and this was on a Monday out of season. However, we decided to book in for the night, park the car with our hosts, then get the measure of the place on foot. So we rang, we rang more than once, but answer came there none. Of course it was Monday and, as one comes to learn in France, there is quite a lot that does not happen when it is *lundi*. It is perfectly possible that some people may not answer their telephones on Mondays and (who knows?) those running Bed and Breakfast establishments may be high among them. Pornic? *'Non'*! Time to move on again. Now with rather less sunshine of spirit we paused for a drink in a big, busy spa hotel, which certainly did not feel like our sort of place, but at least gave us the chance to park and to look at the map. So far our success in following our noses had not been resonant with success. This time we decided to get the bed safely booked first, then travel in the direction of our overnight stay. We had had enough of our bed and breakfast guide so reverted to *Michelin*, where at least the recommended hotels tended to answer the phone and were usually traceable without the aid of either psychic powers or that new-found invention – Sat Nav.

As we came into the flat marshland of the Vendée, with its big skies and little muddy creeks, I began to recognise in this new landscape similarities with Mersea, though the cattle grazing on the reclaimed land were that creamy, beige colour so often seen in France and I had never seen a white egret on the Essex marshes. We had great hopes for Beauvoir-sur-Mer, but it proved to be a rather glum little town which seemed to be anything but 'on sea' for *la mer* had apparently found better places to go; beaten off by silt it had retreated towards the Île de Noirmoutier hundreds of years before, leaving the town dry if not high. The hotel was basic, with bedroom furniture that looked as if it had recently been badly assembled from a kit from MFI. But the room was spacious, the water ran hot in the shower and the welcome was warm. In addition, the food in the restaurant was surprisingly good and no one blinked too hard at my vegetarianism. After dinner I pored over our new large-scale map and noticed several patches of green only a few miles further on. Could this be forest? Was this a breakthrough?

It was Tuesday morning and we would have to head north again on Thursday afternoon. The most any sensible person could hope for now was to identify our looked-for setting. The sun was shining as we drove through more flat landscape, with more cream-coloured cows, and arrived in the village square at Fromentine. This had character, charm and several tempting little shops, and also boasted the ferry service across to Île d'Yeu. We parked easily and, exploring on foot, found a short pedestrians-only prom lined with delightful houses, some small, some larger, all in the prime position of the beach and the sea, which lay directly ahead of their front doors. We wandered to the end of the prom and, 'Eureka'! There was the forest, enticing us into its green and distant depths.

We took a short walk, drinking in the smell of pine trees and wallowing in our eventual success. We gave Fromentine a large tick, then drove five miles further south to somewhere called Notre Dame de Monts. Here the forest comes to meet you as you drive down through the village to the sea. The beach is forever golden and the apartments on the modest prom have no bosoms. At either end of this prom area, which admittedly carries parking as well as pedestrians, the forest meets the dunes and the dunes meet the eternal spread of beach. We looked at each other and headed for an estate agent.

Charles was young, tall, dark and good-looking – no Belle Hélène this one. He was charming and knew his job. He listened carefully to our requirements and, within minutes, we had appointments to view half-a-dozen properties next morning – three in Fromentine, two in St Jean de Monts (a town a few miles further south) and the one in Notre Dame which we had already spotted in the window. Having left Charles' office we drove onward to have a look at St Jean, which is very much a resort but has plenty of forest and an attractive older part of town. We liked it and, though the pull was back to Fromentine and Notre Dame de Monts, decided we ought to back some more horses, so made further appointments with two agents in St Jean for the Wednesday afternoon. After a cursory look at the port of St Gilles, even further south, we found ourselves back in Notre Dame, walking the length of the prom to where it petered out and there, among those apartments which had only dunes and beach in front of them, was the manifestation of the photograph we had seen in the agent's window. From the outside it looked good and the position was perfect.

Next morning, Wednesday, was a heavy viewing day. The properties were mostly holiday homes to which the agents had keys and, in marked contrast to our Cumbrian experience, where this situation had seemed a problem and had slowed things down, here in the Vendée viewing could not have been made easier or faster. We saw four properties with Charles in the morning, then two more with him in St Jean de Monts late that afternoon. Between our two sessions with Charles we had the statutory pause for lunch, then honoured our appointment with the two agents in St Jean. These latter agents conveniently scooted around the brief we had given them and must have shown us properties they were desperate to shift, none of which remotely tempted us. With Charles, however, it was a different story. We looked at three houses in Fromentine, two in St Jean and the apartment in Notre Dame. From these six properties we were able to make a shortlist of three, not a bad score, which left us scratching our heads, but not for long.

We had booked to spend the night in a little hotel situated in the forest at Notre Dame and, that evening, wandered down through the trees to the beach, discussing our options. The house in Fromentine, though on a quiet cul-de-sac, was marginally bigger than we wanted. The pretty little thatched house a mile from the sea, set in the forest at St Jean, was on a road which might get busy in the season. Anyway, did we really want the commitment of a thatched roof? If you contorted your neck from the balcony at Fromentine you could catch a glimpse of the sea but this house could not truly claim a sea view either. Graham had always favoured the idea of an apartment as he reckoned it was more secure. Therefore we took ourselves back through our visit to Manureva of that morning.

There are only six apartments in the block and there is a neat courtyard for parking. Because of the fall of the land, from the entrance to the building you go up a staircase to a landing which holds three apartments, so you think you are on the first floor but, once inside, realise that to seaward the apartment is only a metre or so from the ground. Like all French holiday properties this one had been left with its blinds down, and water and electricity off. It took Charles a few moments to click on the lights, then to roll up the big blind to give us a panoramic view of dunes and sea. So far, so very good. The decor was less so. The apartments had been built in the early 1980s and were a monument to those years and to the French style holiday home. There was a heavy-duty, dark and greenly sinister fabric covering the walls, and seriously nasty, beige, spotty tiles on the floor. The kitchen had been adapted (or botched) to take a massive fridge-freezer and, in estate agent's speak, was 'in need of some modernisation'. The general decor throughout was depressing, though the bathroom was not too bad and there was a separate loo. The living space was dominated, of course, by the inevitable huge, rectangular table, where we supposed the family had spent endless hours, deep in philosophical discussion over mounds of *moules marinères*. The apartment needed extensive cosmetic surgery but its 'Location, Location' was faultless. It had two good bedrooms and a well-kept secret at ground level; if you came in the main door and turned right you discovered the important world of the *cave*, where the true Frenchman keeps his wine. But our predecessors, having the privilege of a large garage on the corner of the building, had had the foresight to keep the garage space and *cave* interconnected, the whole area being tiled to rather pleasanter effect than that of upstairs. Moreover, they had turned the intended *cave* into a shower room with loo, washbasin and plumbing for a washing machine. A bonus feature.

As we wandered down through the forest, then onto the beach that Wednesday evening, not too surprisingly our steps led us to take another look at the apartment from the outside. It was not much of a contest after all. We would make an offer.

Next morning we went to see Charles as promised. The apartment had been on the market for a few months so we could indulge in some hard negotiating. We were good at this, the method being, look at the high asking price, realise you need to get things moving quickly before departure, make an offer so close to that high price that only a madman would refuse, and Jean Paul's your uncle. At 2pm, our offer readily accepted, we were back with Charles, signing documents in his office to commence our purchase. Apart from the minor glitch that Graham (feeling it might be important to have his title correct for legal reasons) announced himself as *'un cheval'* (a horse) instead of *'un chevalier'* (knight) all went smoothly and, by 3.30 in the afternoon, we were on the homeward journey north with triumph in our eyes.

French law allows a cooling-off period, during which time either party to the deal can change their mind; after that you are committed to completion within three months. So we knew where we were, unlike housing sales in the UK. We had time to go home, tell our astonished family and friends of our rash decision, go to Italy in early June to stay in the medieval mill and prang the hire car, and still leave a short window to fly out to France to complete the deal on Manureva at the end of the month.

There was a heat wave over much of Europe that summer and in France some vulnerable people actually died as a result. In Notre Dame it was hot, but not unbearably so. It made a pleasant change from our Macclesfield summer and we naively thought that Notre Dame would always enjoy this sort of June weather. We were to spend the first two nights in the small hotel in the centre of the village, then three in the apartment itself, which had been left stripped bare as expected but was also spotlessly clean. We moved in with a small, round garden table with two matching chairs, two small cushions as pillows and a couple of long sun-lounger cushions for mattresses. I had brought two sheets and a light travel rug with us on the plane. This was our only bedding and the floor was hard, but we managed and thanks to the heat wave were warm enough.

We had a busy few days and, by the time we left, had installed a neat little dresser to take all the crockery, and acquired a comfortable, blue sofa and a double bed – though not in time to sleep in, as it arrived the morning we were leaving. Visiting the island of Noirmoutier we found, not only the dresser but also a delicious *crêperie* with upstairs flooring of blue laminate – or *parquet flottant*. This gave me the key to the colour scheme for the apartment. We would bring the colours of outdoors, inside, filling the space with light instead of gloom. The agent had recommended an *electricien* and *cuisiniste* to revamp the kitchen and I had homed in on a sign in a local front garden for a painter and decorator. Appointments were made for each of these people to call to see us. They all turned up on time, were enthusiastic about taking on the work, and turned not a hair about picking up keys from the agent when needing access to the apartment. Just before we left on the Wednesday the *cuisiniste* returned with his quote and a carefully drawn plan for the new kitchen. We had lift-off! We were hardly able to believe how fast and easily it was all moving – contrasting sharply with current experiences back home, where plans to develop the barn at Greengarth were on hold for lack of a builder.

Looking out from the balcony on our last morning I remarked to Graham on the number of people passing with their dogs. I was missing Rosie yet was now excited at the prospect of getting a puppy, wondering what we would be sent. We had set ourselves a window of time to find a rescue puppy, to get her settled in and sufficiently well established so that we could leave her with Harry come October, when we would be returning to France to see how the apartment was shaping up. I am a believer in letting fate take its course to some extent when offering a home to a rescue animal but in my head I knew exactly what I was hoping for – a smallish, white with black, fluffy something-or-other mix-up, with a long feathery tail.

Chapter 20

The Kish Factor

The day after our return from France we were on the trail of our new four-leggéd friend. We had decided to have a puppy, partly so that we could train it to our ways from the word go, but also to try to ensure that the four cats would not feel threatened by a strange dog moving in with them. We thought it would be wise to have a bitch again, thus avoiding the risk of any confrontation with Cowley, who could possibly take against a perceived male rival.

Life has its little quirks, one of them being that animal sanctuaries have an abundance of puppies needing good homes, until you ring up to offer one. Sadly, Windyway had to tell us that they had no puppies and we drew similar blanks from other enquiries, apart from a litter of needy Great Danes, but we thought one of these mighty canines in the family was sufficient and, so far as we knew, they could never be called smallish, white and fluffy. We thought we might have to resort to a visit to Manchester Dogs' Home, if we could ever find it again. Then on Friday, acting from a desperate impulse, I bought a copy of *Loot* which advertises everything for sale, including the kitchen sink and animals. Among the used cars, the good-as-new cots and sofas, I found an advertisement for a charity near Wigan called Home Rescue, which operated by fostering dogs in volunteers' homes until the animals could be found new owners. The phone call lifted my spirits. Yes, there were two puppies needing homes, a boy and a girl, whitish with some black. They would be fluffy and sweet-natured. Here was my Kish – for we already had a name, taken from a book by Salley Vickers called *Miss Garnett's Angel*. Although set in present day Venice, the modern narrative of the novel is intercut with an enchanting, ancient tale based on one from the Apocrypha. This is the story of Tobias and the Angel, in which the stranger (in fact the Archangel Raphael) is accompanied by a dog called Kish, who plays an important role in the healing process recounted. Our Kish would be our healing dog.

That was the plan but, within moments of my triumphant excitement, came a cautionary note down the phone, for there was already someone interested in the little female. Would I ring back later to see if she was fatally spoken for? So my hopes went up, down and then sideways for, alas, our intended did prove to be already spoken for. But would we like to consider a lovely lurcher puppy instead? There were seven of them, desperately needing good homes. Mum was a greyhound who had got out and mated with no one knows whom, but the puppies were the brindle colour of many a full-blooded greyhound and no one would mistake Mum's genes in the litter. We looked at the pictures on the website and one puppy in particular seemed to have a broader nose, as if she might have some Labrador in there somewhere. If our window of opportunity for puppy settling was going to work we needed to get on with it so, next morning, we drove up the M6 to Standish near Wigan. The front room of the small terraced house was a riot of wriggling, bouncing puppydom. The young couple who were the foster parents already had two dogs of their own and you could only admire their commitment and generosity in giving over the happy ship of their home to such a demanding crew. The puppy we had spotted in the pictures was the one who came to snuggle on my lap. We had found our Kish. Soon we were travelling home with the prize, now slightly trembly, cuddled up in a towel on my lap. Fortunately, I had taken other old cloths with me as she was sick twice during the hour long ride. While this was far from unexpected it was an early indication that this puppy was not going to be another Rosie, who had been instantly at home in the car. As we put our new best friend gently down in the garden when we got home, Mille appeared to greet us, and Kish set off in enthusiastic pursuit.

By this time in our lives, with a book entitled *A Cat in My Lap* long tucked under my belt, some people had begun to regard me as something of a cat guru, and I would get the occasional phone call from friends or acquaintances asking for advice. Sometimes I could help but, as I was always swift to point out, my knowledge was based on in-depth experience of the cats I had known and loved, not on any scientific or veterinary skills, nor on a very wide sample, and the one thing of which I was sure, was that each cat is an individual, so that there can be as many permutations on the theme as there are cats. When it came to dogs I would rate my expertise considerably lower and it was a long time since we had had a puppy, so I had invested in the help of the splendid Jan Fennell. In her book *The Dog Listener* she relates dogs' behaviour to that found in the social structure of the wolf pack and stresses how important it is for the owner to establish him or herself as the pack leader. Much of this is achieved by ignoring one's dog for any initial contact, for example when you come down in the morning, first come back into the house after an outing, or indeed back into the kitchen after being upstairs. I had read Jan Fennell's book and was determined to put her kind, gentle yet firm ideas into practice with our new incumbent. I would recommend this approach to any puppy or dog owner, the snag being that you have to train yourself as much as the animal concerned. I was not bad at some of it but failed hopelessly in other respects, and, anyway, try as I would, I could not see how ignoring Kish when she chased the cats was going to teach her not to do it.

Our new baby was a sight hound – a natural chaser. After she had come home with us Harry brought round his doggie encyclopaedia, which succeeded in frightening me into thinking that Kish would grow into a cat and small dog killer. True she would be loyal and fine with people but we had four cats to consider. I kept these panicky misgivings to myself for some time and, on the surface, did all the right things by her. She was only seven-weeks-old and newly separated from her family. The first two nights I slept with her in the kitchen, lying on big cushions on the tiled floor. I fed her, cleared up after her as we began house-training, talked nicely to her, cuddled her, but could not love her; something or someone was in the way. Poor little Kish, how was she to know that I just wanted Rosie back? Rosie who had been such an easy puppy, who had hardly made a single lunge towards the cats, Rosie who was a link back to my mother and to Bruno. I had thought I was ready for another dog but I think I had been kidding myself, as I was still grieving too much for what could never be recovered. If Kish had been easier with the cats it could well have been different, but seeing them upset by the constant chasing, and worrying about what this could portend, was too much and I began to think that we had made a terrible mistake and might have to rehome our rescue puppy.

She was extremely lively, which was only to be expected, but in the evenings for half-an-hour she would turn into a werewolf, growling and tearing at us, so that we resorted to a heavy piece of sacking to protect ourselves. We would allow this noble fabric to bear the brunt of her vicious attacks, thus sparing our legs and arms to some extent, though the lacerations to my limbs were impressive as a young puppy's teeth are sharper than needles. Meanwhile, Bernard, who was initially pleased to see a dog about the place again, was trying hard to discipline Kish, and I had thought that this would sort it out. He stood up to her, hissed, spat and swiped at her from the worktop but, far from discouraging her, this only made her the more determined to harass him. On one occasion Mille followed us at a distance into the field. Kish, spotting her, took up the classic hunting stance, still as still, body tense, nose pointed to the prey before launching herself at the innocent Mille, who had to turn tail and flee. Although still so young Kish's reactions looked dangerously threatening.

I rang Home Rescue, telling them that, although she was a lovely puppy in most ways, I was seriously concerned about her chasing the cats. The advice down the phone was simple, 'You've got to stop her!' Unfortunately, the advice stopped there. We were left to ponder how. Shouting at her produced no effect, for her instinct would override any desire to please; she simply did not 'hear' us. Fortunately, our house is long and low, and, with the Mothercare gate securing the kitchen, the cats could come and go through the rest of the house, using the garden room entrance at the back. Mille and Lenni could exit our bedroom (where they had always had feeding stations) by leaping from the balcony onto the lawn, an art Mille had perfected when only a few months old and had then taught her brother. She would also come into the bedroom from the balcony, we assumed by accessing our low-slung roof and then abseiling down the virginia creeper, though Lenni never managed this latter feat. Outside, there is a side gate which can keep back and front garden quite separate. Bernard, being indomitable, was the least upset by Kish, so it was Amber who had the roughest deal. Having eventually made a truce with Bernard, she was used to her main access being through the doorless cat flap (or, as she called it, 'the way-in-way-out hole') into the utility room, and thence into the kitchen. But this was where Kish was based. However, it was good weather, so we kept many doors and windows open, to provide alternative arrangements, and we used the human ferry to transport any stranded feline through the Kish endangered zone.

I felt I was successfully establishing myself as pack leader for most of the time and, in many ways, Kish was a good little dog. She was soon house-trained and could be left for short, planned periods, without any chewing problems as, obligingly, she did her teething with her toy bones and not the furniture when we were out. No one could doubt her happy disposition, her love of people, especially children, or her general enthusiasm for life. Nonetheless, my aching doubts remained and that woeful sinking of the stomach kept me awake at night.

Fortunately, after the initial weeks of bedlam with the cats, we were scheduled to go up to Greengarth, which would give them all a break. We even left Amber behind this time for her own peace of mind. I thought Kish would probably be worse on our return home, having got used to having us all to herself so, while at Greengarth, after a couple of near sleepless nights, I decided some action was needed. I rang Wendy at Windyway, who was very sympathetic, gently suggesting that perhaps the problem was as much with my emotions and perceptions as with Kish herself, but offering to try to find a good alternative home for her which, of course, made me feel horribly guilty. I wrote a lengthy six page letter all about my concerns to Home Rescue, then showed it to Graham, at last managing to confess to him how I had been feeling and the state I was now in. I only wish I had done this sooner. He was astonished, supportive, and began restoring some sensible perspective to the scenario. Here we were with a young puppy, with every opportunity to train her to our way of doing things. No, she was not Rosie but no other puppy would ever be Rosie either and, to his way of thinking, the cats were rather less upset by Kish's behaviour towards them than I was, watching it. The letter had been a therapeutic one to write but not one to send, though I rather wish I had kept it for posterity.

I began to feel a little better with the trouble shared, but I followed Wendy's advice to have a word with the behaviourist at the vet's, so that we might have one or two fresh ideas for coping when we got back home. She was very helpful, explaining that with some puppies a cat's swiping response to their overtures was seen as encouragement to up the game, thus making the situation worse. Try telling that to an irate Bernard! There was a lot to absorb after my conversation with the behaviourist vet who, despite being so helpful, made my level of guilt rise still further by telling me she thought I was being very responsible. In my own book I had marked myself down as 'poor to hopeless'.

Meanwhile, Kish was enjoying her introduction to the Lake District, learning while on the lead that sheep were a definite 'No!' and, when off it, practising the renowned lurcher leap of greeting, on any fellow walkers spotted before we did. This happened more than once for, being a sight hound, her eyes have alpha vision. Fortunately, people were entranced by her youthful enthusiasm and early attempts at singing. Her songs of greeting were to soar to a fine art form over several octaves as she matured. Meanwhile, for one so small, Kish was remarkably good about coming back when called and Graham was convinced she had the makings of an ideal family member.

In my Doubting Thomas hat I was still dubious, but marked my self assessment book 'must try harder', feeling ashamed of myself for being such a wimp but expecting to find inter-feline-canine relationships worse on our return home, with Kish thinking she was Queen of the May after a week of being our sole focus. Again, how wrong I was! The first week back was indeed a watershed but not as I would have predicted. Though far from a model of good behaviour Kish was, in fact, a little calmer with the cats. Jan Fennell's methods are all gentleness and patience, and much of this worked well for us. But then you have to adapt to find what works for you and your family in particular circumstances. Kish had regarded as a joke the intended deterrent of a little water pistol, recommended in the pet shop, but we brought on the big guns in the shape of a powerful Super Soaker with a range of 30 feet, thus enabling a shot to the back of a cat-chasing head. A jet of cold water succeeded where all else had failed. Riotous pursuit screeched to a puzzled halt, a turn round and quizzical trot back to the cruel marksman.

There was an irony here as I have always hated the idea of any firearm in the house and, fortunately, though Graham was an A1 shot when in the army doing his National Service, he had never wanted to do any shooting subsequently. I felt so strongly against firearms (along with a phobia of sharp knives) that when the teenage Harry announced that he wanted an air rifle, saying that, if necessary, he would buy one with his own money and I couldn't stop him, my reply had had precisely that effect. 'No,' I said, 'but if you do buy an air gun I will throw it in the reservoir.' Thus, visitors knowing my views on blood sports, and some who might, in the past, have struggled to cut up a carrot in my kitchen with a near blunt knife, were astonished and alarmed to hear Kish threatened with 'the gun' if she did not calm her enthusiastic greetings.

That first week back from the Lakes our newly acquired weapon proved an invaluable training tool. Eventually, true to Pavlov*, it would come to the point where spraying Kish was unnecessary; the mere sight of it, or latterly the mere mention of the word 'gun', was enough. However, at this early stage the snag was that you could not always have the weapon to hand in a cat protecting situation. So, alongside the gun, we put the behaviourist's advice into practice, instigating a definite training programme. We did not think it was much good trying to explain to Bernard that swiping at Kish was counter-productive but we found we could often avert trouble. By now, Kish was well-used to her soft-loop lead (as recommended by Jan Fennell) so we would ascertain the presence of a cat, safe on a high surface, then take Kish on her lead to the potentially hazardous confrontation, making her sit, rewarding her for doing so, while all the time talking gentle reassurance to both animals. After a few minutes we would then remove Kish from the situation, lavishing her with praise for good behaviour.

We were only three days into this new training programme when Wendy rang to say that some very nice people (a mother and daughter) would be interested in coming to see Kish, with a view to offering her a home as a companion to their dog who, they felt, needed a friend. Here was a 'how-de-do'* for, having made such a fuss previously to Wendy, I did not feel I could say 'No' to them coming the next day and bringing their own dog with them to see how he got on with Kish. Graham, being Graham, said that the decision was ultimately mine but that he would be very sad to see Kish go. I doubt if I could have gone through with it but, as it happened, the fates were particularly kind for, on the very evening of the visit, Kish rushed to the front gate to greet some passers-by, one of whom was a very large, grey-blue lurcher called Jack. I got chatting to his owner, confessing the trouble we were having with Kish and the cats, which produced an amused reaction, as she had been there too – with Jack and her cats which, like mine, had been sacrosanct. She did not reveal exactly how, but things had slowly calmed down and all her cats now adored the dog.

The mother and daughter interested in Kish arrived just a little later that evening. Kish played beautifully with their Jack Russell and was generally better behaved than I had ever seen her. How could I think of parting with her? Fortunately, our visitors put the same question, adding reassuringly, 'She does you credit; you've done really well with her.' They were kind enough to sense that the crisis was more about me than a difficult puppy so it was left that, although they would love to have Kish, they thought she was already in the right place and unless I contacted them again, that was how it should stay.

The events of that week, and especially of that evening, helped to bring me through my cold slough of confused emotions (where I had been stuck yearning for the past) into a warmer, sunnier place, where I began to feel the stirrings of real affection for Kish, realising the mountains I had been making out of small molehills. The family mountain was surely Great Uncle Cowley, besides whom Kish was indeed a tiny molehill. Fortunately, despite his early tendencies to alarm her by virtue of sheer strength and size, he took a benign view of her and she came to hero-worship him.

Alongside some considerable progress made with the cats there were encouraging developments in a different quarter as I began taking Kish a short drive in the mornings up into the Rainow hills, where several dog owners met up each day for an hour's walk. I had made this discovery when I used to walk Bruno with Rosie, returning to my mother's for breakfast.

Kish with Great Uncle Cowley

We thought it was important that Kish socialised early with other dogs and this ploy worked well as she learnt her place in the hierarchy, would romp and play, accepting it if one or the other told her to cool it, and finding no temptation to stray far away, as all we had to do was call back the older dogs and, automatically, she came too. Kish and the rabbits began learning about each other while the two-leggéd walkers swapped views on books, films, theatre productions and world events.

We saw the wolf pack social system in action when our basic team of four women and five dogs met another walker with two smallish, wire-haired terrier types. Brother and sister, at that time they were a size or two larger than Kish. Teddy, the male, would brook no nonsense from Kish, putting her firmly in her place, which was a fully submissive one, crawling on her stomach and then rolling on her back to expose the vulnerable throat. Even when she was nearly twice Teddy's size and could, herself, be edgy with some other dogs, Kish would defer in exactly the same way to this dominant power of her youth, proving that it is not only elephants who have long memories.

Most days Harry would collect Kish and take her to the 'afternoon play group' on the Congleton side of town, along with Misha the German Shepherd, so there was no shortage of activities or companionship. Harry built a strong rapport with Kish and she spent a lot of time with him, becoming a two-home dog, for when we were away or out too long, there was always Uncle Harry's house with its willing dog-sitter.

It probably took a mere six or seven weeks for Kish to settle with the cats and for me to start feeling for her as I wanted to, but it was a long six weeks at the time and is a reminder that bringing a new animal into your home is not always straightforward, for it can drastically change the dynamics. My sister was to experience trauma in a different way when they first got their inoffensive, eight-week-old, chocolate Labrador puppy. Tilly had only been in the house four or five hours when Chester, their large black fluffy cat, suddenly flew across the room without warning and clawed the puppy's eye so badly that, for a few days, the vet thought she might lose the sight in it. The other cat, Gromit, who had adored the previous dog, went into nervous retreat after the new one arrived, and would hardly come into the house at all, needing lavish and constant reassurance that this terrifying canine interloper was harmless. It took Gromit two years to accept Tilly but after that would snuggle up to her as if they had been lifelong friends from the word go. Time can often work as much healing in difficult situations as all our own best placed efforts, but effort is still worthwhile, if only to assuage guilt.

We were fortunate; our own crisis was sharp but relatively short. Once over, all the cats thereafter were completely at ease with Kish, indeed they decided she was an asset, and she, in her turn, came to respect, not only her own cats but also ones she met outside the family. Of course Bernard put it down to his special training programme and we would never have disabused him . . .

Training the Puppy

1. Dominate.

2. When the puppy creature first arrives make sure that you look down on it from an impressive height.

3. If, at any time, its nose comes level with yours take a swipe at it.

4. Eat your food salaciously, glancing down to say how superior your meal is to anything the creature itself is likely to get.

5. Move slowly, and with menace if on the ground, indicating (even if walking away from the creature) that you will not be messed with.

6. Advise less confident colleagues to move through the puppy creature's territory only when it's asleep, in this way familiarising themselves with its presence at no inconvenience to themselves.

7. Should the puppy creature interrupt your own sleep in a sunny corner of the garden sit your ground and spit fiercely.

8. Demonstrate by purring frenetically around Her that She is foremost your person, shared with your colleagues and that the puppy is last in line.

9. Impress on Her that your daily routine must not be upset by the puppy and that She should make proper arrangements with security gates, wiring off half the garden and anything else it may take to ensure your continued comfort of lifestyle. Indeed, make it known you expect extra fuss and attention.

10. Never let on that you might be pleased to have a dog about the place again.

Bernard
CFPT
(Chief Feline Puppy Trainer)

Chapter 21

Magicking the Barn

Kish grew rapidly, retaining her considerable exuberance but shedding her torturing milk teeth for gentler, mature ones. The *Mothercare* gate, guarding the entrance from the lobby to the kitchen, became a joke for, if she knocked it over, far from being intimidated, Kish rejoiced at the clatter it made and sped onward to make merry on the other side – quite unlike her predecessor, for Rosie could have worn a label saying 'Beware of the Gate,' remaining frightened of it from that first rattling tumble in puppyhood through to old age. We had to improve our defence system, so enlisted the help of Simon the gardener to design and make a robust, high, wooden stockade-type gate which satisfactorily contained our live-wire puppy, but had the important concession of a strut cut away at the base, so that the cats could pass unimpeded.

We had decided to be a little firmer with this new dog than we had been with Rosie, who, bless her, had tended to festoon the whole house, beds and all, with clouds of her creamy gold hair. We began as we meant to go on. Kish was not allowed on beds and, although not forbidden upstairs, was not encouraged to be up there – certainly not when very young. To give rabbits and other wildlife a sporting chance when she was out and about we fitted her collar with a little bell. The healthy jingling of this bell alongside her disc resulted in the nickname of Tinkerbell up in the Rainow Hills. The garden was, of course, dog-proof, or it was until her full leaping powers were revealed, when some extra high wiring was required to discourage any Houdini attempts. Fortunately, Kish has never shown any tendency to wander but even little sorties into our lane to greet passers-by were not encouraged.

Kish is not a stick person. Her forté is football and she would make a fine goalie. Harry seems able to find abandoned footballs of the sort she likes - semi-squashed and easy to carry. He keeps her well supplied. She has had many of these over the years and soon came to regard any visiting window cleaner, gardener, plumber or electrician as part of her football team, or possibly an opponent in a 'friendly'. She attacks the ball with such ferocity that, on several occasions, has actually injured herself and had to be on sick leave with football banned for a couple of weeks. It does not do the lawn a huge amount of good either but we have always taken the view that a garden is primarily a place for the family to relax, enjoy and play in, so if football is your thing, so be it, except for a few short periods to give the grass a chance to recover.

We had signed a pledge to have Kish spayed as part of the deal when we took her from Home Rescue and, anyway, the thought of our over-enthusiastic youngster on heat was daunting. Veterinary advice now seems to be that the bitch does not have to have had a season before spaying so we were able to have it done around six months, with no ill effects. A few weeks before this, when she was largely through the chewing stage, we swapped her cardboard box for a proper dog basket. It had belonged to Rosie but this was not a problem to Kish, and she now revealed an endearing aspect of her nature for the first time. She is a dog who seems to understand and relish the concept of being given a present. In this first instance it was the new bed and she danced underneath the exciting wicker offering, nose-up and mesmerised till it was placed in position in the kitchen, then sat in it before I had had the chance to straighten the bedding. She had 'Look At Me I'm a Big Girl Now' written all over her face.

Thus, by early 2004 Kish had settled with us and made fond relationships with all four cats – Bernard, Amber, Mille and Lenni – so we could safely turn our attention to other matters. We returned to France at the beginning of March 2004 to see how the apartment was faring and came off the boat at St Malo in snow, which made our normal route too slippery and dangerous. We fumbled our way south, trying to explain to our patient, recently acquired Sat Nav lady that there were complicating weather conditions. There was also obliterating snow covering many of the road signs, making it a challenging journey. When we arrived in Notre Dame it was to find the beach sporting an additional, unusual band of colour. The grey sea was edged by the gold of sand, but this was then met by the white of snow, which had spilled down from the dunes above as if an artist had carefully created the scene, to stunning effect. Nothing like it had been seen in Notre Dame for about 15 years.

When we entered the apartment it was to find it transformed into a light, airy space, fitted not only with a kitchen to be proud of but, fortunately, with electric radiators. There was more good news, for our thoughtful *electricien*, knowing of our scheduled arrival, had switched on the radiators and the super efficient water heater, so that we were welcomed by warmth and scalding hot water. For this we were duly grateful and, as we inspected the details of what had been achieved, were hugely impressed by our French team, who had effected everything we had wanted, exactly to 'spec' and not leaving a speck of dust to betray the amount of work done. We could hardly believe our luck. Just one concern remained – the Battle of the Basin.

There are many differences between French and British homes, one of them being common to many other countries – the notable failure to have the sensible device of an on/off switch on wall sockets. This means that, if you are ironing and want to leave the task for a break, you have to heave the plug out of the wall instead of being able to flick a switch. The French system of shutters on windows I applaud, but their bathroom arrangements leave me puzzled. In a UK home, where there is a loo, there is normally a hand washing facility. Our bathrooms usually have the loo included. In France, the bathroom often excludes the loo, which is separate. This would be fine, except that there is no hand basin, well hardly ever, and the logic defeats me. A person does what a person has to do in that small room and then most of us, whether French, British or from further afield, like to wash our hands. So why not have a handy basin within that room? I had conveyed my concerns to our obliging *cuisiniste* who gave me a quizzical, if not pitying, look and explained that it would mean some ugly extra piping, could only be a very small basin and would cost us a lot for *très peu**. My moderate French could not rise to combat these arguments quickly enough so I retreated, but only to regroup and, like the best of generals, attack again on a different front. We had discovered that our *electricien* was also a plumber, so I asked him about the basin and, if the dear man thought I was 'funny English' he did not let it show. By the time we came over again that summer a little corner basin glimmered white in the corner of what was now a proper cloakroom. So each time I wash my hands I experience a glow of satisfaction – a small triumph for British determination working with (eventual) Gallic flexibility.

Meanwhile, back in the Lake District, the plans for the conversion of the derelict barn had gone through in 2002, thanks to the good offices of Phil, who is not only a family friend but an architect who has the tact and persuasive powers of a Nelson Mandela, when dealing with local planning departments. Work should have begun in spring 2003 but had foundered for lack of a builder, the problem being that our gold-plated men of yesteryear had decided to retire. We had therefore needed to find both a good local builder and a dry-stone waller who would have access to a supply of the necessary stone. The planners are no pushover and, quite rightly, were insisting on local materials in keeping with the area. Fortunately we have a contact in the village who is the fount of all local knowledge. Indeed it seems fitting to describe Barrie as having lived there since before he was born. He was kind enough to tell us of the unbeatable George, the Master Waller who, in turn, works with reliable Sid, the builder and his team. We had reached the starting post and a new date was planned to begin work – spring 2004.

The barn was to have a totally different feel from that of the cottage. I was aiming at a decor with a touch of the magic cabin. In many ways its look is minimalist-contemporary, with plain white walls and an ambience that sprang from a chair I had seen, fashioned in pickled oak. This was one of the artefacts made during the *One Tree Project*. In 1998 a large, ailing oak tree was felled in Tatton Park, Cheshire, with the aim of asking skilled arts and crafts people to create as many objects as possible from its wood. The results were dazzling and an exhibition of this talented artistry eventually toured the country, staying for several weeks at Tatton itself, where I visited it twice and fell in love with the said copy of a pickled Welsh stick chair made by Neil Taylor. The chair struck that fine balance between furniture resonant of the past, yet somehow undeniably of the modern era. I felt it could belong to an enchantress for there was a magical feel about it, and it triggered my conception of the decor for the barn.

This particular chair was already sold but, with the generous final payment from Halton Borough on my retirement from work with the Disabled Writers in December 2001, I bought myself a leaving present, commissioning Neil to make me another chair just like the one in the *One Tree Project*. The enchantress's chair arrived early in 2002, somewhat ahead of the development of the barn, so it sat in our drawing room at Throstles' Nest for nearly three years until it could go to its spiritual home in the Lakes in 2005. Neil knows his wood, having helped with the building of the new Globe Theatre in London, and proved to be an invaluable asset to the barn project, providing sturdy ballisters for the stairs, topping them with a pickled oak bannister, glowing deep and black and smooth. He made quirky tables and three-leggéd stools, then Hansel and Gretel twin beds to fit the small dimensions of the downstairs bedroom. The upstairs living space had a Neil Taylor, wedge-shaped desk specifically designed to fit into a weirdly shaped corner, for the original zany outline of the barn's walls had been kept, at the planner's insistence. All in all we were delighted with the finished barn, rating it something of an improvement on its previous incarnation. Many passers-by seemed to think so too, though, in order to have enough internal height for upstairs living space, it was now about a metre taller than it had been previously, which led some disapproving local to mutter about 'that skyscraper'.

One of the more mundane reasons for converting the building was to have proper laundry facilities but the utility room's black granite has sparkle, and its lighting includes a lampshade glowing in beads of bewitching colours, for which we had cantered the streets of Prague. There may be a modern electric kettle but tea is made in an old silver pot which was once part of an infestation of teapots found in the Cornish cottage bought by Phil, our architect, and his wife Claire, who is Graham's cousin. They thought that I might like this collector's item and I proved them right by having it re-silvered and then installing it in the barn as Aladdin's lamp. The little bedroom has Hedwig among its cuddly toys, while Cinderella's broom sits on the stairs.

Upstairs in the main living area, the two single beds double up as couches by day, softened with thick, mock bearskin throws. Ultra-modern and zany Swarovski chandeliers throw bright (or dimmed) light from crystal droplets, while casting shadows like wavering branches on the ceiling. Once, hay would have arrived in the loft of the barn through a doorway facing the fell. Now, while the plain white walls provide the perfect background for contemporary artwork from young painters trying to make their way, the best picture of all is seen through that same doorway, which has become a small French window framing a view of the fell, with its changing weather, colours and seasons, and the oriental rug, set on the natural boards, could levitate at any moment and fly through that window, up into the sky above the hills.

This is a picture which we like to think the enchantress enjoys from her special chair whilst drinking tea poured from her silver teapot borrowed from Aladdin. Of course we have never seen her but we sense her presence, for the walls exude good vibes and the power of white magic practised in this Cumbrian cabin.

The Chair

She was here

     the enchantress

    her chair

      empty

is warm

     and you can sense her

            being

               in the air

             there is the print of her

            and you can hear

            the silent echo of her voice

        mellow as comfort

              her healing

               touch

Chapter 22

Going too Well

As we entered 2005 family life had stabilised nicely. We had an adorable little granddaughter whom we saw regularly. She would be three in April and soon we could look forward to Phoebe being 'the big, big sister' for a baby brother or sister would be born in the autumn. We began practising having Phoebe for 'sleep-overs' in case she should need to stay with us when the new baby arrived. Meanwhile, Kish was well established, though still jumping up too much which seems to be a nigh-on incurable lurcher habit. In line with our policy of not being quite so soft as we had been with Rosie, Kish had also been practising sleep-overs, but hers were up at Windyway. This was to prepare her, in case we did ever need to leave her in kennels for a week or so.

Some people say that they can't have a dog because of the problem when they go away. We have always thought of it the other way round; if you have a dog, then he or she has to be factored into your lifestyle and, with a little careful thought, any problem can be overcome by using various options. There are relatives, friends, house-sitters, reputable kennels, or short-term fosterers, who offer a home-from-home service. In our case we had Harry and, in later years, a professional house-sitting and dog-walking service. To deprive yourself of the pleasure of a family pet, and a needy dog of a loving home, because of two or three weeks in the year when that dog might need to go into kennels, seems to me to be a sad nonsense. Where there is a will there is inevitably a solution.

Windyway offers an excellent kennel service alongside its rescue work; indeed the former helps to fund the latter. Kish greeted everyone up there with ecstatic arias and came to no harm at all, though of course a cushy night or two with Uncle Harry would have been her first choice. She also had to learn her place when travelling in my car. We had started off with her on the back seat (not the front like Rosie) but once I began ferrying Phoebe this was no longer an option. An over-loving, excitable young Kish was not a good mix with a small granddaughter. So we changed to a hatchback with a dog guard, by which Kish was somewhat affronted, and once, when left alone in the car, showed her displeasure by chewing through the top of the rear seat-belts, which she could reach from her side of the guard. Usually she was not a dog who chewed, so she was telling us something and had made her point, for it cost over £100 in each case to replace them.

However, we could not, of course, give in, so my car now sports the creative genius of Simon the gardener, who chopped a wire flower basket in two, fitting these decorous guards to protect the new straps from our determined demi-greyhound. (Sometimes we refer to Kish's breeding in this way, finding 'lurcher' such an ugly word.) In Graham's much bigger saloon car she travels as a full family member, in comfort, on a rug on the back seat, and in what she considers the manner to which she is entitled. In this setting she would not demean herself by even looking at a safety strap.

Dogs know their people, and with whom they can do what. It would not enter Kish's head to jump on our bed or sit on the furniture when she is with us, but at Harry's house she snuggles up to him on his bed all night and makes use of the bed whether he is in it or not, that is unless she is occupying one of her favourite resting positions downstairs – full stretch on the kilim in front of the gas fire or curled into the obliging shape of the velvet tub chair – her own choice entirely, though to the human eye she looks a bit squashed up being, after all, a 'long dog'.

A two-home dog, Kish was well settled in both, and enjoyed the company of all the cats in ours. This gang of four had Bernard as senior and macho cat, now 16 but still indomitable. Then there was Amber, the gentle marmalade (about 14) who had been busy of late writing her book, letters 'back home' from Throstles' Nest. Amber did not enjoy the best of health but medication and a special diet were keeping her heart and kidney conditions well in check. Mille and Lenni, the millennium kittens, were, of course, in peak condition, being only five-years-old. They were both beautiful, sweet-natured and fluffy, with the half Persian fur that is my favourite kind of cat coat. Lenni's distinguishing feature was that he was to Kish's 'long dog' an even longer cat, with a capacity to loll to an unlikely length, his supple body moving in graceful contortions that looked to the mere human eye impossible to achieve.

2005 looked like being a good year. The transformation of the barn in Cumbria was fully completed by the spring and the apartment in France was running smoothly and was much enjoyed over that summer. There would also be events to gladden the heart later in the year, with the publication of Amber's *Dear Dear Mary* and, more importantly, the arrival of the new grandchild. Ruby confounded her mother by being a girl, when Jo had been convinced that she was carrying a boy but, apart from that minor blip which no one minded very much, we were all thrilled, not least Big, Big Sister who was enjoying her sleep-over with us so much that she was quite cross with her father for arriving to take her home, mid-morning next day. But the sunshine warmth of her tender smile and her new-found eagerness to jump into Daddy's car once Hugo had told her she had a baby sister, would have melted an iceberg.

I had also planned to visit my niece Emily in November. She was living and working in Switzerland, teaching at the Geneva English School. I am very fond of Emily, had been to stay before and liked Geneva and its surrounds very much. I knew it would be an enjoyable long weekend, giving me the chance to meet up with my French friend Catherine, who lives not too far from Geneva on the French side of the border. The visit would also include half a day at Emily's school, sharing some poems with the children.

On the Wednesday, two days before I was due to travel, the local newspaper rang to say that they were managing, at long last, to organise an article about Amber's book, *Dear Dear Mary*. They would like to send a photographer next day to take a picture of Amber with me. This seemed a perfectly good idea and I was pleased to fix an appointment for Thursday afternoon. On Wednesday evening Lenni was sitting on the stairs as I went up to bed. I gave him a little stroke, remarking that it was very cold outside and he might like to stay in that night.

Next morning I was up early as there was plenty to do ready for Friday. As I came into the kitchen I heard a pathetic mew from the living room where, to my distress, I found Lenni lying stretched out miserably on the floor, his hindquarters dragging behind him and excrement smeared on the carpet. Yes, Lenni was a long cat, but this was something different. It was clear that something dreadful had happened and my assumption was that he had been hit by a car on the lane, and shock had carried him forward into the house to collapse. On several counts this seemed unlikely but it was all I could think of. He was obviously in deep pain and I was frightened to move him lest I hurt him more. It was too early yet to contact our own vet but I rang the 24 hour emergency service, with half a mind to rush him over to them. An expert voice on the other end of a phone is calming and the advice sound. Bearing in mind the trauma of a 40-minute car journey it was probably better to keep Lenni warm and comfortable at home till our own vet opened in an hour or so. This was sensible, especially as the voice said to keep the patient still and Lenni was valiantly dragging himself around to be near me all the time. (He was currently on the cold tiles of the kitchen floor.) There was no way I could have considered manoeuvring his wrecked body into a cat basket so it would need two of us to take him to the vet's. Fortunately I had a big, flattish box to hand, which was housing the Christmas cards I had begun to write. These were unceremoniously dumped on the dining-room table, a cosy blanket fitted into the box and Lenni eased, oh so gently, onto this make-do stretcher. He did not complain, sensing that I was trying to help and, once settled on his pallet, seemed calmer and happier. I could then sit by him stroking his head and offering what reassurance I could until it was time to ring our own surgery. The nurse was there before 8.30 and said she would ring the vet, asking him to come at once. Meanwhile, we should bring Lenni straight down to her. I nursed him, lying on his stretcher on my knee, while Graham drove us the short distance to the surgery. Here we split forces so that he could get back to walk Kish, then travel to a business meeting.

The vet came as soon as he could but, inevitably, it felt like several hours, while the nurse and I comforted Lenni as best we could. The diagnosis was not good. Far from having been run over, the vet thought Lenni had suffered a massive thrombosis, from which recovery would be very slow, if it ever came. However, the first step was to give him pain-killers and put him into the equivalent of intensive care for several days. I was relieved to know Lenni would be so well looked after, but had a weep on the walk home to think that one who had been so beautiful was now so broken, and that he might never be the same again. I was still hopeful that we would have Lenni home eventually and, meanwhile, I would go to Geneva next day as planned, though with an aching heart. I was also grateful that my handsome boy had not collapsed outside, in the cold of a bitterly frosty night.

The photographer arrived about two o'clock and swiftly took pictures of an obliging Amber, being held by a less than jolly looking me. It reminded me that when Silvester and I had been photographed for the launch of *A Cat in My Lap* it was possible to detect in the newspaper photograph a faint milkiness to his eyes, just before he actually went blind. This time it is not the cat's eyes which look strange, but mine, which look decidedly strained and weepy round the edges. In fact I was lucky, for the door had just closed on the photographer when the phone rang. Lenni had died.

At least I was alone and could collapse in undignified sobs. Lenni was not quite six-years-old and, as always with sudden death, it is hard to believe. To my eye he was the most beautiful of all our cats, with his glorious colouring, half Persian coat and pretty face. Realistically, perhaps it was a mercy that he did not survive longer, or have to lead a sort of half life, taking medication every day which he would have hated, being the only one of our cats to become wild and distressed at the sight of a pill. Now he was safe from suffering. The ground was too hard to bury him, so Lenni was cremated and his ashes found their eventual home under a small fir tree, where he had often lain . . .

Haiku for Lenni

Sun lights his colours

white and gold blazed to the tree,

a green remembrance.

Chapter 23

A Taste of Travel

In time, we would try to find a friend for Mille who was missing Lenni very much. She may possibly have known how ill he had been, but his total disappearance was another matter and she was both subdued and in need of comfort from us. However, apart from a preliminary call to Cats Protection, we could do nothing about a kitten until we returned from our trip to New Zealand early in 2006. We were no longer keen on long haul travel (indeed airports have generally become a turn-off for going anywhere) and we usually prefer to go to our own homesteads for holidays, but we did want to experience the splendours of that country Down Under, and were giving ourselves a month away in order to see something of both North and South Islands. We would break the long flight in Singapore. The whole experience was to prove a splendid one and we would certainly go again, if only New Zealand were not so far away.

However, as is so often the case, it is not the famous sights which leave the strongest memories but personal incidents and small discoveries made oneself. This was certainly true some years earlier when we went as VIPs to Kuala Lumpur, in the days when Graham was President of the International Co-operative Alliance. I was greeted with a bouquet of flowers and we were installed in a suite that was embarrassingly large and opulent. Our hosts could not have been kinder or more eager to please and this was our undoing, for I had done some background reading on Malaysia and discovered that they boast 'the king of fruits' otherwise known as the durian. The fruit, about the size of a small football, apparently tastes of nectar, food indeed for the gods, having only the slight disadvantage that, when you cut it open, it smells like nothing else known to humankind – worse than drains, decaying matter or suppurating wounds. But the Malays are proud of the durian and we presumed that they were also proud of their ability to battle through the pong to the reward of the taste of its flesh. I made the mistake, and it was entirely mine, of politely enquiring about the durian from one of our many new acquaintances.

On our last night, at the end of the evening, someone slipped into my hands a mysterious package. This was done secretively and with the caveat that we should not open it until safely back in our hotel suite. When we did so, it was to find no less than the king of fruits in all its majesty. As so much trouble had been taken we thought the least we could do was to cut it open, brave the smell and savour the nectar. So we slit it open and were nearly knocked across the room by what exuded from it. Indescribable is the only way to describe the stench which assailed us. However, we had been warned, this was only as expected, so we screwed up our courage and our noses, and each scraped out a spoonful of the foul smelling fruit then, simultaneously, put it in our mouths awaiting an explosion of ecstasy. Unfortunately, this was where events differed from the expected script. Yes, the taste was unbelievable – unbelievably awful. In fact it had to be worse than the smell. It was a race to see who could spit out all traces of his majesty the fastest. We then looked at each other and wondered what on earth to do with the ghastly thing, for the smell would have kept us awake all night. In desperation we bundled up the mutilated beast as best we could and shoved it in the fridge till morning.

In the light of day, with the taste still blighting our mouths, we decided we would have to get the wretched thing properly disposed of, so I rang down to reception and said we had a little problem we would like to discuss. An anxious staff member knocked at our door, obviously expecting a complaint. When she heard our actual concerns, she looked rather solemn and said we should never have been given the durian as they are illegal. In whispered tones she spirited it away, leaving us with days of putrid flavour lingering in our mouths, and desperate feelings of guilt about that unfortunate fridge. Was it ever usable again? I think we were lucky not to have been arrested.

This time, our visit to the Far East was for less then 24 hours and we were not lured to try anything illegal. Our scheduled hotel in central Singapore was overbooked, so we were taken out to Sentosa Beach, which we thought was much pleasanter. We had dinner on the terrace close to the water and were enchanted by the local cats. They were presumably feral, yet fairly tame, very dainty and certainly very well fed, not least by us. There is, of course, a recognised breed called the Singapura. Recently, my niece Emily (of Geneva fame) inherited two of these cats from friends who had to move away. It seems that they are affectionate and mischievous, and she could recognise her own cats from my 2006 description of their feral relations.

On the last leg of the journey to Auckland I had unpleasant confirmation of one of my pet theories, that flying is not good for you. What had been a miniscule niggle back home grew, with rapid ferocity, to raging toothache and I am convinced this was from the pressurised cabin of the aircraft. I had taken the precaution of visiting my dentist before departure and had antibiotics with me but had obviously not started taking them early enough. Hence, my memory of Auckland is somewhat blurred as I spent much of that first morning having a tooth extracted, then, as I developed a painful dry socket, it took all of New Zealand's charms while the wound settled down, to make the holiday hugely enjoyable. But it is a wonderful land and successfully worked its enchantment. Quite apart from an excellent personalised tour of some of the locations for the filming of *The Lord of the Rings*, in this landscape it was easy to imagine hobbits, elves, Aragorn, and Gandalf on Shadowfax. But the best magic occurred unexpectedly when we arrived at Panukaiki Beach on South Island where I recorded my impressions at the time . . .

Sentosa Cats

Sentosa cats are small and neat
Egyptian triangle in face
Falling glossy on their feet.

Sleekly watch us where we eat
Sneak a chair - impose their space
Sentosa cats are small and neat.

Cool cats in the tropic heat
Exploit the feeding in the place
Falling glossy on their feet.

Coats are grey or golden wheat
Exotic dainties of their race
Sentosa cats are small and neat.

Their moves are secretively fleet
They're there, then disappear - no trace
Falling glossy on their feet.

A privilege such cats to meet
Our evening touched with feline grace,
Sentosa cats are small and neat
Falling glossy on their feet.

Panukaiki

You wonder why the hotel is here, built low, almost sitting in the devastation, for your first thought is, 'What a mess, why doesn't someone clear it up ?' The sand is dirty grey, the vegetation a dull, blue-green with leaves that would be spears if more upright, but fold over from the stems like unenthusiastic mop heads.

Strewn everywhere, as if hurled by a petulant giant, is the twisted debris of driftwood, bleached almost white or still darkened with its life-blood – a dead zone, not helped by the greyness of the sky. On the edge of the shore it is no longer sand but the tiniest of pebbles; another few thousand years and they, too, will become sand. The sea hisses into the beach striking the granules like an angry cobra, and this on a calm day. No place to swim, for the undercurrents would have you before you were knee deep.

A quarter of a mile away are the famous Pancake Rocks and the Blow Hole, which bursts into the air like a geyser when tide and wind are right. All this we duly admire, yet it is not the renowned sights of the prescribed trail which would call me back but the exploration and awakening discovery of what the 'dead beach' really holds.

Take a long, slow walk and its secrets are revealed, maybe like coming to understand the work of a modern artist. But Nature has been at it a long time, sculpting the wood into textured shapes, turning holes through some of it, churning and smoothing till it becomes a challenge to refine a choice down to three or four, or yes, a final indulgence of five pieces to bring home. The scrubby vegetation is flax – *harakeke*, a plant essential to Maori life, used to roof their huts, weave baskets to catch fish or birds, or lower into hot pools for cooking. It was useful to bind wounds and, when woven finely, became clothing. *Harakeke*, a genus of 60 plants coming in many shades and sizes.

Walking further, as far as the beach allows, you come to a rocky headland and the lagoon, where you witness the tension between river and sea, the waters pushing and swirling against each other, smashing on rocks, hurling spray. To me this was much more wonderful than the temperamental Blow Hole of the tourist trail. Here in the lagoon the great sculptor begins her work, for the fallen pieces of forest travel down the river's force and are pushed towards the sea, a sea eager to take and shape them, then in thunderous storms throw them back, high onto the beach in twists and shapes of exhibition standard.

The lagoon is blue and cool, safe, yet deep enough to swim away those first impressions, of which you feel ashamed. This is a place to honour. It gets my Turner Prize.

Panukaiki beach

Chapter 24

Enter a Diva

Once returned from New Zealand in February 2006, finding a kitten was a priority, but cats tend not to breed in the cold months of the year and we were limited to a choice of one. She was currently being held for us, fostered by Cats Protection under the name of Bubble, for she was white with big bubbles of tabby, although to assign the word 'big' relating in any way to this daintiest of cats is a misnomer, unless you are referring to attitude. Phoebe was then a fan of *Dora the Explorer* on *CBeebies*, so I had been considering calling the kitten Dora but, on hearing that she already had a name, and since all kittens are adorable, two words seemed to fall naturally together in the shape of Adora Bubble.

Pretty as she was, tiny even for her young age, this new arrival proved to be something of a prima donna or, maybe more correctly, a prima ballerina, for Adora Bubble's petite form, when in indignant retreat, never ceased to amuse us, with its distinctive outward flout of the back legs, somehow reminiscent of the way ballet dancers walk. All this we had yet to discover when Kish and I went to collect her. The dog was in the hatchback section of the car, for I wanted her to know from the start that this was a new family member, and to feel involved in the welcome. Kish was, after all, huge in comparison to this little mite. She is also a demi-greyhound/lurcher and many of her breeding could have proved lethal.

Even if the sight of the kitten in the cat basket, together with her scent, had not given Kish all the messages she needed, the resentful protests from the front seat would have alerted her to a small someone to be reckoned with. Once back home we put cat basket with kitten safely on a high surface, then allowed Kish an enquiring sniff. This she did very gently, then lost interest and retired to her bed on the far side of the room. Adora Bubble had made an arch of her back, combined with one spitting hiss, but then seemed reassured that Kish meant her no harm. Within minutes of her arrival, therefore, our dainty diva was exploring not only us and the room, but sniffing warily at Kish's extended feet. From that moment Adora decided 'to do dogs'. She has never failed to be delighted by Kish, or indeed by any visiting dog, whereas her future history in relation to other cats was to prove more tricky.

I have always believed in introducing new animals to the household carefully. Ask yourself how you would feel if one of your family suddenly arrived home with a new friend, moved that person in without so much as a by-your-leave, whilst dropping a casual, 'Don't worry, you'll really like him/her.' Introductions are usually much easier with a kitten or puppy than with another adult, but not to be taken for granted. So the first day or two with Adora Bubble were planned carefully, so that she could get to know us, and the other cats could become aware of her presence without any confrontations or feeling pushed out of their normal routines. By now Bernard was the grand old man, slightly apart from the others, spending a lot of the day in the kitchen and much of the night snuggled up to me on our bed. Amber was gentle and motherly, but set in her ways, and still regarded the spare room as 'her room'. Mille often slept on our bed close to Graham, and there were feeding bowls on the window ledge, a station established when she and Lenni were young and stayed in the bedroom with us at night.

None of these arrangements could be disturbed without putting whiskers and noses out of joint, yet Adora Bubble must have the comfort of close contact for her first nights with us. The solution was a futon mattress on the floor in my study, where I slept with her for the first couple of nights finding, to my anxiety and astonishment, that her ideal resting place was between my feet, deep down under the duvet. I went to sleep worrying that she might suffocate, but there she was perky and hungry in the morning, tucking into her biscuits and demanding action. I was somewhat nonplussed, when I went to give her a cuddle a little later on, that she growled at me, but this was just Adora establishing boundaries. The photo I love best of her from Cats Protection, is of a cross little face peering from inside a china ornament, plainly saying, 'Who the heck thought I should be in here?' Of course we all know whose idea it was, but you would not dare say that to her.

Mille is cat perfected – beautiful, with an even temperament and, though sometimes shy with strangers, devoted to Graham and me, always greeting us with a friendly chirrup, a willowy waft of warm fur round our legs, then amenable to a brief cuddle. I rarely enter a room where one of our cats is present without saying 'Hello', and Mille has always been one to make a chirrup of greeting in reply. She has a tiny miaow but a big heart and was missing her brother. We hoped that she and Adora would bond. It took a mere three days for Adora Bubble to settle in. By the end of this time Amber had got over her slight displeasure at having her quiet life disrupted by a frolicking youngster, and seemed happy to have Adora aboard. Bernard had given her one reproving biff, then decided he had made his point and regarded Adora Bubble quite benignly, and Mille took to her as a playmate. They did not bond closely but kept each other company and having a kitten for a friend certainly seemed to help Mille. Adora Bubble continued to build on her relationship with Kish and they would play games of peek-a-boo round the sofa.

On the third night we took Adora Bubble into the bedroom with us, the only complication being that, when Mille or Bernard wanted to come or go, one of us (actually me, because Graham was pinned down by Adora Bubble) had to get up and open the door to the landing, or indeed the door to the balcony, from which Mille was used to leaping to the garden below. Normally our home operates on an all-doors-open policy where cats come and go at will. But of course a tiny kitten must be protected and kept indoors for several weeks. Meanwhile, this particular kitten had decided that Graham's feet were better than mine and demanded them as overnight sleeping quarters for a long time.

The only behaviour we found Adora Bubble shared with Lenni was her pleasure in drinking fresh water from a dripping tap, otherwise there was little comparison. Smooth coated and svelte, she had high standards and was strict with us. On the other hand, she could be very affectionate and, even when annoyed and taking a swipe, her claws were always sheathed. She was not spiteful but could be moody, and had very definite views. She became fond of Amber and, when in April chaos broke out as we knocked our bedroom and both bathrooms around, she and Amber both surprised us by rather enjoying the experience, which is more than could be said for the rest of us.

Recently we had been preoccupied with work on the barn in Cumbria and the apartment in France, small wonder that Throstles' Nest had been somewhat overlooked. It was time to give it some overdue attention, and besides, our pieces of Panukaiki driftwood needed a decent display space in a smart bathroom. Our project would come as considerable relief to my good friend Hazel, who is the kindest and least critical of people, but for years had been puzzled and irritated by one aspect of our home, saying in no uncertain terms that she could not understand why we did not have our bed facing the balcony and the hill instead of looking at an uninviting blank wall punctuated with three doorways – to the landing, our bathroom and a poky walk-in wardrobe.

The first reason we had done nothing about it was that, because of the lay-out of the room with its three doors, there was not room to place the bed on the wall with the view. The second reason was that it would be expensive to make the necessary changes. The third, discovered too late, was that the work was absolute hell while it was going on. Hell for everyone, that is, except Adora Bubble and Amber, who thought that the game of exploring under floorboards, and helping Dave the plumber, was very entertaining. They took the banging, crashing, dust, and general destruction of bedroom life as we knew it, completely in their stride, and Amber was thrilled that our temporary nightly headquarters were in 'her' room. Both cats seemed quite sorry when it was all over. We were not.

Fortunately, it was worth it. We could now lie in bed with our morning tea, watching the trees and the sky and the cows in the field. This view compares favourably with tea taken at Greengarth, where 'curtain up' reveals a small amelanchier tree hung with bird feeders, alongside the dry-stone wall, beyond which the fell is a backdrop. In the early morning light we await 'beginners please'. This is usually a greenfinch but sometimes a tit and even, on occasion, the extravagantly costumed spotted woodpecker. We enjoy

Cyril

pampering the Cumbrian birds with expensive seed from the Birds' Bistro* and it does not take long for the dawn chorus to throng the stage of our very own Birds' Theatre. Top of the bill though is the red squirrel, travelling along the wall separating us from the fell in search of his box of nuts, fixed on the big pine tree outside the kitchen window. This area of Cumbria is one of the few places in England where the indigenous reds hold on against the threat of their grey cousins, and much is being done to protect them. The sight of these pretty animals is irresistible and we find it even more endearing to talk about them since our little Ruby, while unable as yet to say 'squirrel' called her mummy to see 'Cyril'. We feel privileged to have these little charmers at Greengarth, sometimes seeing two together playing chase-me on the big pine tree. The very best of nuts being provided here, it is not unknown to be washing-up on our side of the window while Cyril, on his side, engages in fine dining, sitting on the platform of his specially designed box, unconcernedly chomping a hazel nut.

The new style bedroom at Throstles' Nest is (for us) uncluttered, for the music centre, television and vital tea-making gubbins are all secreted in a cunningly devised cupboard (unashamedly copied from a hotel room in New Zealand) which boasts double-jointed hinges on the doors, allowing them to fold right back against the outer sides of the furniture, so that the inner shelves can be extended into the bedroom. The room is very light and I had thought a white bedspread would be gorgeous, provided I protected it with a little quilt (matching the curtains) to take the feline tread, as the cats make their way to their bowls on the window-ledge, or settle on the bed beside us. It was a beautiful bedspread, the best that John Lewis could supply. I bought two so that we could have one off and one on, to allow for frequent washing. What I had not allowed for was the weight of the wretched things when wet. That first one seemed to weigh several hundredweight* as I struggled to manoeuvre it out of the washing machine, and hanging it on a line would have needed a six-man tug-of-war team. It had to go, and so did its companion, still lying virgin white in the cupboard. They were replaced with a complicated arrangement of a crisp, designer sheet, courtesy of Jasper Conran, and sporting Damien Hirst dots, covered by a flimsy Indian throw (featherweight even when wet) topped by the little quilt. This system worked. There were still plenty of paw marks and cat hair, but the washing was easy and we could all relax, rejoicing in our new space, with its scenic view enhanced by the warmth of a small cat between our toes.

However, there was also sadness in 2006. Great Danes do not live long and, at only seven years old, Cowley became ill and left us. It was a bitter blow for the whole family and hard to take in that the mighty had so fallen. True, he had always been a handful when out and about and, during 2004, had even sparked a glorious headline in the Macclesfield Express: 'Cowley Causes Chaos for Co-op Chief Executive'. The chaos was actually more experienced by Harry than by Graham (already two years a 'Woz-Been'* as Chief Executive) but the alliteration was superb. At home, however, Cowley had always been the gentle giant, totally trustworthy with the new baby, Ruby, as well as with Phoebe, who could roll all over him. She adored her 'Cow Cow'. Sometimes children seem less affected by death than adults, perhaps because they do not understand the finality of it, but Phoebe, at four years old, was deeply upset by the loss of Cowley and missed him dreadfully. She needed to keep talking about him and would still mention him years afterwards, believing him to be in heaven watching over her. He was an indelible part of her early childhood.

There was no question of the family being without a dog and, after two unsuccessful attempts at finding a suitable rescue animal, it was decided to buy a golden retriever puppy. So Buster joined the family fold, though he was more of a silver than a golden retriever, being very pale in colour. He arrived as the cutest bundle of little doggydom and has never given a moment's bother. Even as a puppy he was calm and biddable. He is the easiest, most placid and loving dog you could wish to meet; a personality we are glad to walk and sometimes to have as a lodger, even though his choice of perfume is sometimes hard to take. His favourite is a roll-on called 'Fresh Spread Slurry' which even a swim, followed by desperate shampooing and hosing down, fails to eradicate. It is a perfume which is as long lasting as it is powerful, qualities which many a house of fashion would like to emulate, though perhaps not in this precise fragrance, for only 'Enduring Durian' could outshine it for awfulness.

For Cowley (and Phoebe)

Cowley would watch over me
When I was small as small,
For he was big as all my trust
And more than twice as tall.

Our Cow Cow would protect us
With his voice both loud and deep,
Mummy, Daddy, Ruby too,
He'd guard us in our sleep.

But one day Cowley went away,
So strong yet old and ill,
And how we missed his handsome face
And how I miss him still.

A little cuddly puppy came
And he is growing fast.
He is our good and happy friend
But I don't forget the past.

For Cow Cow is in heaven
And wherever I may be
At home or walks with Buster
Cowley watches over me.

Buster

Chapter 25

Grace and Vegas

Meanwhile, other events began to unfold through the year. My sister's elder son William, was to marry his lovely Laura in October and, for various reasons, they had decided this should take place in Las Vegas. To be honest, this would not have been our own choice of venue, and Graham opted out, but I was looking forward to a bit of an adventure, keeping my niece Emily (William's sister) company, with a slightly over-the-top glitzy frock, fit for the desert lights, stowed in my luggage. Emily would travel from Switzerland over to London and we would then fly together direct to Las Vegas.

This was the best laid scheme but, unfortunately, Laura became ill and, though making good progress, by August it was clear that a long flight and the American adventure were not to be. The plan, anyway, had been to have a big party in a Chelmsford hotel when the bride and groom were safely back from America, so William, ever resourceful, was able to stitch a Registry Office ceremony and a family lunch to the earlier part of that same day. True, it would leave some of us walking up Chelmsford High Street on a busy Saturday morning looking incongruously sparkly and over-feathered in our fascinators, but worth it to see William and Laura so happy. When Laura threw her bouquet, we were all glad that Emily caught it. She was single at the time, with no man on the horizon, but the flowers worked their magic for, within a short time, she had met her Paul and they were married in Geneva in the summer of 2008.

When William and Laura had decided to pull the plug on their Las Vegas wedding they awarded themselves the consolation prize of a sleek, black kitten, whom they could not call anything but Vegas. She brought great comfort to Laura while she was having to rest up so much; a small purry person is a good healer.

Vegas

Emily and I had been looking forward to spending time together, so we decided that, on the weekend of the cancelled Las Vegas wedding, I would travel instead to Geneva and we would treat ourselves to a pampering weekend in a spa hotel in the mountains.

Two days before the trip I had been out shopping early and was driving home in the thick of the rush hour when I saw a smallish, grey-tortie cat 'bumped' by the car coming towards me. She paused in that long, low position that a cat will take when terrified, before taking off across the road in front of me, disappearing under the nearest parked car on my side of the road. Fortunately, there was room for me to park, which I did, rather inelegantly, in the hope that some friendly passer-by would help while I tried to encourage the cat to come to me on the pavement. I was nervous of frightening the cat back into the path of another car, so someone guarding that side would have been useful. As luck would have it the only person to appear had a discontented small child and a yappy Jack Russell in tow, hardly the ideal cavalry, so I had to manage alone.

Frightened and distressed, the cat began moving up and down the road under the parked vehicles. I tried to keep her in my sights, talking to her all the time, and eventually she seemed to settle under my own car. My soft talk probably degenerated to the soppy but she was not a critical audience and, to my delight, began to come to me. However, the moment I made a move towards her she cowered back under the car. I took a gamble. Just behind me was a breakfast bar called Nosh and Breks, where several kindly women feed many a hungry man. I made a lunge through the door and pleaded some bacon, which was readily given, especially as one of the staff had seen the cat hit. I was horribly afraid that, in those few seconds, she would have disappeared, but she was still there under my car and the smell of bacon proved irresistible. She came out, I moved, she retreated. But the next time I got my act together, gathered her into my arms and managed to slide into the car on the passenger side. The cat made no resistance once I was holding her. I put her gently onto the back seat while I slid to the driver's side, then took a proper peek at her over my shoulder. She was so pretty, so thin, so full of purrs, a mixture of grey and ginger, her face mask half-and-half, the colours neatly divided down her nose. You'd have thought she was in heaven she was so rapturous. Even though the saving bacon had not made it into the car she was ecstatic. I can only think it was because she suddenly felt safe.

Maybe you should not drive with an injured, stray cat loose in your car but no alternative scheme presented itself and, as it happened, she was no trouble whatsoever, though she did end up purring ferociously on my lap. A nurse soon had the little cat installed in a warm, cosy cage awaiting the arrival of the vet, to whom I spoke at midday. The assessment was mixed. The damage from the car had been minimal but she was about 15, drastically undernourished, with an eye infection and a very dodgy liver. She was now on a drip to try to re-hydrate her but he feared she could be suffering from a condition which, while not a death sentence, was very serious and could be passed to other cats. So we could not offer her a home. She was not chipped and had obviously been fending for herself for a long time, while growing more and more frail. It seemed a miracle that she had survived thus far and she developed quite a fan club at the surgery, under the name of Grace. She was only alive by the grace of God, yet her hold on that life was amazing.

I visited Grace on the Thursday (eve of departure for Geneva) to find her attached by a blue bandage to a tube and a drip, but purring fit to bust, which the nurse said she had done continuously, despite the pricking of needles and being pulled around so much. Nor could she stop eating, for she had been starving. She was in safe and loving hands, but I went off to Geneva with mixed feelings, only too well aware that Lenni had died less than a year ago on the eve of my previous journey to this destination. Now I grieved for all that this poor little cat had suffered, and worried as to how we might be able to rehome her, especially if she could not be with other cats.

Over the weekend Graham related the story to Harry, who nobly offered to give Grace a home, providing she did not freak out when Kish visited. The news got better, for the latest blood test showed Grace to be clear of the feared infection. However, since she was still too fragile even to withstand inoculation, a home with Harry still seemed the best option. Thus, on my return from Geneva, together we went to the surgery so that he could meet Grace and begin some bonding. I like to think she recognised me. She was certainly thrilled to see us both and was still eating like a mini-horse. If she continued like this she would be well enough to come to Harry in a week's time. I was able to return to the bacon donors, thank them properly and give them the good news.

A day or two later however, the picture changed. I had called on the Wednesday morning, had a cuddle and taken photos of Grace on the surgery table. As always she was hugely affectionate, but now she was stronger she was beginning to be stressed and a little stroppy when yet another needle had to be put into her. Moreover, despite all the eating she had not put on weight and, in the last 24 hours, had been drinking a lot. A further blood test resulted in a call from the vet next day with the sad news that Grace had severe diabetes. He thought this was the underlying reason for her liver being in such a bad state. Jaundice and her general weakness had been masking the problem. Grace would need daily insulin injections at approximately the same time each day, which would stress her out and be a huge commitment. I did not feel this would be fair on Harry, who would soon be working shifts. In these sort of circumstances I think you can only be guided by professional advice, especially when it comes from a committed, kindly vet who has done so much to try to save your animal, and who is also a personal friend. The kindest thing was to let Grace go.

I asked to be with her and an appointment was made for late that afternoon. Meanwhile, the nurse had been giving her cuddles and lots of food, and Harry had come round and made a beautiful place for her in our garden, under the birch trees and near our little fir tree. I could not bear to think of her being anywhere but in our garden.

Grace came to me and purred and purred as I fondled her then, gently, the vet tranquillised her and she became sleepy, still purring as I stroked her and talked to her. Her poor little front legs were sore from previous injections and blood tests, so I suggested a back leg for the final shot. Usually the veins are not big enough there, but

Grace was a trooper to the end, the vein was available and she slipped so gently from us, still purring while I continued to rub her head and talk soothing nothings to her. We then placed her in a basket as if curled asleep, wrapped in a woollen shawl.

Poor little Grace. The vet said that to have had such severe diabetes she must at some stage in her life have been plump, therefore pampered and loved. Whatever can have happened for her to have been found so ill, frightened and abandoned? However, I think she thought she had gone to heaven when she arrived at the vet's. Perhaps now she is truly there.

I had not yet scattered Lenni's ashes from the previous year so it somehow felt the right moment to put them under the little fir tree, close to Grace. A comfort (however silly) that these two cats, who had never known each other but were linked by my love and journeys to Geneva, should, in some way, be together. The autumn sun was still glowing warm and the leaves lay golden on the grass as Harry arrived to give Grace a final caress and help me to bury her. Despite the sadness of it, we felt that we had given this little cat of our best. Amazing Grace, who had suffered much but, at the end, had a home to go to, and people to love her and weep at her passing.

Grace

Chapter 26

A Bear Essential

However careful a dog owner you think you are, you can still be caught unawares. In Rosie's middle years, for example, at a time when the nation was neurotic about dangerous dogs and over-reaction was rife, Rosie was accused of biting the paper boy. Rosie would never knowingly have attacked anyone but she did have an aversion to large bags. We knew this and usually kept her indoors when papers or post were expected. On this particular day however, she and the paper boy coincided on the front path. I saw Rosie make an aggressive lunge at the bag, called her off and checked that the bag bearer was unharmed, which he said he was. But late that afternoon I was accosted on the doorstep by an embarrassed son, and an irate dad complaining loudly that our dog had bitten his boy, necessitating an anti-tetanus injection and, more importantly, ruining a brand new pair of jeans.

A vision of Rosie bundled away for instant destruction swam into view and I was not going to argue. A profuse apology and a £20 note produced calm, while a placid and friendly Rosie probably helped our case, for she loved people, especially youngsters, who no doubt reminded her of Harry and Hugo. I made it clear that we would not expect the young man to come into the garden again and we promptly installed a box for papers and post at the gate. Lesson learned.

The experiences with Kish were different but nonetheless unnerving. One morning, while out with the Rainow Doggie Playgroup, Kish sighted a large Bernese Mountain Dog in a field about 300 yards away and set off to say hello, taking a dry-stone wall in her stride. What she did not know was that, between us and the other dog, a main road was hidden behind the wall and that next field. Her programming was on 'go' so she failed to respond to the anxious shout which went up from the horrified band of watchers. She cleared the wall, made it safely across the road and arrived, delighted, to greet the large Bernese, whose owner would have caught hold of my dog except that his own dog told Kish, in no uncertain terms, to push off. Disappointed, and a bit frightened at the reception, she turned tail and ran back across the road. This time she was not so lucky. We saw the car, heard it brake hard behind the wall and held our breath for anxious seconds. The next moment Kish cleared the wall and was back with us, far less shaken than I was. We heard afterwards that the car had seemed to hit Kish quite a blow, and the poor driver was terribly upset, thinking she might have killed her. A check at the vet's proved that Kish had escaped with a bruise to her shoulder. He gave her a mild sedative for shock, but I think I was more in need of it than she was.

This event did make Kish more aware of traffic dangers, which had to be a good thing, though hardly the best way of learning. The next time she frightened us was on a routine visit to the vet. I opened the hatchback and out she leapt. Normally we are somewhere traffic free when opening the car so this had never mattered, and this time it was a quiet little road outside the surgery, but she took off round the corner to the busy main road. It was heavy rush hour traffic, which in a way was fortunate as the cars were hardly moving but, for a few minutes I had that dreadful feeling that I might never see her again. This was not typical Kish behaviour at all but then, like most dogs, she had come to associate the vet with some marginally uncomfortable experiences and thought she had found a good way of avoiding them. An RSPCA inspector was just coming out of the surgery and, for a moment, I thought he was going to help me, but that was short-lived as he had to go to an emergency. And this was not? I dashed through the door and asked the nurses to keep an eye out for Kish there, then used my mobile to ring Graham. He and Harry said they would both come immediately. There was no sign of Kish on the street outside the vet's but, as I turned the corner back onto the main road, guess who was trotting along the pavement towards me. We greeted each other with mutual relief. My guess is that she did not cross the main road because of her previous experience with cars and the same veto had operated when she reached a junction further on. So here she was, returning to Mum, just as Dad and Uncle Harry arrived to help.

The next fright happened when we were staying in the Robert Owen World Heritage village of New Lanark in Scotland. We were halfway round a longish walk by the river and the Falls of Clyde when Kish suddenly sighted a deer in the trees and was off. We were not too worried about the deer as we felt certain it would outrun her, but Kish was gone a long 15 minutes, during which time we had convinced ourselves she had run so far from us on strange territory that she would be lost or caught in barbed wire, or had fallen into the fierce current of the river and been swept away. The advice if you lose your dog is to stay in the place you last saw it, as it is likely to try to return to you there. Anyway, there seemed little else to do, apart from call Kish now and then and make desultory attempts to eat our packed lunch. At last came that faint chink of a bell, signalling a panting dog's return. Kish was tired but cheerful, having enjoyed the last few minutes rather more than we had. The lesson from this experience was TTAD – Try To Anticipate Deer!

The following summer Graham and Harry had their chance to share a crisis with Kish. Harry was helping with an RSPCA event in a park on the other side of town and Graham took her down there for a look at the fun. She was much more interested in some young lads who were running remote control cars, which have the effect of an electric hare on Kish. She had an exhilarating time chasing these things, cheered on by Graham, Harry and the owners of the cars, who thought it was hilarious. After a while Harry had to return to his stall and Graham decided to bring Kish home, even though she kept looking over her shoulder, both at the cars and at Harry. Once home, Graham assumed she would have forgotten all about the afternoon's excitements and that she had followed him, as she would normally do, back into the garden from the drive. It took a few minutes for him to realise that Kish was nowhere to be seen. I was out that day so was spared all the trauma, for traumatic it was. It did not take long to work out the most likely scenario; Kish, annoyed at being dragged away from her fun afternoon, had decided to go back to it under her own steam, crossing goodness knows how many roads along the way. The mobiles were humming between Graham and Harry. Graham set out to drive back to the park while Harry was on red alert to spot Kish if she made it back to him. By the time my menfolk met up they must have both been feeling panicky for there was no sign of the dog. Harry decided to abandon the RSPCA at this point and join the hunt in his own car, while Graham returned home to see if Kish was back at Throstles' Nest. His heart hit his boots when there was still no sign of her. However, there was a message on the answerphone. Had we lost our dog? If so, she was safe at our local Co-op corner shop. The relief flooded over him like a tsunami. Our great adventurer must have scared herself at the first road she had had to cross and gone into the shop to seek some human comfort. Fortunately, the staff had had the wit to look at the disc on her collar, make the contact call, then secure her outside the shop until there was a response.

Some dog owners seem to think it is only important to have their dog chipped but that pre-supposes that whoever finds your animal has the necessary equipment to read the thing. Imagine, if Kish had had no disc that day it could have taken many long and agonising hours for us to be reunited with her. Whilst chipping is an important back up to your dog's safety it is no substitute for an easy read of a contact number, and now it is a legal requirement to have a disc with the relevant information on your dog's collar. The advantages of 'disc on dog' had certainly been reinforced by Kish's escapade, just as it had been a lesson to me the previous year that Kish must not be allowed to leap at will from the car when the back is opened, but be made to 'stay' until given the signal to come out. She must have agreed with me as she was very quick to get the hang of the new system.

Kish is quick at a number of things, for example, the sight of Graham in a suit in the morning tells her immediately that he will be a washout for a walk that day, so she had better focus her attention on me. Her sense of smell is far from her biggest strength, but her eyesight is remarkable even for a 'sight hound'. On one occasion in the Lakes, when she and Graham had just stepped out onto the fell, she took off like a rocket, responding to something she had seen nearly half a mile away. Concerned, Graham came puffing up behind, to find Kish on the top of the hill in confrontation with a fox. It was actually more of a stand-off, as neither would move or risk turning their back on the other. It was only when Graham arrived that the tension was released, the fox taking its opportunity to flee and Kish to bask in praise for having been so far-sighted.

In recent years we seem to have devised the maxim, 'A project p. a.* keeps boredom at bay.' In 2007 it was the garden that was our focus. The conservatory at the back of the house led on to a narrow strip of paving with steep steps up to the lawn. It was too small to sit out on and the steps were almost dangerous. It was a nothing kind of area and had been bothering me for some time. I had been lucky to have a legacy from my father's sister Stella, known as Ban or Aunt Ban. She had died two years before, and Graham and I missed our trips to Louth to visit this eccentric, highly intelligent woman of whom we were very fond. Ban was generous, both to my sister and to me in her Will, and I was sure she would approve of some of this money being spent on our garden.

The landscape designer had imaginative ideas for a semicircular patio which would have much shallower steps, and flower beds banked with walls terraced up to the height of the lawn. He also engaged the necessary workforce and undertook the overall supervision of the project, and, since all the disruption would be external this time, it would be an easy ride compared with what we had undergone the previous year with the bedroom. Part of the idea for the design was to lead the eye up the garden towards some statue or sculpture, which would stand between the birch trees in the longer grass. As soon as this idea was mooted memory's bells began to chime:

In 1999 we had been on holiday in the Canadian Rockies, where we hoped to see some black bears among other wildlife. Bears are very appealing animals, helped by the ever popular Teddy Bear and Pooh. Appallingly abused in certain parts of the world, bears are holding their own in North America despite the hunting season, and we thought we stood a good chance of seeing one or two. However, we were not anxious to meet one face-to-face while walking in the forest, so took the advice to purchase and wear 'bear bells'. These could be worn on wrist, shoe, rucksack, or indeed your dog's collar, giving gentle warning of your presence and thus avoiding confrontation. We think they must have worked because we did not see any bears . . .

Bear Bells

A hairy bear
can be a scare
if you should meet one
unaware,

and if you meet one
unaware,
you may scare
the hairy bear.

So wear your bear bells as you go
to let your hairy bear friend know
that you are coming by his way,
then no one gets a scare, okay?

Never scare
a hairy bear,
or ever meet one
unaware.

Wear the tinkle of the bell;
the bear's aware, and all is well.

In fact, we never saw a bear at all in Canada, even from a safe distance, but we were to have a memorable encounter elsewhere a couple of years later. Both Graham and I love London and always enjoy staying in our tiny Camden flat. One of my favourite places in London, or indeed anywhere else, is the wonder that is Regent's Park. Apart from the zoo, now doing valuable conservation work, this park has everything, from clouds of daffodils and crocuses in the grass in spring, to the colourful planting of the long herbaceous beds and the splendour of Queen Mary's Rose Garden. Then there is the ornamental lake with its unusual wildfowl, including black swans. The Open Air Theatre also provides great entertainment in summer and the children's playground is fun all year. Jogging, football and rounders live happily alongside babies in their buggies. Dogs can bound joyously over most of the park, and it is a pleasure to see the professional dog walkers sitting in a group at the café, gossiping away while their charges wait patiently.

We had gone for a walk in the park that early spring day, merely to enjoy the sunshine, the crocuses and early blossom, but stumbled on an exhibition of sculpture which moved me greatly. There were about 12 pieces, strategically placed over one area of the park. The work was by the Scottish sculptor Ronald Rae. Once in a while, one is lucky to stumble on an artist whose work, for whatever reason, touches the soul, whether it be a composer, singer, actor, painter or sculptor. Who knows why we respond emotionally to some pieces of art and not to others? Even experts, with their vast knowledge of art or music, will ultimately have favourites which cannot be explained in technical terms.

Ronald Rae is possibly the only sculptor in Europe to work with granite on a grand scale using nothing but his own strength. Wielding only the hand tools of hammer and chisel to shape the rock, he punishes his own body in so doing. In a quarry he finds a stone, which he swears already knows what it wants to be. He is just the medium or agent who releases the spirit and he actively encourages people to connect with that spirit, by touching, feeling, or indeed climbing on, his sculptures.

A very spiritual man, several of Rae's works relate to Christ. All his sculpture appeals, but his *Wounded Elephant*, *Tyger Tyger* and vast *Lion of Scotland* speak to the animal lover in me. On this March day in 2001 it was *Bear*, set under a blossoming tree, which captivated. Graham took a photograph of me caressing *Bear*'s uplifted, mighty head with one hand, the other tickling it under an irresistible, craggy chin. I joked that, if ever I could afford it, one day we would have a Ronald Rae, and preferably this one. I then made a note in that important little notebook always in my handbag, and we passed on.

Six years later, as we were planning the improvements to the garden at Throstles' Nest, thanks to the internet I was able to track down Ronald Rae, look at his work again, this time on his website, then rather diffidently make contact. My original plan had been to make a commission for a smallish piece that would have been placed according to the design, in line with the patio steps. My approach to Ronald Rae was nervous, for this was a Great Artist and I was prepared for a snooty reaction, but I could not have been more wrong. Ronald Rae's delightful wife, known as Pauline MacDonald, keeps the practical side of the show on the road, so that Ronald can concentrate on being the consummate artist that he is. Consummate, but warm and approachable, particularly to those who favour his 'babies'.

Pauline could not have been kinder or more helpful as we discussed the various possibilities. Because he works from the heart and soul Ronald does not take commissions, so it was a question of what was already for sale. I could hardly believe it when Pauline said *Bear* was still available. It threw a rather large spanner in the works as, at seven tonnes, it would be far too big for the position designated, but I was so excited at the prospect of having a dream come true that I was not going to be thwarted by such a minor detail. At the top right-hand corner of the garden, still near the hedge bordering the field, was an uninteresting no-man's-land where the children's metal swing had been, until it rotted away. Very little would grow there as it was too shady, almost like a forest glade. Suddenly it was obvious. What this dull space needed to light it up was the massive form of a granite bear, its nose uplifted to the hill, the stars and the rising moon.

The garden designer took my new tack on the chin, especially once he had checked out *Bear* on the website. We agreed that, with such a large sculpture installed at the top corner of the garden, a simple stone birdbath would look right in the other position. Meanwhile, Pauline invited Graham and me to go up to Edinburgh where Ronald had a large representation of his work in the grounds around Holyrood Palace. With typical thoughtfulness, they wanted me to see *Bear* in the granite once more before finally committing myself, and they invited us to spend a day with them in April.

Two weeks prior to that visit we went up to Greengarth, taking Amber with us as usual. She was 14 going on 15 although we did not know her exact age. Bernard would be 18 in July and had mellowed, the two cats having learned to live alongside each other amiably enough. They were now both on medication for kidney problems. In fact Amber had not had very good health for three or four years, and there had been a time when we thought we might lose her before she could even reach twelve but, with good veterinary care and the right food, she had come through the crisis. We knew she was vulnerable, was becoming a bit thin and was on borrowed time. But she was happy, cheerful and had had her book published. No bad record for any cat.

The weather that last March weekend was fine and warm in the Lakes and we were able to sit outside. Amber joined us, sitting on one of the garden chairs, purring contentedly, but on the Sunday afternoon there was a sudden change and it became clear that she was not at all well. She wanted to be picked up and cuddled, and slept close to me on the bed that night, still purring, but she looked frail, was not eating and was bringing up bile. I rang our vet on the Monday morning and made an appointment for the afternoon surgery, nursing Amber on my knee all the way home, sensing more and more that there could soon be a final parting. At home it was still warm and sunny in the early afternoon and Amber wanted to be in the garden, just outside the back door. I kept a close eye on her but suddenly she was missing. When I found her, which took a few panicking minutes, she was in the dark of the bottom of the airing cupboard. When a cat seeks out such a place, yet still looks restless and uncomfortable, I think it is a sign that they are nearing the end. Some cats, of course, choose to go away to die, which is distressing to owners who want to be with them in this final phase of life, but if that is your cat's decision you can only respect it.

Amber never minded going to the vet's and was still relaxed and purring as she finally left us, knowing that we were there, loving her to the end. Her final resting place is by 'her wall' where she used to like to sit, basking in the sun, a dear little friend whom we miss still. Yet our grief was tinged with the comfort of knowing that we had done all we could for her and that fate had been kind, her last days spent with us at Greengarth, her 'No Other Cat House' where she was always happiest.

There was more comfort when we went up to Edinburgh. Pauline and I already knew we would like each other from our emails and telephone conversations, but Ronald greeted me with a hug as warm and enveloping as that of any bear. Then, to have a tour of each of his breathtaking sculptures, with the thinking and emotions behind them explained by the artist himself, was a rare privilege. I was reintroduced to *Bear*, this time situated on a green sward a few yards from a roundabout near the castle. Seeing the sculpture again I had no doubt that this was the piece which would be perfect for our garden.

Ronald also makes a mean soup and it was over lunch round our hosts' table, while making plans for *Bear*'s new home with us, that we explored our mutual love of cats. I was glad that I had thought to take Ronald and Pauline a copy of *A Cat in My Lap* and of Amber's *Dear Dear Mary*. Pauline herself has to be a 'cat lady' for she has the greenest eyes of anyone I have ever met. We were told of a neighbour's cat called Toby Jug, who was trying to adopt Ronald and Pauline in the wake of the death of their much loved Bramble. In our turn, we had just lost Amber, so there was shared empathy in the pain of loss.

It was about a week later, back home, and still feeling sad about Amber, that a mysterious envelope arrived containing just one piece of paper – the most rewarding letter that any writer could hope to receive in response to a book . . .

Dear Dear Jenny,

It seems a long time since I last saw you and I am missing you dreadfully – as much as I used to miss Dear Mary so you will know just how bad it is for me. I never thought I would ever be without you. I am not sure where I am or what has happened or how I got here. I don't think I came in the moving room. All I remember is being asleep. Now I am awake but I feel that I am dreaming.

This place is like a magnificent garden full of beautiful flowers that seems to go on forever. There are no houses like Throstles' Nest with rooms and doors – only garden rooms, plenty of them so there is space for everyone. There are no bumpy roads with big roaring machines that do Terrible Things to cats. Everyone seems to be well and happy and there is no fighting. Some cats call it paradise. But there is no Jenny and that is what upsets me. Yet, there is a feeling of love all around – the same love that I felt when I was with you.

The sun seems to shine every day and the sky is blue with only a few puff clouds. It is not cold and it never rains, so in that respect, you can imagine that it suits me very well. You know that I like to be warm and am at my best being an outdoor cat. So I no longer need to worry about the warming heart* breaking down, or me being on the wrong side of the door, although I do miss the velvety room, the big bedroom and, most of all, your lap.

My first surprise on arrival was Silvester being here to greet me, and, would you believe it, he could see again! I thought there must be an even Cleverer Vet here, but apparently there isn't a vet at all as everyone is well and it's not needed. Silvester was so happy to see me. He was not alone; Aaron and Moses are here too and all the other cats that you have looked after and loved. Some days we sit and reminisce and your name Dear Jenny always comes up. We talk about the old times and how kind you were, and we all agree that you are the best mother a cat could ever have, along with my Dear Mary. I always add that because I have not forgotten her either and that special day she came to see me in your garden. I shall never forget that.

So you see, Dear Jenny, you must not worry about me as I am well now and find myself purring a lot, up to level ten some days, and even more when I dream about being on your lap.

Loving you and purrs forever,

Amber

Chapter 27

The Lull Before . . .

There were no clues within the envelope as to the source, but a close perusal of the exterior revealed a faint Edinburgh postmark which told me whence it had come. Pauline subsequently told me that, after reading *Dear Dear Mary*, she woke from a dream with the words pouring onto her page as if sent to her. I have doubts about the afterlife myself, but if there is one for us, then why not for animals? The thought of it is comforting in bereavement, and it brought Pauline and me close.

In May work began on the garden. It meant a small digger coming across the lawn and a skip in the field to take quantities of earth away. By now Bernard thought such activity beneath his notice, and Mille was mildly put out, but Adora was fascinated, thinking that the new stone terraced walls were being built especially for her entertainment. She also enjoyed chatting to the men at work and showing off how she could climb the little malus tree on the edge of the lawn, though the men were more impressed to see Mille perform one of her leaps from the balcony. Adora appeared up there soon afterwards and I had hardly said, 'I'm afraid Adora Bubble can't quite copy Mille doing that yet,' when she promptly proved me wrong. It became her party trick.

A great leap for Adora Bubble.

The landscaping was progressing well and would be finished by the time we came back from our first French holiday of the year. It was also the first time we would be taking Kish with us to France, and we were anxious that it should all go smoothly for her. Accordingly, I took her to the vet for a last check before our departure and happened to meet Wendy from Windyway in the waiting room, where she told me how worried she was about a little kitten who had had to have her leg amputated. The mother cat, Spud, had been brought into the sanctuary from an unsatisfactory home, together with her kittens. These had all been placed easily enough, and a young couple had been keen to take both Spud and little Lottie until the problem with her hind leg manifested itself. On hearing that the leg would have to be removed they took fright and were never seen again. Wendy thought the mother cat could be rehomed without too much difficulty as she was 'so sweet', but there was serious worry that no one would want the disabled kitten, now almost four months old.

Graham and I discussed the kitten and decided that, since we were about to go away, we should let fate take a hand. If she had not found a home by the time we returned from holiday we would go to see her with a view to making an offer. However, for the moment we had to concentrate on our first attempt to take our dog abroad. In theory Kish was all ready to go, with her smart blue passport and the chip safely located in the nape of her neck. I had even organised a separate French collar with our details on it to use over there, just in case she should get lost. But the window for the return trip was then a narrow one, a visit to the vet being necessary a full 24 hours ahead of leaving French soil, yet arrival in the UK essential before 48 hours had elapsed. I was already having nightmares about getting it wrong, with Kish marooned on the wrong side of the Channel for several months.

We couldn't know how she would react to the overnight crossing on the ferry from Portsmouth either, but had taken the precaution of arming ourselves with a sedative pill for her, and were lucky to find the perfect place for a good pre-ferry walk at Speen, a small village just off the A34, only an hour from Portsmouth. Kish has the tank of a camel so we knew this exercise should suffice until the morning, especially if she was sedated. We also knew that she would be happier within the familiar setting of our own car rather than in some tin can of the kennel on offer, but we still felt horribly guilty when we abandoned her to the clank and clatter of the boat's hold while we went up to enjoy a fine dinner and a good night's rest. We left Kish food and water, and the windows open, so felt we had done all we could. Moreover we had followed instructions and not set our car alarm, but I was horrified to learn later that many people's are left on and, once the ship starts to move the noise is horrendous until the wretched things wear themselves out. Poor Kish.

Next morning we got to the car as quickly as we could and I peeped in at the spacious back seat. My stomach swooped to the bottom of the sea. No Kish. Next moment there was movement and she revealed herself, sitting on the driving seat still half asleep. She was perfectly all right but almost as relieved to see us as we were to see her. Within 15 minutes we had found a footpath by an estuary to give our confined traveller a run, though she was still fairly quiet, perhaps sensing that she was on foreign soil. However, after a day or so she adjusted to the new terrain. Though not overly impressed with the sea, she enjoyed greyhounding on the low-tide sands, as well as paddling and retrieving sticks from the shallows, but was disappointed with the water's taste. Having been brought up in a landscape with streams and pools for snatched drinks she found both the beach and the forest (which she much preferred) a big letdown for liquid refreshment. However, she valiantly made do with the bottle of tap water which we lugged around lest she dehydrate.

We had taken Kish's secondary bed from home, which is big, soft and easy to transfer, so she soon felt at home in the apartment and settled very well, though insisted on the bed being moved close to ours at night-time. A visit to the local vet's, to register her with him and make an appointment for the return journey, put our own minds much at rest. At first we did not leave her alone in the apartment at all but, after a few days, felt we could begin to do so for short spells when necessary, and were pleased to be complimented by our fellow apartment owners on our 'very quiet dog'.

The previous year we had decided it was time to transform the garage space below our apartment, known as 'the barn-garage'. Accordingly, we had set work in train to be done over the winter months. We were looking forward to seeing the new developments and our *electricien/plombier*, the *cuisiniste* and the *peintre* had all done us proud. We now had a sort of studio flat, with fitted cupboards disguised as beach huts painted in jolly stripes, and an upgraded shower room. This boasted the posh, frosted glass door recycled from our apartment above, where, if left in situ, it would have scraped the blue of the now laminated floor. In its new position it added a touch of unexpected glamour. Our curtain order, placed the previous September, was fulfilled within two days of our arrival, the colourful check curtains softening the two windows which look out at ground level. The other full length set, in a suitably maritime design, hid our bicycles, providing them with the kind of privacy accorded a patient in a hospital bed. From this bay they could also easily be accessed from outside, through the up-and-over door.

However, the pièce de resistance was the transformation of the aggressive concrete pillar which, placed off-centre like a mast in the main space of our 'studio', was essential to the structure of the building but, being armed with vicious corners, could seriously damage your health or land a small child in hospital. I had been determined to tame this creature's sharp edges so enlisted the help of the *cuisiniste* – he who had scorned the installation of the cloakroom basin. As it turned out he might have been justified in telling *madame* that her current idea was even more daft, but this time he was very obliging. The plan, I thought, was a simple and inexpensive one, merely to wrap some natural-fibre rope around the pillar. It would look good but, more importantly, would gentle it down to a safe level should anyone have a close encounter with it. Easy and effective once achieved but, as we discovered when we got the bill, a long and winding road to get there, involving 160 metres of rope and the *cuisiniste*'s dizzy hours installing it for, as he said, once he had begun he dare not stop lest he lost the thread. Fortunately, we all saw the funny side and the finished effect was superb.

178

We had (and still have) much to learn about living in France, including the mysteries of opening times. Lunch is, of course, a serious matter, and one of the best value eating experiences is a midday meal at a good *routier* or *relais*, sitting among the local white van men, some in their traditional blue overalls. The three courses are simple, tasty and inexpensive. Moreover, no one bats an eyelid at my vegetarian needs. For the *Plat du Jour* I just order, 'Vegetables only please', and a delicious mix arrives.

Disembarking at 8.30am in St Malo we have always tried to do a supermarket shop before arriving at the apartment around one o'clock. This has been done with varying levels of success over the years, with the goalposts appearing to change for reasons we can only half grasp. For example, a supermarket might close for lunch at 12.30 one year then, by the next spring, it would be 12.15 and we would arrive to closed doors. Our local supermarket (before its reincarnation into a bigger and grander form) would close on Saturday afternoons and remain shut until 3.30pm on Monday. Now it is open every day, except that it shuts at 12.30pm on a Sunday, presumably so that the staff can enjoy the all important family lunch. In the week it is open from 9am till 12.30pm, then from 2.30pm till 7.30pm. However, the supermarket we favour en route seems to be miraculously open all day, at least it is in the summer months, but we once tried it in early May when it was closed for lunch.

As a general rule most places stay open more in the high season, but that is a very short spell over an indefinite period. Broadly speaking, the season builds slowly from Easter to a peak, lasting from 15th July to 15th August, then dips away again until mid to end September, when the beach cafés are dismantled for the winter. But even in high season you may find your favourite eating place shut because it is Monday, or Tuesday which seems to be becoming the new Monday. Some decide that, as they are shut on Tuesday it is not worth opening on Wednesday either. I recently saw a Bar/Café closed at 12 noon on a Saturday, presumably to suit the management. Take nothing for granted and beware of trying to eat out on Sunday evenings as most restaurants have exhausted themselves on the great ceremony of Sunday lunch and need to rest up.

Notre Dame de Monts is a different place in the season when there are literally thousands of people around instead of a sprinkling. We try never to arrive until the crowds have begun to recede but, at the end of August, most of the seasonal shops are still open, which makes it fun. These include a useful baker's shop only four minutes walk away for the breakfast bread, instead of the more usual 20 minutes to the parent shop up in the village. If you are clever, from some uncertain date in June, you may catch our handy baker's shop open at weekends (not Monday to Friday of course) but remember, it doesn't open till eight, whereas the parent shop opens at seven.

The French are justifiably proud of their country, and this extends to their particular local area, so it is always a pleasure to explore regional specialities. But the down side of being more parochial is that, in our local tourist office, information is willingly given about every minute detail in Notre Dame itself, but try to find out what is happening in St Jean de Monts or Fromentine, each ten minutes away, and you might as well be enquiring about Brighton or Moscow. And did you ever try to post anything in France?

The staff at *la poste* in Notre Dame despair of this Englishwoman's stupidity. With letters I have been reprimanded for failing to write the French post code within the specially prepared boxes on the front of an envelope. With parcels I have used the 'wrong kind' of brown paper, then sticky tape allegedly unequal to its task, attempted to send an item in a box apparently unsuitable for purpose, and compounded all felonies by tying a parcel with string, which any fool should know is a crime in France. Thus, on one occasion, determined to get it right, Graham sent a bottle of malt whisky to his French friend for a special birthday. At huge expense we bought the proper box from *la poste*, filled in the form and paid for guaranteed 48 hour delivery. It never arrived.

But what is the point of being abroad if everything mirrors life at home? The French may be strict about their post and are certainly much more rigid about who can sell what; Graham was greeted with amazed looks when he asked for a comb in a pharmacy and the supermarket does not sell newspapers, thus sensibly protecting the local newsagents. However, French people can be much more relaxed on other matters that we British have become ridiculously twitchy about. In Britain if a law is there we think it should be obeyed, however silly or inconvenient. In France, if it does not suit, they tend to ignore it or go round it, *'on s'arrange'*.

When it comes to dogs France is a paradise for the British dog owner. I remember a notice at one of the Loire chateaux to the effect that, so long as you could carry your dog you were welcome to take it on the tour with you. This approach may explain why so many French people have small dogs, but their attitude to the larger variety is also much more relaxed than ours. Used to the prissiness of eating establishments back home we began diffidently with Kish, asking if we could bring the dog in with us. But we were always greeted with a surprised 'of course' usually accompanied by the offer of a bowl of water. Naturally, whenever possible we sit outside with Kish as there is usually more space, but indoors is never viewed as a problem, even though Kish (being a long dog) takes up a fair bit of floor when crashed out. The staff just step over her, cheerfully telling her not to move. From the start Kish appreciated the privilege of being with us and this has applied to every dog we have seen in restaurants. French dogs, like French children, accept the discipline of the dining-table and behave themselves.

Some French beaches ban dogs but, in our part of France, even if not allowed in the day, you can exercise them early morning and from seven in the evening. I am surprised this does not also include the lunch break as most people seem to depart from the beach between 12.30 and 2.30, including the lifeguard, who has a far, far better thing to do during that period than prevent you from drowning. In Britain everything may stop for tea but in France lunch is sacred.

On the beach in front of Notre Dame's short prom there appears to be some limiting of dogs, but our stretch of the beach is just beyond that area and boasts the wildness of the dunes that travel all the way to Fromentine in the north, so we have never been sure if any restrictions apply. We are not great beach sitters anyway and it is certainly not Kish's favourite activity but, when we do all go for an hour or two, she is content to sit under the shade of the umbrella, on her lead, and is no bother to anyone nor they to us, and some people have their dogs loose anyway – *'on s'arrange'*!

Of course, having a dog with us makes the holiday different. Kish is not delighted to visit busy markets or go clothes shopping, and is rather too large to be carried round chateaux. In warm weather, leaving her in the car can never be an option, but she is very good about being left in the apartment so long as we make her our priority on our return. She travels well in the car and, if we take a holiday within a holiday to a different part of France, we have found it the norm for French hotels to welcome dogs. Some posher ones even provide a bed and doggie bowl.

Like most dogs Kish loves to be with her pack and, being in France gives her a better than average opportunity. Moreover, there are few dogs of her style over there and she arouses interest and admiration, which does not go amiss with any of us. We explain that she is a *demi-levrier* (half-greyhound) while her vibrant singing and keen football skills cause amusement, and even the accolade *'adorrahble'*. Kish and France like each other and she has become an essential part of our French holidays. With the help of our local *vétérinaire* we quickly established an anxiety-free routine for her return journeys and, with the first of these safely accomplished, we could turn our thoughts once more to that three legged kitten.

Chapter 28

The Tortie Wars

When I rang Wendy at Windway on our return from France the relief in her voice was palpable. The valiant little Lottie certainly still needed a home but fears for her general well-being had faded. She was now a perfectly healthy little cat on three legs, though several times more terrified than the saying 'nervous as a kitten' could imply. She had been given the same affectionate handling as her siblings but, because of her congenital problem with the leg this same handling had hurt her, so she had come to associate human contact with pain. Once the reason had been recognised for her being 'hissy and spitty' when cuddling attempts were made, she then had to undergo investigation by the vet, followed, eventually, by amputation. It was enough to give any kitten psychological problems. Describing her, Wendy assured me that Lottie was a very pretty, dark tortoiseshell. We had never had a tortie cat but, of course, we had known Grace and for her sake I was more determined than ever that this little tortie should be offered a good home.

Next day, Graham and I went up to Windyway to meet her. She was housed with her mother in a spacious, comfortable pen, and the mother cat, Spud, greeted us enthusiastically. She was also dark tortie but with some white on her face and chest. Lottie looked at us suspiciously and moved away, with a pronounced dipping movement where her fourth leg would have met the floor. But she allowed her main carer, Claire, to stroke her reassuringly. Meanwhile, Spud was busy telling us how nice we were and Wendy was tentatively asking whether we would consider taking her as well, as there was serious worry about Lottie's ability to cope in new surroundings without her mum. This came as a surprise to us and I was well aware that, although Graham had always left important feline decisions to me, it had been strictly on the understanding that 'four's the limit', so I was particularly glad that he was at first hand when this challenging situation arose and could prove himself every bit as soft as his wife. In a quick exchanged look the answer was 'yes' and collection was arranged for a few days later. We needed time to make our care plan and Claire needed time to make her farewells to this little kitten who, as she said, 'had been through so much' and had won a special place in her heart.

By now I considered myself an experienced cat owner, even able to offer several good guidelines to those less so, for example, if your cat becomes overexcited when you are stroking it, rolls and grabs you by the wrist, starts to bite and kick hell out of you with its back legs, don't try to pull your hand away but relax and let your hand go limp so that there is no resistance to work against. Similarly, if your cat succeeds in entering the one room in the house that is forbidden, don't waste your energy trying to catch it or entice it out. Simply close the door firmly so that the cat is trapped in there, then return a few minutes later and open it. Your cat will be delighted to see you and to make an exit. It was true that we had never had five cats before, nor a terrified kitten on three legs but, with all my experience, plenty of patience and careful planning, we would soon have everyone settled down nicely.

Our spare bedroom (Amber's old room) would, as usual, be our holding bay for a few days. It is often recommended that a cat is kept indoors for a month when they come to you. I have always found two weeks to be sufficient but knew that, this time, it could be longer, as we did not want the mother cat going out until the little one had been safely spayed and they could explore the garden together. However, after a few days they would be able to have the whole of our upstairs (bar the balcony) for exercise for a few hours at a time, since we could use our dining room/hall as a sort of airlock between upstairs and down. Until all the cats had been successfully introduced we would have to keep the resident brigade downstairs while the newcomers were making their exploring upstairs, but the hope was that, within a few days, when the cats all knew each other a bit, we would be able to open up the door onto the balcony. Mille would then hardly be inconvenienced, as she tended to use the balcony access to come in and out of our bedroom, and Adora Bubble could be ferried upstairs, then exit by that same route if she so wanted. We were confident that neither Spud nor Lottie would be capable of leaping off balconies for the moment, for it is an acquired skill, which certainly requires four legs. At 17, Bernard, though often snuggling up to me at night, by day would choose either to be outdoors or in the kitchen, where he reckoned he could keep a close eye on Mum. The new arrivals would not, initially, disrupt his lifestyle at all.

There were decisions to be made on names. I could not live with 'Spud' and thought 'Lottie' should be something more significant. We decided to avoid paired names this time as it had not proved lucky in the past; with Moses and Aaron, the latter had been killed, and with Mille and Lenni, that massive thrombosis had taken him from us. I thought the mother cat deserved a really pretty name and we settled on 'Hermia' from *A Midsummer Night's Dream*. Little Lottie required something to reflect, not only her need to balance but also her courage in coping with all that had befallen her. So she became 'Odette', taken from the prima ballerina role in *Swan Lake*, and from Odette Churchill who parachuted so bravely into France during World War Two.

We had a plan. The cats had new names. We were ready for action. Kish came with us to collect Hermia and Odette, as they now were, and Claire was there to bid them a tearful farewell. I promised to keep in touch, telling her she would be welcome to visit anytime. They were soon installed in Amber's old room, with the dual offer of a cosy box on the floor or the use of the bed, both options provided with a hand-knitted blanket. My mother had been a good knitter and, when pullovers were beyond her, she took to making small blankets for the cats. We have several, the cats love them and I treasure them as a little piece of Margie still with us. I had been concerned lest Odette could not manage the journey up onto the bed but she proved remarkably agile and, when we peeped in later, mother and daughter were side by side on the woollen blanket. I visited them a great deal, each time being received rapturously by Hermia, but Odette would hide under the bed if I moved in her direction. Needless to say I slept in their room so that she could accustom herself to me while I was safely in a recumbent position. On the second morning I woke to find both cats on the blanket at the end of the bed, with Odette actually purring and allowing me a tiny stroke. By the third evening I was confident enough to carry them down into the living-room in the cat basket.

Kish was asleep on her bed so we put the cats on a high surface where they could peer down at her. She then woke up and went to sniff them. Neither of them seemed alarmed, so we slipped Kish's lead over her head and gentled her, then opened the cat basket to let Hermia and Odette come out, if and when they were ready. It did not take long for them to start to explore, and little Odette was surprisingly brave, going almost near enough to the dog to sniff her tail, which was quietly wagging. Everyone settled down. Kish, now free of her lead, lost interest and went back to bed as the cats wandered round this new space, which included the garden room. When it came to bedtime Graham slipped out into the garden with Kish for a few minutes while I began taking the cats back to base. Since Hermia was on my lap by then it was easy to reinstall her upstairs, but then I looked for Odette. Could I find her? I could not. And, by the time Graham and Kish returned from the garden panic had set in. Despite all Graham's sensible reassurance that she could not be far away, desperate hunting by both of us proved futile. Of course, we had had panics before with Adora Bubble, who makes an art form of disappearing into tiny hidey-holes but is always there, somewhere. However, she is white and shows up, whereas Odette wears dark tortie camouflage. After ten minutes or so I began to wonder if she had somehow slipped out behind Graham into the garden and began a totally useless hunt with a torch. By now our nerves were in shreds and there was only one thing for it, we made a cup of tea, sat down and tried to calm down.

Realistically, Odette had to be somewhere in the room. Perhaps terrified by the hunt for her she had retreated to some impossibly small bolthole. We began the search again, this time using the torch indoors. It was Graham who found her, in a place I had already checked several times. She was behind the small wicker sofa in the garden room, curled up, fast asleep, which at least paid tribute to our tippy toe approach to our frantic searching. All we had to do now was gently extricate her and return her to Hermia at base camp. Since Odette knew me better, and was less frightened of me than of Graham, I said I would manage alone, went into the garden room and closed its sliding doors. With the concentrated care of a child trying to remove a pick-a-stick without disturbing any other in the pile, I began to ease out the sofa so I could reach behind it, only to achieve a thunderous crash as the high chair, stored in the corner for small visitors thumped to the floor. Odette flew out and fluttered like a desperate bird against the big glass doors. Cursing myself (very quietly) for my clumsiness, I somehow managed to scoop up the trembling kitten and, hugging her to me with Graham acting as doorman, returned her to Hermia, the only one able to give effective reassurance to the poor little soul. It made us rejoice in our decision to give this wonderful mother cat a home.

However, other family members were to view that decision differently. Bernard, although now an elderly gentleman, was still very much the senior cat. Within two days of the newcomers' arrival he had chosen a spot on the landing close to the door of their room to sleep, as if assessing them without the bother of them. Mille chose to ignore their presence until such time as she would actually meet them. Adora Bubble, on the other hand, was instantly resentful of them being in her home. The day after Hermia and Odette arrived I went to stroke Adora as she lay on a shelf in the airing cupboard, and was greeted with a growl. This was our first hint of what was to come, early rumblings of The Tortie Wars.

Up to then I had always believed that, if animals were introduced carefully they would get on. It was true that Amber and Bernard had taken time to settle down together, but we had persevered until they co-existed peacefully. It had never occurred to me that, in introducing Hermia and Odette to the household we would be encountering an intractable problem, but then I had never heard the expression 'naughty tortie' either. With all my so-called experience with cats I still had much to learn.

Although we thought of Odette as a kitten because she was still so dependent on her mother, she was now about five months old and, in theory, old enough to become a mother herself. The vet said it would soon be safe to have her spayed. It therefore made sense to keep both Hermia and Odette (now known as the HO team for short) indoors until that operation was over. We were scheduled to go up to Greengarth during this waiting period, so took them with us. Apart from Odette demonstrating by the resonance of her yowling in the car, that she must have some Siamese ancestry, the HO team's visit to the Lakes went smoothly. Hermia seemed unfazed by anything, so long as she had human companionship, and Odette could cope so long as she had her mum. Hugo, Jo and the little girls were to join us at Greengarth, our two holidays overlapping. When the family arrived, Kish and the cats moved across to the barn to sleep, along with Graham and me, leaving the cottage bedrooms to the family. This meant an added disruption for the cats but, again, Hermia was unfazed. We began calling her Imperturbable Hermia.

What was perturbing, though, was Hugo's state of health. He had arrived somewhat under the weather and had progressively become worse, his illness deepening after we had gone home. The eventual diagnosis proved to be a very rare condition called dermatomyositis, which causes nasty skin problems, but even more seriously attacks the muscles, preventing them from replenishing their strength – akin to a car battery unable to recharge. Obviously, the end result is that the battery drains completely, the heart stops and the lungs cease to breathe. It was a worrying scenario. Thankfully, he was soon in hospital. Medication halted the crisis but, over the next few years it would be Hugo's own determination, coupled with his knowledge of the body from being a personal trainer, that returned him to a normal lifestyle. However, he will always have the condition and it had a disruptive effect on his family life.

The week after we returned home, and despite what was going on in respect of Hugo's illness, Odette was safely spayed. She came through the operation remarkably cheerfully and Hermia's affectionate welcome home to her daughter was touching to see. After 24 hours recovery time there was no longer any reason to keep the HO team indoors, but we began cautiously. I carried Hermia down into the garden and had a good walk round with her in my arms so she could begin to know the lie of her new land. Then I took her into the utility room, put her on the worktop near our flapless cat flap known, since Amber's day, as the way-in-way-out-hole, went outside and called her through. This was considered a good game and, like Eeyore* with the balloon, Hermia happily practised 'in' and 'out' for an hour or two. Any lingering doubts there might have been about her disappearing into the yonder were rapidly dispelled as she reconnoitred the territory, yet constantly checked back to me.

The next step was to reunite mother and daughter upstairs, then release the airlock of the dining-room so that Odette could follow Hermia outdoors when she felt ready to do so. This did not take very long. Being summer, both kitchen and garden room doors could be open, and the ramp in the utility room, which had served the blind Silvester so faithfully, was ideal now for Odette. She was soon beginning to explore the garden with as much enthusiasm as her mother. We already knew from the skitterings and galumphings round the upstairs play area that, once travelling at speed, Odette's limp disappeared and she seemed to move as fast as any other cat. She now demonstrated that she could climb the little malus tree favoured by Adora Bubble almost as well as our diva. Indeed, apart from the deep limp at slower speeds, the only real manifestation of her disability came in terms of lift-off, for she was not able to leap up to a high surface. Amber used to say that Bernard could fly, whereas most cats have to pause and concentrate for at least a moment before they leap upward. Odette simply did not attempt this particular move. Otherwise, it became clear that, if she could only come to relax sufficiently to trust us, she would be able to live a full life, even if her hunting skills would be impaired, which was something we could not feel too upset about and, anyway, she was soon demonstrating that she could kill a biggish feather as well as any other cat, catching several for our admiration.

During the initial settling-in period we had had to operate a closed door policy, foreign to our normal modus operandi, but had tried, nonetheless, to effect brief introductions between the cats. Bernard had largely deemed the HO team as beneath his notice and, after their curfew, when they were shut back in their room for the night, continued his normal pattern of coming up to our bed, if and when he chose. Mille had shown some alarm at Odette's unfamiliar gait, but saw Hermia as no threat and went on much as before. Once or twice Adora Bubble had been in the same room as the HO team, sitting on a high surface at a safe distance, flicking her tail and looking disgruntled, while Hermia purred on my lap on the sofa. As it turned out, both cats were probably using this time to assess the opposing force, so what we blithely saw as the good news of a return to our normal open house, meant that, for Adora Bubble, the skies were darkening over her small piece of Europe. We knew she had not been pleased that these invaders were in her world but had assumed that she would gradually get used to the idea, failing to anticipate the outbreak of open hostilities.

The first skirmish occurred when Hermia and Adora Bubble met one-to-one in the dining-room. We heard an indignant squall of rage, and I was in time to see Adora Bubble in infuriated retreat, returning to higher ground upstairs. Hermia turned her imperturbable, affectionate green eyes back to me, calmly announcing that it was first blood to her then. More than that, her dominance had been established. I went to comfort Adora Bubble, now safe in her foxhole in the linen cupboard. I leaned in to stroke her and was rebuffed with a growl and a swipe of her claw that drew more than metaphorical blood, 'This is all your fault. Don't you come here being all nicey-picey!' I sympathised with her point of view, felt very guilty and, from then on, with only occasional moments when we deluded ourselves that there was at least a truce, the war had begun.

Hermia was a skilled general. She kept her supply line of affectionate response to us always intact, never grumbled if I confined her for a while to give us all some respite, but was determined in the line of battle. She would rush the enemy from across a room, or the garden, with a speed unlikely for her howitzer* build. Adora Bubble's only defence was her rocket speed, accompanied by explosive noise, which alerted us to another battle in progress. Adora was courageous in that she did not succumb easily, but she could do nothing about her own small force, nor the superiority of those ranged against her. She desperately found new redoubts where she felt safer, yet still within her familiar territory, like the adopted 'tent' in the utility room, where she began hiding on Graham's tool box, hidden behind a draped towel. Once or twice she even sought refuge in the garden shed, so we put a bed and some food for her in there. She used every alternative exit she could find, including the leap from the balcony for a while, but this soon ceased, presumably because of an ambush following a lawn landing.

We were interactive observers in The Tortie Wars, trying every strategy we could think of ourselves, then desperately seeking outside advice. I was very conscious of how pathetic I had been when Kish was the new arrival, and was determined that, if properly tackled, we could bring this current onset of troubles to a peaceful resolution:

The amount of shutting and opening doors became worthy of a French farce, and we were taking a security risk by always leaving the door to the balcony open an Adora-sized crack, to provide her with some escape lest Hermia got her pinned down in the bedroom. It was unfair to expect a visiting cat carer to cope with these ever increasing tactics so, if we went away for a night or two, Hermia was boarded with Harry. Hermia was happy enough there, but he found her constant need for affection 'too full on'. There were other knock-on effects to the household. True, Kish remained an ally to all the cats and Bernard generally ignored the situation, just putting Hermia firmly in her place when the need arose. But Mille, upset by the storm in her usually calm environment, would now sometimes turn on Adora Bubble and chase her round the bedroom, causing her to retreat yet again into the watchtower of the airing cupboard.

Odette meanwhile, became her mother's first lieutenant, despite being walking wounded herself. However, as the young cat matured, so Hermia grew less tolerant of her daughter, sometimes batting her away. But this is only normal behaviour for any

Odette

mum who feels it is time for an offspring to stand on its own feet, even if it does only have three of them. In fact, Hermia had long exceeded the normal call of duty and was up for a Mother of the Year award, something which her daughter would certainly have supported, for she continued in affectionate admiration of her mum, slowly becoming more independent of her, yet remaining a committed member of the HO team and imprinted with Hermia's views of the battlefield.

The Tortie Wars took over our lives. With all the trauma Adora Bubble began soiling, so we had four trays placed strategically in the house, one of which was provided for Hermia when we decided to impose a curfew on her in the evenings. After a big cuddle she was shut in the downstairs study till morning, to give Adora Bubble a rest.

Relations between Bernard and the Hermia battalion remained neutral and once Mille had grown used to Odette's strange gait, the same was true of her. Neither of the older cats gave ground to the forces of invasion and Hermia respected them for it. With people, Hermia was as affectionate as any cat could be, loved to be picked up and cuddled, and was always delighted to see the grandchildren, of whom she would make an extra fuss. Having termed her Imperturbable Hermia, we moved on to referring to her as *Ubique**, for she patrolled her newly acquired territories with relentless efficiency, managing to be everywhere, notably at strategic points such as the cat flap or the landing, in readiness to ambush poor Adora Bubble, who was becoming more and more neurotic.

I was beginning to run out of ideas and would have felt horribly guilty if it had not been obvious that we had all been doing an excellent job by Odette, who was much more confident and well settled, even allowing Graham to stroke her (well almost) so long as he remembered to speak to her in his best counter tenor voice. It also seemed that the hostilities were as much a result of Adora Bubble's tricky personality as of Hermia's bullying tactics. Quite simply, the two cats had taken an instant and profound dislike to one another. However, knowing that was no help at all in achieving the much looked-for truce so, wearing my blue peace-keeping beret, I rang Wendy and Frank at Windyway to put them in the picture. They did not have any solutions but kindly offered to have Hermia back. However, I was very fond of her and felt I should try to do better by her than that. Besides, in the light of my performance with Kish, you could hardly blame Frank and Wendy if they thought I might be exaggerating the problem and that, given time and more effort, peace would descend. How I wanted them to be right.

I hoped fate might take a hand, that I would just happen to hear of somebody, somewhere, desperate for a cat, for whom Hermia would be perfect. A forlorn hope, for rehoming mature cats is never easy. I also asked advice from all the cat minded people I knew, including the vet. It made me feel less inadequate to talk to friends who, for many years, had taken in those cats hardest to rehome – the elderly, the ill, the just-gone-blind – caring for them to a peaceful and much loved end. They had looked after many cats over the years and, in all the time they had been offering this great service, had never had any trouble, until recently when they took in a tortie. Now they were experiencing their own Tortie Wars and my friend was feeling as helpless as I was. They had been enduring hostilities longer than us and were coming to the regretful decision that the newcomer would have to be rehomed. I said I was still half-hearted about accepting defeat and would battle on, trying to achieve a resolution of the conflict.

I reviewed the intelligence gathered from many sources . . .

1. Have plenty of space for your cats.
    We thought we more than qualified.

2. Have separate feeding stations for your cats to avoid confrontation.
    We had five, three of these having two separate bowls, thus a total of eight dishes.

3. Have more than one tray, placing them where the cat does not feel threatened when using them.
    We had four, for use of only three cats at maximum, for Bernard and Mille never needed them and, latterly, it was really only Adora Bubble who did. She even had one in our bathroom lest she get trapped up there in her cupboard watchtower.

4. Try to have more than one entry/exit to the house.
    In half decent weather we can manage at least four. I would also seek out Adora Bubble in order to ferry her to a safe haven.

5. Hostilities can be caused by one or other cat feeling insecure and unsure of its territory. Give plenty of reassurance to all parties.
    This went without saying, but Adora Bubble blamed us (especially me) for the situation, making her views plain when we tried to comfort her. She was having none of it.

6. Buy expensive Feliway units and plug them in around the house to release soothing pheromones into the atmosphere.
   We tried this with absolutely no effect.

7. Rub each of the combatants with the same towel so that they grow accustomed to each other's scent.
   We tried this too with no effect.

8. Bring both cats into the same room, but with one or the other in a carrier so that no one can get hurt.
   I was very dubious about this and it was a complete failure, whichever way round we tried it. With Adora on a high surface in the basket, Hermia was poised to loom, gloat and throw grenades into the pill-box if allowed to do so. When the positions were reversed Adora Bubble refused to stay in the room, making an instant retreat, her eyes flashing wild ack-ack as she did so.

9. Be patient.
   We were trying.

Ye gods we were trying, employing every tactic and manoeuvre we could think of, including giving Adora Bubble respite care with us up at Greengarth, something which had done wonders for Amber's confidence. But madam only half enjoyed it and, once home again, remained unhappy. Oppressed, traumatised, she was losing some of the little weight she had. Hermia, meanwhile, was implacable, though she had her lighter moments, enough to con us into a mistaken belief that one day it would all come right, but only till we were disillusioned by the next outbreak of battle.

Hermia

Chapter 29

The Day of the Bear

The ongoing feline warfare, plus the continuing worry of Hugo's illness, meant it came as more than light relief to be able to plan the October arrival of a new family member, one who would bring us nothing but joy. The exact position for the sculpture had been prepared while the landscaping was taking place, since it required a sunken concrete plinth, otherwise *Bear*'s seven tonnes would slowly sink into the ground. Ronald Rae always likes to be present when one of his sculptures is being installed so he and Pauline would be arriving from Edinburgh the morning of 5th October, having watched *Bear* lifted by crane onto the lorry at Holyrood the previous day.

It made it extra special to have the sculptor and his wife with us for this memorable occasion. Ronald thoroughly approved of the site but paced anxiously like any expectant father awaiting the delivery of his baby, and this one was an hour or so overdue. At last the moment came. The large lorry trundled slowly up our tiny lane, squeezed through the farm gate into the field and onto the tracking laid carefully to take it. This was the only possible way for *Bear* to make its entrance into our garden, so we were lucky that our farmer was obliging. Once lined up with the hedge, the crane lifted *Bear* over it and the mighty form hung, suspended above the plinth, while Ronald supervised, narrowly avoiding injury when one of the supporting straps snapped back. My job was to ensure that the sculpture was placed exactly as I wished with its nose pointing up to hill and sky. I wanted this same outline to greet me from the bedroom window each morning as I drew the curtains then sipped my tea in bed. While *Bear* was hovering an inch or two above the ground the position could be finely tuned, but once it had landed and the straps were removed it was installed for good. We had to get it right. In the event it was not difficult and we all relaxed and stood back to admire the effect, which was magnificent – an unlikely ambition fulfilled.

One of the joys of sculpture in the open air rather than in a gallery, is its freedom to respond to the elements and the changing light. You can watch the varying moods of *Bear*'s Kemnay granite as it darkens in the rain, or sparkles in the sun or moonlight. However, discoveries were ahead of us. Over a wet winter we were to find lichen beginning to turn *Bear* green, attractive in its way but the brightness of the stone when pristine lights up that corner of the garden, and this is how we want it to be. So *Bear* has the occasional scrub down, as indeed it had enjoyed before coming to us. I purred my way round my new friend, rubbing and embracing its stony charms and looking forward to its first meeting with Phoebe and Ruby. Big Sister Phoebe was introduced a few days later when we collected her from school and brought her home for tea.

Now it has to be admitted that some adults just fail to 'get it' in relation to *Bear*. I have seen a puzzled flicker cross the face as they try to be polite but fail to understand what they are meant to be appreciating. There is never any such problem with children, even at a very young age. Ruby, at two, was as enthusiastic as Phoebe when her turn came to meet *Bear*, and was just as eager to climb on its back and go for a magical ride to the moon and stars.

Bear had to have a name, something which reflected the spirit of all bears but was as grand, impressive and eternal as this one's beginnings – born of stardust. I had assumed it was a male and decided to call him *Ursus* Bear after the Great Bear constellation, only to discover that the more formal name for this is not *Ursus* but *Ursa* Major. Fortunately, the Latin genus name for bears, being *Ursus*, is more obliging and solved the problem. Thus I had told Ronald and Pauline that their *Bear* would henceforward be known as Ursus Bear. However, we had reckoned without Phoebe. At this first encounter, she climbed the steps up to the lawn, paused to take in the mighty stone beast in the corner of her grandparents' garden then, captivated, before running to ride bear-back she made her announcement, 'Grandma, I love your bear, but it's not a boy . . .'

Great Bear Day

Bear swings in at seven tonnes,
a little late, but heck,
when you are 470 million years old
what's an hour here or there?

He hovers in his slow trapeze,
clears the trembling hedge, and
nose uplifted
chooses his position;
precisely where he'll stay.

Majestic, he allows his carers
to grunt round him,
releasing his protective harness,
risking themselves
in service of his freedom.

Thoughtfully he scents the air
deciding
this will do.

'...spake as a child...'

How do I name this *Bear*?

This great *Bear*

living ancient in the rock
discovered
by the thunk of hammer
coaxing on fire-tempered tools.

His conjured bulk is power-packed,
his granite muscles rippling
under rain
or sun
or children's scrambling limbs.

He is magnificent,
born of stardust
gazes to the sky.

What name reflects this grandeur?
For here is Spirit Bear.

He is genus *Ursus*
yet has a kindly eye
which Phoebe finds,
and riding happy on his back
with easy wisdom of her own small years,
informs me I am wrong,
Bear is not a boy.

Her name is Emily.

Bear-Back Riding

My grandma's got a big, big bear
And she is old as old,
She lived full deep inside the rock
Her secret name untold.

But came a strong and magic man
To cherish out her form,
So she could lift her lovely head
To where the sun is warm.

So she could trundle through the trees
And sparkle in the light,
So she could fly into the blue
And round the moon at night.

And we ride safe upon her back,
The wind calls in our hair
As we hold tight to loop the loop
On Emily the bear.

Photograph taken in summer 2011

Chapter 30

Five, Four, Three

Emily Ursus Bear was an instant favourite with the children and many was the time that autumn they insisted on having their tea seated in the dark, on a rug draped over Emily's broad back. Fortunately, we have some outside lights, including a couple of small spots focused on the bear, but even so the experience had the taste of adventure, and the cooked tea itself had to be something practical, like hot dogs. After they had eaten, and before they got too cold, Phoebe would then insist that I climbed aboard as well, using the little step ladder which we kept hidden behind Emily's granite bulk. Sometimes Grandpa and/or Kish would join us, then we would go on an imaginary ride around the sky, being told to, 'Hold on tight, Emily's going to loop the loop!'

From Emily Bear's back Phoebe would sometimes see Cowley up among the stars and reassure him that she still loved him. Kish, meanwhile, loved the children but was also rather taken with Emily Bear, and it became her special trick to leap onto the platform of Emily's back and sing a song about what a clever dog she was. Hermia also loved the children and would usually appear to make a fuss of them, sometimes joining us for a starlit ride. She was the only one of the cats to acknowledge the arrival of the sculpture and enjoy sitting on it from time to time. Bernard was really too old to care, Mille had enough in her world without needing art, Odette had her three-leggéd limitations, and Adora Bubble had virtually ceased to go outside at all, and would soon be living more or less permanently in the airing cupboard.

The Tortie Wars dragged on through the next year until, by the late summer of 2008 I had, with great reluctance, come to the conclusion that Hermia would definitely have to move on. On one of my more desperate days I had bought a book called *Cat Detective* by the cat guru Vicky Halls, in which she offers advice on problems you may encounter with your cat, including inter-cat aggression. It was a surprise, but in a way a huge relief to see that, in her experience, if you have more than one cat you are lucky if they get on. Furthermore, she says that, in many cases where there is warfare, the only possible solution is to rehome one or other of the combatants. This made me feel less guilty and less of a failure, and it gave me the necessary shove to start seeking a new home in earnest for Hermia. Ideally, a home where she would be the only cat and thus Queen of the May. With regard to Odette, the young cat was now as settled with us as she would ever be, no longer needing her mother for constant reassurance, and anyway Hermia was not patient with her daughter anymore, sometimes being quite unpleasant to her, something which Odette accepted with unswerving loyalty.

On this particular warm, early autumn day, the children had been with us and Hermia constantly with them, enjoying their company, joining them on Emily Bear, sitting with them in the tent made by the weeping silver pear tree, and even being delighted when little Ruby picked her up and lugged her about for a while. She was endlessly patient and affectionate with the girls and it was lovely to see. That evening I was chatting to both Hugo and Jo while the children were in the bath. I said I was seriously looking for a home for Hermia now, spreading the word and wondering whether they might possibly know of anyone anxious to have her – a forlorn hope of course. As I put the scenario to them Phoebe burst into tears, 'I don't want Hermia to go. I love Hermia. Why can't she come and live here?' We three adults looked at each other and, despite the fact that Pudding and Pie were already resident, it was agreed to give Hermia a try for a week.

It would be an exaggeration to say that she was an instant and resounding success. Pudding and Pie were not pleased but would brook no nonsense from Hermia, and she accepted that. Hugo and Jo found her overly demanding, likely to be round their feet when coming downstairs and instantly on a lap the moment one of them sat down. On the other hand, the children adored her and she them, sleeping on the bed with them every night. She certainly was no longer the warrior queen, indeed, in a perverse quirk of fate she became frightened of a visiting tom cat. She refused the cat flap, unless propped open so she could check the possible dangers outside. Even then, she did not relax and enjoy the garden unless Buster was out there with her. He became her best friend and protector. However, surprisingly for a cat, Hermia appeared to harbour no resentment towards me for having moved her on, and greeted me enthusiastically whenever she and I met in her new surroundings.

Meanwhile, back at Throstles' Nest, Hermia's departure did not instantly transform Adora Bubble into a happy bunny of a cat. After all, she had known short times of respite before, perhaps this was one of them. She had been heavily traumatised for too long and was taking no chances. Similarly, if Odette missed her mother it may have also been on the assumption that she would be back one day soon. As the days and weeks ticked by and Hermia did not return Odette showed no visible sign of distress; after all she was over two years old now. Moreover, Hermia had taught her daughter well. Among the skills learned from her mother was the intimidation of Adora Bubble. Given less than half a chance Odette would charge Adora with as much determination, and rather more speed, than Hermia had done, the difference being that she was smaller and lighter than her mother, and had limited lift-off. Fortunately, despite Adora Bubble being even smaller and lighter than Odette, she was also faster and could leap to safety in one lightning spit of yowling rage. Thus alerted to the single combat taking place, one of us would administer the ultimate terrifying deterrent to Odette – a sharp clapping of hands.

Adora Bubble was no longer hopelessly outnumbered and, because the enemy force had been reduced by 50% the encounters were also rarer. She began to recognise that we were on her side and, after emitting sounds like purple murder, she would recover her good humour remarkably quickly. Slowly, over the ensuing months, she became more relaxed. She was not going outdoors but no longer confined herself to the airing cupboard, for she also favoured the window-ledge and the top of the old pine sideboard in the living-room, both heated by a cosy radiator which lay between the two. This was also a good vantage point. Odette could not approach without being sighted if she attempted to climb up there and this seemed sufficient to deter her from trying. I cleared the chosen area of ornaments, providing one of Margie's knitted cat blankets in their stead so that Adora Bubble could be truly comfortable. We were back to our optimum of four cats and life was easier again, but far from perfect.

Mille

Mille was still our same equable Mille but Bernard was becoming very old, deaf and frail, needing more medication, frequent visits to the vet and much loving care. Odette continued to be nervous much of the time but, endearingly, wanted to be called in at night, then insisted on stroking and tummy tickling in her room to settle her down as she throbbed an approving purr. Often I would take my bedtime reading onto her bed, where she would not exactly cuddle up but risk lying near my feet. I would stay with her for 20 minutes or so before returning to the marital bed and Bernard duty. I was, of course, very fond of Odette, and thrilled that one so disabled and frightened had been brought to a full and happy life. Nonetheless, a bit of me resented her continued persecution of Adora Bubble, who would soon be revealing a different and more endearing side to her tricky nature.

As the autumn of 2008 deepened into winter Bernard grew more gaunt and his kidneys weaker, needing to be closely monitored both by me and the vet. Fortunately, we were going away very little at this time but I would no longer think of leaving him alone even for a night, and our reliable animal and house-sitter would come to stay to enable us to go up to Greengarth for a weekend. Bernard did not go out much but, right to the end, he preferred to potter into the garden to do the necessary rather than suffer the indignity of using a tray. In November his mouth became very smelly and probably uncomfortable. He should have had some teeth removed but a preliminary blood test showed that his heart would not stand the anaesthetic. Instead, he was put on a drip for several hours at the surgery and this worked wonders for a few weeks. There are, of course, proprietary veterinary foods for many conditions and we tried them all, finding that Bernard would eat one or other for a short while, but then refuse it. He continued to like fish, with its strong smell, and would lap up the liquid it was cooked in even if he could not manage the flesh. But he grew thinner and thinner.

Earlier in the year we had been greatly saddened by the death of the vet who had cared for our animals for most of our time in Macclesfield. Ian was Amber's Clever Vet, and he and his wife Corinne were also our good friends. When Ian had to give up work because of illness we obviously had to look elsewhere and were fortunate, for we found someone else who was not only a good vet, but sympathetic and caring to owners coping with the sadness of impending loss. I remember our new vet, Nick, saying to me something in relation to Bernard which I already knew, but was good to hear again from a professional, 'You will know when the time is right.'

During the last weeks of his life Bernard became ever closer to me. He needed the reassurance of my presence and came inside the bed each night, snuggled against me on the outer edge. As we moved into December he seemed to lose his purr, but could still chirrup and was content enough with his life as a stately old man. The entry for the diary of 9th December says that the vet and I agreed Bernard was doing miraculously, despite having lost a little more weight. After two injections that day he was 'brave and cheery', and remained so for a few more days. By night he slept in our bed with me. By day he either stayed on the bed or came downstairs to settle on a lowish table under the other window in the living-room. I put a hot-water bottle and blanket there for him and it was also close to the radiator. It was during these last days that Adora Bubble showed her adorable side, crossing the room from her sideboard to come and sleep curled up close to Bernard, as if to watch over him.

By Friday 19th December Bernard was going downhill once more. He was given intravenous fluid again that day and sent home with two separate medicines, to be given by syringe into his mouth. As with most of our cats, pills had never been a problem with Bernard, but the syringe was different. His trust in me never wavered but he was plainly discomfited by the experience. When I took him back to Nick on the Monday he said that this time Bernard had not responded much to the treatment and we agreed that, despite Christmas being so near, to prolong his life any longer would be more for our sake than for his. An appointment was made for a home visit the next day.

A little restless overnight, Bernard enjoyed some juice from the turkey giblets next morning, a last treat, too late to do him any harm now. He then curled up on our bed for a while before wandering downstairs to sit on my knee in the living-room, afterwards going to the table by the radiator. Adora Bubble kept him company until the vet's arrival, when she shot out of the room as if sensing what was going to happen. But it was a beautiful moment, which could not have been gentler or more peaceful. The nurse held Bernard on her knee, still on his favourite blanket, and I stroked his head while Nick sent him kindly to sleep.

Harry had called in to say goodbye the previous afternoon. Now we made sure all the animals were aware, though I think Adora Bubble already knew. Surprisingly, it was Odette sitting on her landing who sniffed Bernard the longest and, in the most lingering, seemingly affectionate way. We had prepared a worthy place in the garden and, as we planted the early blooms of hyacinths and daffodils above him, I felt less in pieces than I had expected. It was good to know that, after a long and happy life, Bernard was safe. It was simply his time to come to a graceful end . . .

For Bernard
24th July 1989 – 23rd December 2008

When my time comes

may it be as easy passing,

gently held by those I love

with all my home around me.

Nor would I be averse

to the kindly needle path

that brings starlight oblivion.

May I have as fine a resting place

and be as well remembered

as this our loyal lion of cats.

Chapter 31

Gulliver Travels

We entered 2009 with our cat count depleted from five to three, a trio living an uneasy truce, for Odette would still chase Adora Bubble if she saw an opportunity and Adora would respond with her familiar indignant shrieks of rage. The difference was that she only had Odette to contend with and knew she could get out of the way. Slowly, she recovered some confidence so that, just before Christmas, I could make a cautiously optimistic diary entry, 'Adora Bubble almost went out today'. She progressed to making very brief excursions outside, beginning with high places like the arch over the side gate to the back garden, where she felt safe from Odette. Life was bearable again for all of us, but still far from ideal, especially as we were a cat down. We wanted to restore the number to four but were wary lest we made things worse again. I thought we should get a kitten, that it should be a boy, and that his temperament would be the all important factor. We were due to go to France in May so would wait till we were back before trying to find the perfect candidate. Fate had other ideas.

Not only were we a cat short but, sadly, I was also lacking an illustrator, for Jo Berriman had died suddenly and unexpectedly the previous February. I missed her, both as a dear friend and a skilled artist, for she had the gift of going beyond the physical attributes of animals and capturing character. I would need someone else soon, for a new book was beginning to form in my mind and needed to be written. I had had the good fortune to meet Josie through various unconnected circles in my life rubbing together. Now the same thing happened. When I had been working with the disabled writers I had met a splendidly resilient disabled artist called James Robert Duncan. I had helped him to write his courageous and remarkable story *Art Found Me*. James had stayed in touch through the years and we came to call him The Good News Man, for his frequent phone calls usually began with, 'I've got some very good news for you'. Not only did he defy his double vision sufficiently to achieve a BA in Art and then remain a keen painter, but he was an avid reader, despite the problems it posed for him. If he had particularly enjoyed a book he would sometimes send it on to me. Thus it was James who had introduced me to the delights of *The Cats of Moon Cottage,* the first of four books written by Marilyn Edwards about her cats. This accomplished author is as warm-hearted as her books suggest, responding to my appreciation of her work by contacting me, which resulted in an invitation to lunch, then a valued friendship.

Marilyn and I not only shared a love of cats but also the sad loss of our respective illustrators. It had happened to her a year or two before it happened to me and she told me she had been fortunate to find someone else. France Bauduin had initially contacted Marilyn as an appreciative reader of the *Moon Cottage* cat books. Coincidentally, she had recently taken up serious drawing in her spare time from teaching and welcomed the opportunity to try her hand as an illustrator.

When Marilyn learned of my own predicament, with typical kindness, one weekend in March she invited me to her Cumbrian home to meet France who, together with her husband Mark, was staying with Marilyn and Michael. Prior to the meeting I sent France my two cat books to read and she came armed with her artist's drawing book, showing examples of her work. We soon found a mutual respect and had much else in common, not least a normal quota of four cats in the household. Naturally, I told France the story of The Tortie Wars, of how we were down to three cats but wanted to go up to our optimum number again, providing we could find the right character. As it happened France's cat Spooky, elegant and semi-long-haired, had had kittens. The little male, she said, would have been ideal for us in our situation, for he promised to be laid-back and gentle, but he had already been spoken for. I thought this was just as well since it avoided any awkward decisions. We would be going away for three weeks from early June and he would be ready to leave his mum at the end of May.

I had found my new illustrator. She would be very different from Josie, for France warned me she can only draw what she sees, but she is a biologist by training so has a true eye for accuracy. Moreover, her internet and computer skills more than compensate for her self-confessed lack of ability in imaginative drawing. I think she and I were to learn from each other. As the working relationship developed I became a little better at computer literacy and her drawings grew more adventurous.

But I had found more than an illustrator. Three days after we met, France was in touch to say that the male kitten's intended owner had changed her mind, so he needed a home after all. Would we consider it? At first glance it seemed madness to take on a kitten and then go away for three weeks but was fate taking a hand, sending us the sort of chap we needed, just as Silvester had been sent to help Moses all those years ago?

One alternative would be to wait till we came home from holiday, but then the kitten would be bigger and possibly more daunting for Adora Bubble. We would prefer to have him at ten weeks, which is the youngest France allows her kittens to go (inoculation done) but the decision would hinge on our cat-sitter Leo, whom I knew I could trust completely. Would she be willing to look after an eleven-week-old kitten along with her other charges? I need not have worried. Leo was not only willing but keen, seeing it as our loss to miss the kitten's important early weeks at Throstles' Nest.

Still wondering if I was doing the right thing by Adora Bubble, but working on intuition and France's reassurances, the deal was struck and our newcomer given the name that had been awaiting a cat to fit it. On a journey to a children's theme park known as *Gulliver's World*, Phoebe and Ruby had decided that if Grandma ever had a boy cat again, 'Gulliver' would be a good name. Now it made even better sense, for our little Gulliver would be travelling all the way from Bristol.

I was able to meet Gulliver in early May on a return journey from Devon, where Harry and I had been to visit the wolves at Combe Martin. I was not likely to have changed my mind on seeing him, but he was everything I could have hoped for. He was almost exactly like Adora Bubble in colouring but, whereas she has her signature bubbles of tabby, Gulliver wore a mantle over his back. The markings on the face were also not dissimilar but, while Adora always has a tendency to look a bit cross, it was clear that Gulliver's natural expression would be that of serenity and contentment. He could easily have been her cousin, but was going to be one cool cat, and it was this that was so vital. France had to break the news that he would not grow to be fluffy-coated like his mother, which was a minor disappointment, but the promise of an easy-going nature more than compensated for this, and it fascinated us that he had Maine Coon in him somewhere, so he would certainly be a big boy. (There have been rumours that this breed can continue growing until they are four-years-old.)

Three weeks later I drove down to collect Gulliver, spending the Saturday night with France and Mark before bringing our new family member home on Sunday morning. Shortly before leaving, Gulliver climbed up to the wooden sculpture of a unicorn made by France's father. Though hardly on the scale of Emily Bear the unicorn seemed protectively large against a small Gulliver, who gazed up at me from between its hooves. I hoped this augured a unicorn's blessing, together with a touch of magic, something the kitten would bring with him to our still uneasy, feline household.

Gulliver travelled well, with only minor protestations, but was as relieved as I was to reach our destination. As usual, introductions were carefully made, but we were aware that we only had a week with Gulliver before going away, so felt we had to take the settling in process faster than usual. Because it was summer and doors were often open, it was not going to be easy to keep Gulliver indoors for long, for we could hardly use Odette's room as his holding bay. We would have to make do with the downstairs study and our bedroom.

On arrival, seeing Kish for the first time from the safety of his carrier placed high on the sideboard of the living room, Gulliver gave a big jump and spat at her, but Kish had seen it all before and, nothing daunted, a little later came to talk gently to him when he was on my knee on the sofa. This time Gulliver hissed again but with much less alarm. In the evening I brought Mille in to say hello. She looked a great, black, fluffy panther seen against him, and he seemed a little nervous of this, our senior cat, but she reviewed him graciously and then withdrew. Later, Odette came into the room, glared at Gulliver and then limped off, slightly huffy we thought.

And what of Adora Bubble? She was up in our bedroom sitting on the window ledge when she first met Gulliver. She stared down in blatant disbelief at yet another intruder in her world, as he began exploring the room seemingly unaware of her presence. When she saw him settle down for a big sleep on a strategically placed hot-water bottle on the bed, where he would spend the night, this was too much and she retired to the airing cupboard. However, she emerged in the night to eat some biscuits and, once I had taken her downstairs in the morning (grumble, grumble, when I picked her up) she enjoyed

Gulliver

the garden briefly. The body language was saying 'displeased', but there seemed to be no danger of her leaving home.

Monday was Gulliver's first full day and he had a good time exploring the kitchen, then had a sleep on Bernard's old cushion on the window-seat. While the indispensable Sandra was helping in the house that morning he managed to escape into the garden, where he was accosted by an amiable Mille. Gulliver was impressed with the big outdoors but, while having a little walk round, Odette appeared and stalked him threateningly. However, Gulliver knew about older cats who were less than welcoming. France's household had been a good training ground. He was totally unfazed, just glanced over his shoulder at her then carried on exploring. Next, Odette tried to intimidate him by looming over him on the patio steps, but he calmly stood his ground until she felt rather silly and backed off. As the day progressed Gulliver became more and more used to Kish and stopped hissing at her. Adora Bubble seemed to be avoiding him but that evening went to sleep on Bernard's old cushion in the kitchen, where Gulliver must have left his scent. We decided to leave her there, absorbing that scent for the night, rather than attempt to take her upstairs with us, only to be sworn at.

The next day Odette's attempt to bully him resulted in Gulliver dancing up to her with a gentle 'Boo!' This was sufficient to frighten Odette who ran away. Gulliver was already establishing boundaries in his relationships. He was certainly no coward but not aggressive either. He totally failed to see why everyone could not get along together happily, a point of view we had been trying to get across to Adora Bubble and Odette for some time.

As expected, Gulliver was a huge hit with the grandchildren and with friends who came to see him while he was small, but by the time we went away on 8th June, Odette was threatening to leave home and live in the shed, though at bedtime she forgot, reverting to her normal delighted cuddles in her room. Adora Bubble was severely displeased. She would not stay in the living-room with us in the evenings, retiring to a box in the utility room. However, her displeasure seemed to be mainly aimed at us rather than at Gulliver, whom she was keeping under review before coming to a decision about him. He, meanwhile, was already growing fast – a fine, strong young chap, safe to be left in Leo's care for three weeks while we went to France. By the time we came back, towards the end of June, Leo had much to report, adding to the information we had received by telephone during the interim. After a few days at home I stitched the experiences together as best I could, then wrote the following . . .

1st July 2009

While Graham, Kish and I were away the cats would play, and the name of the game was All Change. Gulliver's arrival has totally altered the dynamics of the feline household. He has the sweetest, gentlest nature and will surely grow to be a real gent. From the moment he saw her, he decided to woo Adora Bubble and took all her grumbling, hissing and spitting as symptoms of someone who was actually longing to be loved – shades of the prince and princess in 'Turandot'*. 'Vincero' he said to himself, and he surely has for, to her own astonishment, Adora Bubble found herself responding by playing with him, and we had reports from Leo of what our sons would have called in their boyhood 'funny fights' – quite rough stuff, from which Adora might flee, only to return for more, followed by a deep and exhausted sleep, sometimes side by side with Gulliver in the vacant dog's bed.

Mille continues to be Mille, largely unfazed by the new arrival but conscious of being the senior cat. She has formed the Mille Association, of which she and Odette are the Chair and Hon. Sec. with Gulliver and Adora Bubble being welcome members. Leo reported a few occasions when Mille had 'had a go at Adora Bubble', springing on her in a semi-aggressive manner. Fortunately, Adora Bubble will take this from Mille and it is reminiscent of how Mille behaved once or twice during the early part of Hermia's reign of terror. This renewed phase had passed completely by the time we came home. Mille has, however, largely relinquished her claim on our bedroom for the moment, though will drop by from the roof in the early morning, for a quick hello and a snack. She then leaps from the balcony back down into the garden. Otherwise, Mille is content with the chair or sofa in Graham's study, or the 'warming heart' basket in the utility room, where she is able to offer support to Odette.

Leo reported that Odette took to sleeping in one of the boxes in the utility room, she being the one upset by Gulliver's arrival – an arrival exacerbated by Mum and Dad's audacious departure, leaving her to cope all on her own with this serious crisis. All alone and by herself. Well all right, admittedly with Leo and Mille there, but that was hardly the point. Once home, we have seen for ourselves her disapproval registered in several ways. She tries to be unpleasant to Gulliver, but he dumbfounds, annoys and slightly unnerves her by being disarmingly cheery about all her moodiness. The worst aspect for her, we suspect, is that she senses he can see through her protestations and that it will only be a matter of time before he wins her round. All the time we were away she refused to come in for Leo at night, and hardly made use of the spare room, which has always been 'hers'. She did, however, allow Leo to make a fuss of her in the garden, which can be counted a large feather in Leo's hat, as usually Odette will not even allow me to do this. When we came home, far from being the one most pleased to see us, rushing up to her room to be loved, Odette did not appear for several hours. She then kept her distance, with much loud pathetic miaowing.

Could this have anything to do with the sudden appearance of Adora Bubble on the spare room bed? Our diva had, to my knowledge, never previously been in that room, certainly not since the arrival of Hermia and Odette. Now, here she is on the hand-knitted blanket, curled up as if she owned the place, often with Gulliver nearby. She knows how to make a statement – the revenge of Adora Bubble. She has put on a little weight too, enjoying the garden (helped by the good weather) and has virtually abandoned the airing cupboard, where she had spent most of her life during Hermia's reign. So Adora Bubble is in Gulli's Gang and content to be so. It is wonderful to see her playing and even going outside a bit. We are more than vaguely aware of the huge night-time galumphings of the Gulli Gang all round our bedroom, over and under the bed, and us, which probably lasts an hour or so around 2am, but, like the sound of children playing happily in gardens or school playgrounds, this performance only provides us with a feel good factor.

So, all was going very well until yesterday when Gulliver disappeared. One moment he was there playing in the living-room with Adora Bubble, the next gone, vanished. Big panic. I hunted everywhere, getting more and more frantic, for he had never been missing before. He is always in evidence. Adora Bubble was helping me look for him and seemed worried too. I checked the same places half-a-dozen times and called all round the garden. No Gulliver. I began to have nightmares, after all he is only three months old. A long hour went by and I was feeling sick with worry. Then, into the kitchen he strolled, 'Just been on some travels,' he said, cheery as you like.

Later in the day, when he had had a big sleep on the sofa, and I had recovered my equilibrium, I followed him outside. I registered that Gulliver is beginning to go further afield, still safely within the garden but into dark corners and exceedingly leafy trees, where he can disappear very successfully despite his colouring. I shall not worry so much when he does it again. Cats have to learn their territory, but it will mean allowing extra time to call him in if we are going out, for he is far too young to be left unattended for long. I have the feeling that, if he is busy, he will not instantly reappear just to please me and I may have to indulge in heavy bribery to encourage him to come more quickly. But, all in all, we seem to have made excellent progress, just needing to work on the somewhat discountenanced Odette, for it is her turn to be outnumbered – by the Gulli Gang.

A few days after this it was Adora Bubble I could not find. I don't spend my life worrying about the exact whereabouts of my cats but seem to have a sixth sense which tells me when I have not seen one of them for too long. It was only a minor panic as I know Adora Bubble does not go anywhere much and has always had a talent for hiding away in impossibly small places. After hunting for half an hour, I eventually found her buried deep in the airing cupboard, somewhere we thought she had abandoned. Never underestimate any cat's ability to confound.

In mid-July Gulliver spent a weekend with us up at Greengarth, as he was still too young to be left at home without a full-time cat-sitter. We let him go outside but only under strict supervision. He took his new setting in his stride in his usual calm way, enjoying the stone wall onto the fell just as Amber had done, and Mille and Lenni as kittens. When Kish and Graham went for a walk Gulliver was game to go under the gate and explore a few feet of fell for himself. He also did a great deal of bird-watching, though fortunately was not yet competent enough to catch anything. He enjoyed having us to himself on the bed at night, purring hugely beside us, but we got the impression that he was even more delighted to be home again, where Adora Bubble gave him a royal welcome. Her prince was back.

When introduced to our vet Gulliver was pronounced 'a splendid little chap' and having a micro-chip fitted seemed a further step towards maturity. Far from being upset by the experience, when Adora Bubble was due for her annual check-up a week later, Gulliver wanted to get in the carrier with her. She too passed her medical with flying colours and her weight had increased by 10%, which seemed a sure sign of a happier cat. In her case the only snag was a migrating identity chip. After a long, fruitless search it was decided she must have a new one, emphasising how important it is to have these devices checked on a regular basis. We had already noticed that the authorities at Portsmouth always ask, before we board the ferry, when Kish last had hers confirmed. Since I make a point of going to the vet's a few days before each departure it is never a problem, but the possibility of chip migration must be taken seriously.

The weather was warmer and Gulliver was enjoying the great outdoors. We have three so-called cat flaps, two of them being mere square holes, but the utility room door has a cat flap proper, normally propped open to give clear access, but closed while Gulliver needed some restricting. Early August saw Gulliver break out. He burst through the flap while I was in the utility room, delighted with himself and heading speedily for the way-in-way-out hole and the temptations of the garden. At nearly five months old it was time to allow him his total freedom during the day. We told Leo the new development when she arrived for her next three week stint and we said goodbye to our fast-growing boy once more, leaving him snuggled up to Adora Bubble in the airing cupboard.

Leo, as always, enjoyed her sojourn and it passed uneventfully. Gulliver came in at night for her, which was good, and to use his tray with great commitment during the day, which was less good. Her attempts to encourage him to dig holes in the garden were not a success, which was a pity, as his rapid growth in size was being accompanied by an ever greater capacity to produce noxious pongs when using his tray for serious matters. We resorted to the advice I remembered from a rather prissy television celebrity from days gone by. Her treasured pearl was that one should always strike a match after using a cloakroom in a friend's house as this would dispel any unfortunate odours. It may be prissy but it works. Remove the offending solid first, strike your match, add the afterthought of a little lavender spray, and the room is pleasant again. However, once we were back from France in September I deemed it the right time to encourage Gulliver to perform all ablutions outdoors. Maybe he was just that bit older, or my digging techniques were more impressive than Leo's, but within a couple of days he had got the message and never looked back.

Before Gulliver could be signed off into young adulthood, there was the final hurdle of his operation. These days castration is, mercifully, done under a general anaesthetic, but this in itself makes one a little apprehensive. However, we have never experienced any problems over the years, and none of our cats has ever been as dopey as you are warned that they may be when they first come home. But Gulliver took us totally by surprise. Not very dopey? He was hyper! For once he behaved as we had been warned some Maine Coons may do, rushing round the house at speed, knocking the telephone off the hook and an ornament to the floor. His special invalid food intended to last him 24 hours was gone in 12. There were galumphings round the bedroom in the night and a final burst of speed early morning. Then he crashed out, waking some hours later, his normal placid self.

By the end of September we were wondering how we had ever managed without Gulliver. Not only was he Adora Bubble's best friend but he was also making continual overtures to Odette to play with him. She was not exactly keen but we had the feeling that, eventually, he would win her round. Meanwhile, Adora Bubble, having made her point about her right to go into Odette's room, stopped doing so, but Gulliver continued to wander in there sometimes. He took most things in his stride, even the vacuum cleaner did not bother him, and a trauma with Buster soon passed. It was our fault that it happened at all. We were so used to Buster being a complete softie that we had overlooked the fact that he regards it as one of his duties to chase off any unknown cats in the camp. We had failed to introduce Buster to Gulliver properly, so when the latter tried to join a walk in the field, Buster thought 'I spy strangers' and chased him. Graham was alarmed on Gulliver's behalf, especially when he did not reappear for a while. But Gulliver being Gulliver (and not most cats) was prepared to forgive and forget. Once apologies and proper introductions had been made, Buster was instantly accepted and a good relationship formed.

As we approached the latter part of the year, life was settling down and Adora was behaving much more like her former self. Our little diva had made something of an odyssey – from the moment of the hated Hermia's arrival, through to her departure and then the arrival of Gulliver. Here, she had yet another journey to make, one of changing size. Suddenly she was huge, for a phenomenon of having a kitten in the family is that the other cats become instantly massive, slowly travelling back to their own size as the months slip by . . .

Gulliver Grew

When first he came

the small cat

feels herself

transformed –

a leap

to mighty leopard.

But Gulliver grew

and for a while

they share their size.

But Gulliver grew

so she resumes

her small cat role.

But still Gulliver grew

till more than small

the she cat

sits

diminutive

beside him.

Chapter 32

Losing Odette

Gulliver continued to develop his more mature lifestyle, beginning to hunt, though fortunately mainly mice and shrews, few birds. We never enjoy this aspect of our cats' nature, but he did not bring us many presents, so we hope the kill count was relatively low. Our experience has been that young cats become keen hunters for a while but, once skills are established, interest in blood sports wanes again as they grow older, much to our relief.

Gulliver would come into the bed with us, alongside me, shades of Bernard, though not with his grace, for you could never say of Gulliver that he can 'nearly fly'. Bernard was a macho, muscle-packed cat, but Gulliver, though loose-limbed as a Harlem Globe Trotter, tended to be clumsy and his movements lumbering. However, when he was about seven months old I got up one morning to find him nowhere in the bedroom but greeting me on the landing. Since everywhere had been secure, apart from the patio door, we realised that he was emulating Mille. He must have leapt off the balcony into the garden, just as she had begun doing around the same age. Our mistaken belief that Mille came onto the balcony via the roof was later corrected by Gulliver, for Graham saw him one day, ascending the virginia creeper from ground level. This made much more sense, for cats generally much prefer climbing up to going down, which is why they occasionally get stuck up trees.

Gulliver began coming for walks with us up the field, particularly enjoying the darkness. He continued to come in at bedtime, as if to settle us down and say goodnight, but once he could exit from the balcony he felt, as we did, that he was old enough to please himself about his night-time activity. Many people keep their cats in after dark, for that is when they are very vulnerable to road traffic, being drawn by the lights, as we knew ourselves from bitter experience with Sam. I have never been convinced that I would manage to get our cats in at sundown, but salute all those who can. I would be worried about our cats' safety every night of my life if we lived anywhere near a road, but as we don't we are relaxed about them being out, once they reach a reasonable maturity. There are always risks to free-ranging cats, of course there are, but they are naturally nocturnal animals, their freedom is important and, as it happens, the only accidents that have occurred to any of ours have been in daylight.

France and her husband visited us in October, for she always likes to follow up her kittens to make sure they are happily placed. In our case I hope she had not been having doubts and that it was more of a friend-to-friend visit. There was certainly no hint that she thought Gulliver needed rescuing from our evil or incompetent clutches. He, meanwhile, showed that cats have good memories, for he was thrilled to see France again and made a huge fuss of her, recognising the person who had helped to build him into such a confident, affectionate fellow. France took good photographs of Gulliver on

Emily Bear for, having left home with a unicorn's blessing upon him, he had happily swapped exploration of that wooden sculpture for the larger, outdoor piece, throwing his shadow onto Emily's sparkling granite and sometimes sharing her with Kish.

When Phoebe and Ruby came for a sleep-over Gulliver saw it as his duty to help put them to bed in the spare room, then keep watch overnight. Odette was less than enthusiastic about little strangers in her room, withdrawing to the landing. Adora Bubble, meanwhile, continued to be much more settled, getting up to one of her old tricks, which was to shoot into the drawing room unseen, then get locked in. We had wondered where she was that bedtime but thought she was hidden in a cupboard somewhere, asleep. Frantic miaowing next morning alerted us to her plight and, once released, a desperate rush to her tray brought relief. The next night there were no mistakes. Adora Bubble slept deep inside our bed, and so did Gulliver.

Odette was still the odd one out. Though she half wanted to be friends with Gulliver, who was certainly stretching out the paw of friendship, she was still rattled by his arrival. Finding not only Gulliver, but also Adora Bubble, claiming rights on what Odette had considered to be 'her bed' was hard to take. However, we had a strong feeling that Gulliver would not give up on her, and that all might yet be well. Then the crisis occurred:

It was the second Monday in December and would be a busy day. I had to take Graham to the station for the seven o'clock London train, next there was a walk in the dark with Kish and Buster, followed by a drive to the Trafford Centre to test the enduring patience of the young Applemac instructors in a one-to-one computer lesson. There would then be Christmas shopping, a two hour German lesson and sprucing up Harry's house before arriving home in something of a worn-out heap.

Going downstairs that morning at 6.15am I gave Odette a light caress, drawing no sense of impending crisis as she sat on the landing outside her room. Do we ever say to ourselves, 'Could this be the last time?' Could we do much about it if we did? I thought nothing of it when Odette was not around on my return from the dark fumble of the dog walk, as Sandra was vacuuming – a sure-fire way to make all the cats except Gulliver skedaddle. So everything seemed normal as I left for the Trafford Centre. It was six o'clock when I returned that evening. Gulliver was sitting on the railing by the drive waiting for me, as was becoming his habit. Often there would be an Odette yowl from the little gully below the drive and she would limp out, almost greeting me before scuttling off, semi-scared as always. However, I had a lot to catch up on that evening so registered only vaguely that I had not seen her. It was not till her bedtime call that the first alarm bells began to ring. She is the only cat to require me to call her in last thing and usually comes within a moment or two, but tonight there was only a cheerful Mille to reward my efforts. Admittedly I was very tired and needing my sleep so, when I could not find her anywhere in the house either, I told myself that Odette is nearly as good as Adora Bubble at hiding herself away and must be in the depths of some cupboard somewhere. Thus I was not sufficiently alarmed to lie awake worrying. However, when there was still no sign of Odette next morning, anxiety began in earnest. Yet I told myself I had been here before, allowing alarm to set in only to find the missing animal strolling in an hour later. I tried to keep calm and decided to walk the dogs as usual, in the hope that Odette would have appeared by my return. No joy. I did then begin to panic and extended the search into neighbours' gardens, alerting them to the situation.

Soon after 10 o'clock I was to leave for a lengthy hair appointment and just before I did so there was a ring at the doorbell. My heart simultaneously rose, in case it was good news, then fell, in case it was bad. This was not a comfortable sensation and, when I saw who the caller was, my emotions were even more confused. It was my dear friend Hazel (who used to live next-door-but-one) bringing me my Christmas present. Usually I would have been delighted to see her but old memories stirred. It was poor Hazel who had found Aaron stretched out stiff on her doorstep all those years ago and had then had the horrible task of breaking the news to me. She now lives a few miles away and seldom arrives unannounced, so it seemed too much of a coincidence that she should come today. An omen? Being the sensitive friend that she is, Hazel was quick to notice that I did not seem quite myself, and when I told her Odette was missing, she must have made those same connections. It can't have been an easy moment for her either. We gave each other a brief hug, then had to dash our separate ways.

My hair appointment was one of those interminable ones involving a rubber hat and fronds of hair waving through it like a sea anemone, so that colour can be applied. Today I was not the most chatty or relaxed customer. I was torn between wanting to stay away from home, because at least that way I could kid myself that Odette had safely returned, and wanting desperately to get back there to do everything I could to find her. As I sat there waiting for golden brown to cover the grey I became more and more convinced that she had been hit by a car and then crawled away to die. What if the car had injured her one remaining back leg, leaving her only the two at the front? She would be helpless. My imagination ran riot, so that by the time I got home I was visibly shaking as I checked the undergrowth on both sides of the lane, and the neighbours' gardens once more.

Again I drew a blank, but found a kind of negative comfort from the lack of a dead or dying body. In the house the lack of her presence was haunting. Every moment, I met her failure to miaow piteously, demanding attention. I imagined her limpitty-hop form as she dipped and dived ahead of me to her food bowl. There was a cat-sized space on the landing where she would often curl up, hoping for passing attention. I could not concentrate on anything sensible, except that Kish was telling me she needed her midday walk and fancied a run with her new friend Renée, a border collie working nearby. I took Kish on her lead across to the neighbour's courtyard, the last house on the lane and on the opposite side to us. Alan, the waller, was hard at his skilled dry-stoning, his dog in the back of the truck. As I was speaking to Alan before he told Renée she could jump down and come with us, I heard a deep and desperate yowl from behind the closed garage door.

'That's funny', said Alan, 'We've been working here all morning and not heard a sound.' 'No, you wouldn't, I replied, grinning stupidly with relief. 'She would have been too frightened till she heard my voice.' Alan held Kish while I went down on my hands and knees, to find Odette cemented with fright to the concrete floor under

Eric's classic sports car. The irony was, that although she was behind a closed door with a terrifying concrete mixer grinding loudly on the other side, the garage, being a large, double one, has a second door which was fully open and had been so since early that morning.

I weighed up the order of play. I had a cat to rescue but also two lively, impatient dogs to exercise. Since it was extremely unlikely that Odette was going anywhere, and I now knew her to be safe, I decided the priority was to take the dogs for their burst of speed up the field, using this breather to work out how I would extricate Odette without frightening her further. Thus it was, that a few minutes later, with both dogs returned to their respective bases, I was trespassing in Carol and Eric's garage, accompanied by Mike and Joanie, two other kind neighbours, who were available for emergency service, since Carol and Eric were not at home. Armed with soft-headed mops they gently pushed Odette from her glued position under the car into my outstretched hands. I was able to grasp her rigid little body, taut enough to be a rocket launched at the moon, and held her resolutely till she was safe in her own room. As I put her gently on the bed, talking to her and stroking her all the time, I could feel the tension flow away and, within moments, she was purring and pushing against my hand. Soon after this she was eating a large number of her biscuits, then settling down for a big sleep. I left the door on the latch the way she likes it, so she could open it in her own time, and I visited her frequently throughout the day, to be greeted with ecstatic purrs. Tears pricked my eyes, tears of relief and privilege that this small, nervous cat had had sufficient trust in me to alert me to her plight, even though, with all the coaxing I could have mustered, she probably would never have come to me without the encouragement of those mop heads.

By late afternoon Odette had emerged from her room, been in our bedroom and even outside for a short time. That night she was delighted that I slept in her room with her and she snuggled up close. How she had managed to get herself 'trapped' under Eric's car we shall never know. It had certainly not occurred to me that she could be on that terrain, but Carol and Eric have a very large cat called Sniff, built like a bus who could, if he wished, defend his territory with force. For all her nervousness with people, Odette is feisty when it comes to other cats, so perhaps there had been an unwise confrontation in which she had come off worst. Whatever had happened it resulted in Odette staying very close to home after her safe return. The previous December we had had to cope with losing Bernard two days before Christmas but that was a graceful ending to a long life. I could not imagine trying to celebrate Christmas with Odette missing.

Of course, many people have to greet the festive season facing much worse than a lost cat, but when I rang Hazel to tell her the good news, knowing me so well, she commented that I had just had my best Christmas present. A wise as well as a good friend, she is among the first to recognise that we only realise how much we love someone when they appear to be taken from us.

It seemed that Gulliver recognised this too for, after the scare with Odette, he revealed the full extent of his remarkable nature; taking the episode very seriously he decided it was high time to take her into his care as well as Adora Bubble. Thus, he regularly began to sleep in Odette's room with her, giving her preferential treatment. He still found time for his other charge, who was secure in his friendship, so that she could spare him for Odette duty now and then. By Christmas he had it sorted, Odette actually leaping on Gulliver in play and not in the least worried if he chased her, momentarily squashing her with his greater bulk. Far from being left lonely on the sidelines of the Gulli Gang, Odette now felt she had a friend too, and we guessed that, for one of such a nervous disposition, her happiness quotient had reached unlikely proportions.

Of course all cats are different but we had certainly never had one like Gulliver. We began to have an inkling that he feels he is here to look after all of us rather than the other way round. As time has gone on, and family members staying in the house have been ill or in low spirits, he has always appeared, proffering comfort. His is a benign, even an angelic presence, and certainly he is Gulliver the Peacemaker, taking first Adora Bubble and then Odette under his wing . . .

Look Not for Angels

Look not for angels

robed in their expected guise,

haloed blue and gold,

for one may come upon you

an unheralded surprise.

Chapter 33

The Days Peace Broke Out

After several years of winters that were too mild for anybody's good, with the festive season of 2009 the weather had a change of mood, throwing ice and snow at a country taken by surprise. Blizzards trapped cars, ice on tracks halted trains, people fell and broke bones. At home, our little lane was dodgy to negotiate long after the main roads were clear, and exiting the home base safely was our chief concern, determining whether we could reach the Lakes for New Year – that, and the access to the cottage once we arrived. We took my smaller, lighter car, but even so we would not have made it up the track to the cottage without help from neighbours who pushed and shovelled. Once safely ensconced, the car did not move until departure time and, when it came to it, we had to stay on an extra day. Even 24 hours later we only just gained the A66 to head home to Macclesfield before the next entrapping snowfall.

The Lakes under snow, hoar frost and icicles is indeed beautiful and Kish, like most dogs, loved the white stuff, though with her thin coat she has never been keen on a cutting wind, and I sympathise, for it is my own pet hate. When that wind is joined by pelting hail it will drive her to try to shelter in the lee of our bodies, and we know it is time we all threw in the towel and went home. Harry did once buy her a coat to wear, but she thought he was trying to turn her into an old demi-greyhound granny, and looked so utterly miserable that it had to go back.

Mille, Adora Bubble and Odette were not very keen on the snow, but Gulliver revelled in it, enjoying the fun as we struggled to dig out the drive, and wishing he could join in as Kish and Buster cavorted in the field, romping in snowy mock fights. Meanwhile, indoors we were having extended problems with the chimney and roof of the utility room, which in turn affected the boiler. Leaks, condensation, a collapsing ceiling and 24 hours with no central heating formed a cocktail that failed to cheer those bitterly cold days. But it is a good lesson, making you appreciate modern day comforts when you get them back again. Then, not content with one cold winter, the weather threw more of the same at us at the end of the year, and was so enthusiastic about it, that the harsh weather began in late November, 2010. Some plants which had survived the first onslaught, found this double dose of cold too much, and gave up the ghost, but others, like the cherry trees, thrived on weather that made them close down properly for the winter, rejoicing in an extra burst of springtime blossom. Sadly, our own much loved winter flowering cherries had died of disease some years before, only the much larger, wild ones surviving. The cherry tree on the edge of the drive not only survived but rewarded years of waiting with a cascade of white flowers in summer, tumbling from a mountaineering Kifsgate rose.

As we grow older, changes in life patterns and our surroundings are as inevitable as breathing. Some of this we like, much of it we don't, and consequently, we can become dangerously grumpy as we look back at a rose-tinted past. In our own immediate environs there is much to be grateful for, though not without a crisis, followed by necessary adjustments; always vaguely aware that the reservoirs above us could, under certain circumstances, be a threat, it was not until vicious rainfall, accompanied by a blocked spillway in early December 2007, that our little community swung into action. It was a frightening night when Niagara Falls poured down the footpath and in at our front gate, made a lake of the front garden and rushed onward to flood next-door's cellar. Then, much worse, it flooded the whole of the ground floor of the house beyond. The force of the water coming down the footpath that evening was daunting, and Harry was seriously worried about his father as they struggled up against the tide.

We all did our best to pull together but it was our neighbour Carol's quick and determined thinking which probably saved us from catastrophe. By dint of several phone calls we had eventually persuaded the fire brigade to come, but it was Carol who laid down a nine line whip, making them lift the heavy grid cover over the culvert in the corner of the field. This vital drainage feature was almost concealed in long grass and had not been in use for years. Once the cover was raised the threatening flow of water found a new outlet, being instantly diverted to become an underground river. It was not, alas, in time to save Sally, next-door-but-one, from six months in rented accommodation while her house dried out, but certainly rescuing the Melmoths from the growing lake in their garden, which would have been oozing in at the front door given another hour or two of the prevailing conditions.

Several people had to plunge into hot baths to recover from the shivers of the night and the experience was a frightening lesson to all of us, from which we learnt very fast. An association was formed of the eight houses in the lane, with a monthly rota established for keeping watch on the reservoirs and, more especially, on the spillways. The local community police gave good support, in warm weather discouraging youngsters from using the reservoirs as a playground for, sad to say, it was they who had left litter and pulled stone walling down which had caused the blockage.

The farm which owns the reservoirs was inherited by the younger generation in the summer of 2007, and since then has been managed by Stan. He was there on the night of the crisis, helping to divert some of the water down another pipe to a pool much lower down the fall of the land, and he has worked tirelessly on improvements ever since. This work, combined with the efforts of the neighbourhood itself, together with support from the Environment Agency and the Footpath Association, have combined to make us all safe in our homes.

In addition to the reservoirs there is also Swan's Pool. Tucked away from any major roads as we are, the final approach to our little dead-end lane is via an unmade road, passing attractive meadow land running down to a large pond – or very small lake. This edges the road and is a favourite place for people to stop, enjoy the view and feed the ducks. When we moved to Macclesfield in 1975 Swan's Pool was graced by a lone swan. This vanished after a year or two and, for many years, the pool was without its signature bird. But the autumn of 2009 saw the arrival of a pair of swans and there was excitement when it became clear in the spring of 2010 that they were breeding. A stretch of the pool is hidden from the road and runs behind two gardens. The wise young parents had chosen to build their nest in the safety of David and Gitte's domain, where they were watched over diligently and named Gustav and Solveig.

Residents and passers-by alike rejoiced at the appearance of five cygnets and, besides neighbourly personal updates, emails were flying around, reporting any new developments under the title of *Swan Watch*. Unfortunately, there was anguish to endure over this first breeding season, for the male, or cob bird, a very dutiful, protective father, injured his beak, or perhaps had injury inflicted upon him. Had he been left unattended he would have died. Thankfully, the RSPCA were able to capture him and restore him to health in their swan hospital at Stapeley Gardens. But meanwhile, despite all the care of the devoted mother (the pen bird), one by one the cygnets were lost, either disappearing completely or found dead in the water. Botulism was the suspected culprit in the latter case, due to the dry weather conditions impinging badly on a relatively small expanse of water. It is not uncommon for swans to lose all their cygnets but in this case the whole neighbourhood mourned their loss. However, there was rejoicing when the male bird returned. Swaddled in his travelling bag he looked rather undignified and not best pleased, but once released onto the water he soon regained his cool, and his graceful form. Swans usually mate for life but nonetheless, reconciliation after a break in the relationship cannot be taken for granted. Our female had had a tough few weeks without him and you could hardly have blamed her if her reaction had been, 'Where the hell do you think you've been?'

All was well, however. They settled back as a pair and have been with us ever since, apart from taking a brief respite from the inhospitable, iced surface of the pool during the winter of 2010, when they must have returned to their own birthplace of more open water in Congleton. Come the spring of 2011 our swans tried again and, from a clutch of nine, raised four healthy youngsters, which is more than a good average. In time, the adolescent birds will be encouraged by their parents to fly away and make their own lives on waters new. This success story has given many people great joy and the return of swans to Swan's Pool is symbolic reassurance that much is still right with the world.

Gustav and Solveig

On the Pool

The watched pride of swans;

young ones boasting glints of white,

the future signalled,

splendour flexed in full grown wings,

spirits lifted to the skies.

Encouraging reassurance, yes, but it would be disingenuous to pretend that all is right in this, our troubled world. If we tried as individuals to empathise with every agony and anxiety out there on our mightily challenged planet, it would probably kill us (which is perhaps part of the reason why news stories move on so fast) but there can surely be no excuse for failing to have concern for the environment, nor for failing to support selected charities when we can. One resource the world will never be short of is good causes. On a small personal scale there are some aspects of life Graham and I would like to be different. As in most families there is usually one problem or another in ours, whether it is illness or a failure in relationships.

We are both lucky in our own health, though knees get creakier and hills steeper. Jars, bottles, and cellophane round birthday cards grow harder to break into, so that I wonder how frail people living alone ever manage to open their recalcitrant bleach or pill containers. Names of acquaintances, films, actors, books and places slip into the mist beyond memory and have to be dragged back over the horizon. More and more articles go walk-about in the house and require hunting time. The eternal, 'Where are my glasses?' being joined by 'It can't be far away, I had it a moment ago' and 'Who could have put that there?' 'Somebody' gets frequent blame for moving things. It becomes necessary to check the diary daily to avoid missing appointments, and Hugo has given me the useful device of a large blackboard for the kitchen wall, which guards against the danger of having a good idea (like packing the spare car keys for holiday) and then forgetting it again before it has been activated. Making lists is a help, providing you can remember what to write down on them, check them and have them handy for additions.

I have always had a few memory rules, like taking mental snapshots before leaving the house, so that we are not halfway up the motorway when I say, 'Did we lock the back door?' or 'Have we switched the computer off at the mains?' Recently I have made myself some new rules and try to remember to abide by them. When you meet someone and can't recall their name, don't be embarrassed, simply ask them to remind you of it, giving them your own name at the same time. Since nearly everybody has trouble with names it seems silly not to acknowledge the problem and find a comfortable way of settling the matter. The next one is to do it now while you are thinking of it or, failing that, chalk up a memory jogger. I know I am less good at multi-tasking than I used to be, so try to keep the number of balls juggled at any one time down to a sensible number. None of this is foolproof but it helps.

I had grown used to print blurring to obscurity without my glasses, but then people began to mumble in conversation and actors failed to project in the theatre. Someone kindly told me I had dropped my coffee, when she had meant my poppy of remembrance, Swansea became 'swampy' and the 'flag of Greece' I heard as 'police'. Kish's bell no longer told me she was approaching, and that was yet another signal of the need to seek digital help. Although much better than the hearing aids my mother struggled with, they still don't replace my original ears on the world, so I value sur/subtitles, not only for operatic English but also for many a television programme or film, especially those spoken in side-of-mouth American.

After retiring from the Co-op, Graham took on the hugely demanding voluntary work of being Chair of the National Council for Voluntary Organisations (NCVO) based in London. He held this post for the full permitted term of six years, only stepping down to be a 'Woz-Been' for the second time late in 2010. He compensated for this by a new commitment with the Greater Manchester Centre for Voluntary Organisation (GMCVO) and by acquiring the accolade 'The Best Grampar (sic)* Ever' from our delightful granddaughters, who never cease to entrance us.

We have swans with four cygnets on Swan's Pool and four contented cats at Throstles' Nest. Where there are small mercies let us be grateful, as indeed I was in January 2011 when I felt able to write in the animal diary, 'It seems safe to say that peace has broken out'. Gulliver, of course, had been effecting his miracles of peace-making for many months prior to that, but now here we are in a relaxed post-war household:

Mille has moved gracefully into pole position as senior cat, occasionally putting the others (especially Adora Bubble) in their place but, overall, she has good relationships with all of them, and with Kish. Her chief devotion, however, is to Graham and me, giving a reliable chirrup of greeting whenever she first sees us. 12 years old in December 2011 she does not go out as much as she used to do, her favourite resting place being our bed, preferably with us in it. She not only showed Gulliver how to come and go using our balcony but continues to draw satisfaction from practising this art herself.

In her relationship with us Mille's nature is as soft as her gloriously perfumed coat. However, she is properly feline too, for example, if I have to move her from the bed in order to change the sheets, despite my profuse apology and the offer of a comfortable chair, she will refuse to stay in the new situation. She is not cross, for she never is, but perhaps disappointed that I can be so thoughtless, gently pointing this out by retiring to the linen cupboard, or washing thoughtfully on the carpet, until her rightful position on the bed is available again. Occasionally, Mille will be impressed by a visitor to the house, but that person is among the rare and privileged. By and large she is Mummy's and Daddy's girl. Our cat-sitter Leo can coax warm responses from most cats, but reports that Mille is the one to be withdrawn when we are away, though our abandonment of her seems to trigger her old hunting instincts, and several times house-sitters have been presented with unwelcome presents of mice and birds, behaviour she has normally left behind and which disappears again in her delight at our return. Her devotion is touching, and she is the only one of our cats who actively likes to be picked up for a quick cuddle, held on the shoulder with her head rubbing against the cheek.

Adora Bubble, six in November 2011, remains a diva. Once Gulliver had given her the confidence to establish her right to be in Odette's room she lost interest and abandoned it, deeming it no longer necessary. She then moved into a new mode of being a downstairs cat, often sharing the radiator warmth on the window-ledge-cum-dresser-top-space in the living-room with Gulliver, who proved adept at wrapping our expensive silk curtaining round them both like a tent, thereby excluding any possible draught, and improving the warmth factor. They remain close friends despite Gulliver caring for Odette as well. After about a year of being a downstairs cat Adora's behaviour changed again and now she is everywhere – upstairs with me in my study, deep inside a cupboard in Graham's, enjoying the balcony and, most of all, back to diving down under our bed covers at night, her favourite spot being between Graham's feet. She grumbles if he dares to move but otherwise is mainly good-natured with us though, unlike Mille, is affronted if we dare to pick her up. Endearingly, she attaches herself to Leo when we are away and makes more overt fuss of her than she will ever do of us, yet is always the first to greet us on our return from holiday. She remains close to Kish, often taking over the dog's bed if Kish is not in it, or sharing it with her if she is. She is always delighted to receive any visiting dog and relishes the days Buster spends with us, partly for his own sake, partly because she knows (despite him being so harmless) that he is a good Odette deterrent, and that the latter will keep a low profile while he is about. One of the few things Adora Bubbble and Hermia will always have in common is their admiration of Buster.

In better weather Adora Bubble goes out in the garden, perhaps not as much as in pre-war days, but enough for us to feel she is enjoying it again. Over the winter months, independent cat access to outdoors is reduced to that cat-sized square hole in the wall of the utility room. Adora Bubble considers this a danger zone for possible confrontation, hence the one tray we keep in the system for emergency comes into greater play. Post-war trauma has also left Adora Bubble lacking the courage for those leaps from the balcony, despite Mille's and then Gulliver's example. She will pace up and down anxiously miaowing to herself, but even with my encouragement from below she cannot quite bring herself to make that final jump back to her pre-war lifestyle. This is a shame but a minor limitation and, apart from that, Adora Bubble is as contented as her tricky nature will ever allow. We have Gulliver's friendship and support to thank for this, for he is a vital part of her well-being.

Odette is a complex character – brave, timid, affectionate, loud-voiced, velour-coated, three-leggéd, feisty. She does not let disability keep her from doing much. She cannot, of course, manage that leap from balcony to lawn, but her one hind leg must have strengthened well, as she is able, with concentration, to jump from our bed to the window-ledge to establish her right to an occasional nibble at that feeding station. She and Adora Bubble have learnt to live in mutual dislike. Odette will still seize an opportunity to charge at Adora, provoking familiar yells of rage, but this happens less often, and is contrasted by their capacity sometimes to be asleep in the same room, albeit at a safe distance.

Odette loves to be outdoors, even when the weather is not so good, and she must have many special hide-outs. We have never seen her across the lane (apart from the drama of the garage incarceration) but she certainly ventures into the field at the back of the garden. She sometimes comes for a chat outside too, but rarely allows me to stroke her alfresco, or indeed anywhere at all except on the landing and in her bedroom.

In these areas she becomes a different animal, rolling over for a tickle of her apricot tummy, requiring massive stroking, and even allowing me to pick her up for a brief cuddle. Bedtime has become a ritual, in which I have to go to the front door, step out onto the path in my dressing gown and call her. After a moment there is an answering deep miaow and her hoppity form appears, rushes past me, indoors and up the stairs to the landing, where she waits for me to fuss her. Odette has now taken this a stage further as she will often come into the kitchen, yowling to ensure I have got the message, then go out in order that I can do the proper thing and call her in! She reverses the ritual in the mornings, going downstairs ahead of me, then waiting in the dining room for me to open the front door. I must then retreat back up the stairs so that she has a safe run at the exit. One is left feeling that Odette cannot shake off a dreadful suspicion that someone or something horrible might be lurking to grab her from behind, so she must take serious precautions.

Odette's voice and purr are the loudest in the house, her coat deep and soft, her affection for me, in its own way, boundless. If she can, she will entice me to spend the night with her in her room, and I do it two or three times a month to help keep her happy. Of course she is not that lonely, for Gulliver doesn't allow her to be. Now he knows Adora Bubble is fine with us in our bed, he is free to keep Odette company on hers, coming in off the nightshift in the early hours, staying there often until mid-morning, by which time Odette has gone to explore the day.

Odette will usually allow Graham to stroke her when on her designated, safe territory, and long-stay house-sitters report that they are accepted after two or three days, being gentle people. She has proved intrepid in her rough and tumble games with Gulliver, and is unfazed by Kish. The dog can roar across the garden towards her, in hot pursuit of the football, and Odette will sit there calmly watching. Sometimes she will even join us for a short walk up the field. She is as fond of Kish as are all the other cats, but this does not extend to any other dog. In fact, with rare exceptions, any form of visitor

is a no-no-Odette. Like Adora Bubble, but for different reasons, Odette has some limitations on her lifestyle. Some disabled cats can apparently continue to hunt successfully but, as far as we know, Odette's hunting instincts never progressed beyond killing feathers. We can't pretend to be sorry about this and, while we sympathise with her extreme nervousness, we feel quite smug that, given her history, she enjoys life so much. It's good to be able to say, at least most of the time, 'There goes one happy little cat.'

Kish is now in middle-age, greying at the muzzle and much calmer, though still an impressive singer and footballer. She no longer leaps up at total strangers she encounters on walks, though she may lean on a privileged person or two, usually resulting in her head being fondled in an amused response to her charms. She is still not quite cured of leaping up at adored visitors; Phoebe and Ruby have had to learn to 'be boring', standing straight and still, ignoring Kish's rapturous welcome until it subsides. Kish is strong and fit, the only health problems arising when she has overdone the goal-keeping and has to have treatment for shoulder strain. Her metabolism, however, has changed slightly over the years and, after a few unexpected experiences of coming down to find the Mountains of Morn heaped on the kitchen floor, we realised that she now needs a brief walk at bedtime, usually in the dark of the field and often accompanied by one or other cat.

Kish's loyal devotion to family and friends is touching, and her occasional tendency to aggression with other dogs when out and about has waned to almost nothing, though we still take the precaution of lassoing her with the lead if in doubt. There are certainly some breeds she prefers to others. She almost always likes spaniels but often dislikes collies, for reasons unknown. Normally she likes Labradors, but there is one notable exception. Tess is black, a lovely dog, devoted to Rick, her dad. She and Kish used to play happily in the field together, Kish greeting Rick with her typical ebullience. Then Rick had a bad accident which put him out of action for several months and made him less steady on his feet when, eventually, he came back to us. Kish, thrilled to see them both, made the mistake of her usual over-enthusiastic welcome, and Tess, now in protective mode, was having none of it, rounding on Kish in no uncertain terms. They did not fight, but it sounded like it, and they have hated each other ever since. The row that ensues when Rick and Tess are passing our house is phenomenal, but we are on good terms with him, all acknowledging that it is six of one and half-a-dozen of the other with the dogs. Besides, we respect Tess for taking care of her dad.

Kish's territorial behaviour from the car, or at the front gate, tends to remain rowdy. There are a few canine passers-by who must know the password and can go by unmolested, but most people going past the garden with a dog could be forgiven for thinking that a vicious brute lives on the other side of the wall. We usually call her in but don't altogether discourage her, thinking that it does no harm for word to travel that we are protected by a fierce guard dog. People who know Kish also know that any visitor stepping inside the gate, whether dog or human, will be enthusiastically welcomed as a guest. But keep it dark. Fortunately, when we are in France her behaviour is generally much less territorial. If she were to let rip from the balcony there, in the way she does at home at the front gate, it would soon create bad relations with our neighbours. But when she sights other dogs passing her French home, at most she utters a gentle 'Woof' and often only a quiet whine of interest.

Her relationships with all our cats is good and, if we are visiting friends who have cats, Kish is politely deferential, able to reassure the host animals within minutes that she is no threat, though we never dared to experiment with my sister's hypersensitive

Gromit. Kish, being a dog, wants to be the centre of our world, so she relishes having us all to herself when away on holiday. But any jealousy she has of other animals manifests itself not in aggression but by an endearing and pleading thrust of her nose into a lap, or a paw placed on the foot, denoting 'This is my person'. And from our side she is a best friend and great companion, enhancing our walks, keeping us exercised, and helping to make home the special place it is.

And Gulliver? He may, at last, have stopped growing. A fine big cat with the softest, deep plush coat, he is gentle and calm as ever, but exploring further afield, having been seen as far away as the top of The Beanstalk, presumably going mousing on the bank that slopes between the two reservoirs. He has a busy schedule and great responsibilities, as he takes it upon himself to check regularly that everyone is all right. Like Hermia (who is doing fine and always greets me with enthusiasm in her new home) Gulliver could be termed *ubique*; when not on duty he may be found asleep in any room of the house and, when on patrol, though he may be unseen for many a long hour, he can then silently materialise beside you, for his is a quiet presence; he rarely miaows and now he is mature, seldom purrs, but radiates contentment. He has helped with several pages of this book, sitting beside the keyboard, sometimes typing a comment or two as Bernard used to do, and looking up at me with a sweet smile which reminds me of Piedy, all those years ago.

To describe Gulliver as affectionate does not quite catch him. Benign is a better word, for we feel that it is *Gulliver* who is looking after *us*. He is not keen on being picked up, or even stroked, except when he chooses to bestow that favour, but he will suddenly arrive on your lap, staying for a few minutes to satisfy himself that you are fine, before moving on to one of his other charges, notably Adora Bubble or Odette. If I am worried about him because I have not seen him for a while he will waft across the garden, just to reassure me, and once, just before we left the house for 24 hours, I had just said to Graham, 'I have not seen Gulli today, I would like to know he is okay before we go'. I had my hand on the front door handle as I spoke, and lo, the words were no sooner uttered than there was Gulliver, paw on the glass on the other side, come to tell me all was well. He seems to have a sixth sense as to when he is needed. When a family member was having troubles and had to stay with us for a few weeks, Gulliver was instantly there to offer comfort. When I struggled back from a visit to Essex, with a pain in my groin worthy of a broken hip, he was full of concern, staying with me (on me) to help me recover from what was, this time, only referred pain, which he and the marvellous Bev soon cured between them.

On the one occasion that he needed help himself, when he was about 18 months old, he appeared quietly in the kitchen holding up a front paw. A quick glance told me it required treatment and I rushed him to the vet just before closing time. The gash was deep underneath and the bite vicious on top. The vet thought he had been in a cat fight, but this seemed out of character, and I still wonder if the encounter had been with a squirrel. Given a sedative and a pain-killer he was allowed home, but the wound was stitched up under anaesthetic next day, his paw bandaged to keep all dirt at bay and an edict issued to keep him indoors for several days. The bandage must have stayed on a bare half-hour, and our attempts to keep Gulliver in our bedroom also proved laughable:

Balcony door shut. Bedroom door shut. The doors to the cupboards which link the two bathrooms behind the scenes, shut. One cat – escaped. Fortunately I met Gulliver on the landing before he had progressed any further, returning him to base where he settled down again very amiably. I worked out that he had succeeded in opening the sliding doors of both bathroom cupboards, then found freedom through the door of the bigger bathroom. We shut it. Calm, confident and affable throughout his ordeal, nonetheless Gulliver became bored. It was inevitable, and my attempts to divert him with toys, then a smart scratching post with swinging snowballs, he thought ridiculous. (It was recycled to Windyway.) Playing Houdini was much more his style, after all he had duties to attend to and patrols to make. Three days into his confinement, after I had been keeping him company only an hour earlier, I came up at bedtime to find an empty bedroom, those wretched doors negotiated again and the outer bathroom door scrabbled open on its less than reliable latch. I cursed myself for not foreseeing that this might happen and, since Gulliver was certainly outside by this time, I worried that he would damage his paw, or get dirt in it causing an infection which would greatly prolong his imprisonment.

I switched on the security lights and took a look out from the balcony, and there, miraculously, was Gulliver sitting on Emily Bear. In her turn she must have been looking after him. I fully expected that he would have vanished by the time I got near, but he was still there as I came out into the garden, still there as I tried to appear nonchalant as I crossed the lawn, still placidly there on Emily's back, enjoying the night air, as I arrived to gather him up and return him (amiable as ever) to the safety of a more heavily barricaded bedroom. The next day was a Sunday, but I was able to purchase a sturdy hook which Graham fitted to the dodgy bathroom door and, on Monday, the

vet pronounced no harm done, the wound was clean. A new bandage was fitted which lasted all of five minutes, but it was a good try and there were no more great escapes. From then on Gulliver seemed to accept that his confinement was only to help him heal faster. The whole episode lasted ten days. A long ten days but it was worth it when he was signed off with plaudits from the vet for our care and his patience. There were sighs of relief as Gulliver resumed his full range of duties, moving benevolently among us like a good spirit, giving us his comforting protection.

When it comes to our cats' safety I believe in the art of the sensible compromise. Among certain experts there are long lists of possible dangers and, if you were to follow them all you would keep your cat in a padded, sterilised cell. In theory there are vast armies of plants dangerous to cats in the garden. Indoors, elastic bands are potential killers and large, dog-water bowls are obviously plotting to drown all kittens. Much of this information I would treat as unnecessary fussing, but not all. When one of our wooden water butts developed a rotting lid, I was quick to anticipate it giving way under an exploring cat with lethal consequences and, since becoming aware that even a small amount of lily pollen can be fatal to a cat, as there is no antidote to the poison, have banned lilies. If I am given some of these beautiful flowers they are recycled to a cat-free household. However, day lilies (*hemerocallis*) are harmless.

The one area of cat safety where I fully admit to neurosis, is in relation to traffic danger. Several of my friends and relations who have cats live on through roads, but I'm not sure that I could do that any more, after years of living somewhere so relatively safe. Even here we knew tragedy with Aaron, and it worries me when I see a vehicle travelling along our tiny lane faster than I think is wise.

Part of the pleasure our animals give us lies in the knowledge that, as far as we can, we are offering them a full and happy life. It makes *me* glad to see them contented and to feel that our home is their home too, in which they have rights. None of our animals is a hooligan but they do occasionally scratch at furniture or scrabble carpet. We don't get excited about this, merely making good from time to time. After all, human beings create wear and tear in the home, and animals (within reason) can only be expected to do the same. It is certainly true that they make more work, but so do children or visiting relatives, and we would not be without *them*.

Cats can have surprising preferences. Silvester always liked to take his drink from a glass of water by our bed. Gulliver started the same habit, wanting to share our night-time drinking water. We gave him his own glass, as we had done his predecessor. However, this is not a hugely practical drinking vessel for a cat as, halfway down, the going gets tricky. Instead, we offered him a rather elegant glass bowl and this has met with approval. We kid ourselves that Kish makes little mess, with her neat short coat, but when we are in France with that blue laminate floor, this is proved false, for I have to sweep up scatterings of dark hair twice a day, hair which, at home, is invisible on the darker floors. Do we care? Not a great deal, which is just as well since the four cats must also be making a hefty contribution for the Dyson to ingest. Recently a friend said to us, 'Cats are all right so long as they know their place'. I would agree with that but not quite in the way it was intended . . .

Knowing Their Place

Our cats know theirs
    have pride of it

No such concept as
    wrong side of the door

Always correctly placed
    for demanding access
    or egress

Restriction not in their vocabulary
    come the day long night
    go the night long day

Their right to exercise
    in garden, grasses, the landing
    where the pipes run warm,
    best chair or car bonnet
    the cupboard of clean linen

Then our bed:
    on it
    or in it
    curved to our bodies
    folded to our feet
    pinning us still,
    purring the honour they do us
    knowing their place

Our hearts.

There is no escape from growing older and experiencing uncomfortable changes; marriages break up, people grow frail then slip from us, there is heartache as life throws its many slings and arrows. Yet, for every death there is a birth – babies born to parents eagerly awaiting an event which still savours of the miraculous. And despite all the negatives, people still fall in love and find happiness in stable relationships. Some even continue to marry, or commit to civil partnership.

Our animals' lives are, of course, much shorter than our own, but ours, in turn, are mere blinks in the vastness of time – 'our little life'* indeed. Yet there is comfort in knowing, that long after we have faded back to stardust, a rock that had its spirit released as *Bear*, a rock that once I knew and loved, will endure. Emily Bear has been blessed with laughter and the climbing limbs of children, the bounding leap of a happy dog and the soft paws of many an exploring cat – one of whom had invisible wings.

Though it would seem that nothing in our universe is truly eternal, Ronald Rae has a phrase which captures a timescale we can all understand . . . 'till the stars go out'. In those terms Emily Ursus Bear can surely be seen as immortal, and as she stands with her thoughtful head lifted to the moon and stars, perhaps she will carry the essence of us with her – into the beyond of time . . .

Emily's Moon*

Emily's moon lives under the hill,

Rises night-time smooth and still.

Sometimes it's a silver slice,

A curling finger, white as ice.

Emily's moon is on the sky,

Moving softly, moving high,

A silent ball, a gold balloon

Rides dark velvet, Emily's moon.

Emily's moon, awake at night,

Travelling tireless, brimming light,

While far above, the stardust deep

A guardian watch on all will keep . . .

Afterword

The narrative of these pages closes in late 2011, but of course the cycle of life is continuous, bringing the good and the bad. During the months spent preparing for publication, we were glad to welcome back into our lives people we had thought lost to us, but were devastated by the loss of our beautiful Mille to a sudden, fatal heart attack. Yet there is comfort, for from the same family background as Gulliver, comes his great nephew . . .

July 2012

Enter Melvyn

Explanatory Notes*

Page

7   **Shelob** was the gigantic spider guarding the secret way into Mordor in Tolkien's *Lord of the Rings*.

19   **The Queen's House** was built by Inigo Jones in the 17th century for Anne, wife of James I.

23   **Messerschmitt** – a World War Two German fighter plane.

36   **Keith Littlechild**. Engineer, German Shepherd fan. Fellow Ralph McTell devotee.

37   **David Griffiths**. Former civil servant. Attends same French conversation class.

37   **Derek McBryde**. Also attends French. Ex-computer consultant. Likes singing and drinking tea.

37   **Peter Walton**. Former civil servant. Poet, writer and enthusiastic birder.

37   **Jan Shirley**. Children's author and French translator, living in Cumbria.

38   **Ian Slater**. Writer, German language enthusiast. Macclesfield devotee, reluctant exile.

38   **Brenda Perridge**. Valued email correspondent, grandma and cat lover.

38   **Hedwig** is Harry Potter's messenger owl in the books by J K Rowling.

40   **Pennant Roberts**. Former pharmacist. Writer, poet and performer. Great performance colleague.

59   **vile jellies** – a reference to 'out, vile jelly' in Shakespeare's *King Lear*.

66   **bit** – a part or head for a brace or drill.

68   **Goody Two-Shoes** – an expression derived from a character in an 18th century story for children, possibly by Oliver Goldsmith.

74   **Darby and Joan**. According to the Oxford English Dictionary this is a term from a song or poem dated as early as 1735, or maybe even before that. It denotes a devoted elderly couple living contentedly in retirement. Not so much in use today, the phrase holds its own in relation to social clubs for senior citizens.

75   **'hard by the Fulham Road'** – a quote from a poem Graham wrote for me as part of his courtship.

85   **'Gentle'** is a reference to the famous villanelle by Dylan Thomas, *Do Not Go Gentle into that Good Night*.

101   **Northern Writers in Education** has since become part of the countrywide organisation known as the National Writers in Education.

continued . . .

Acknowledgments

I would like to thank the following:

The photographers of long ago who provided the family portraits:
PW Carisbrook in Blackheath   SAJ Quilter in Beckenham
Rowley Studios, Russell and Sons, Portman Square, London

Becca Thornton, for the 2011 photographs of the family aboard Emily Ursus Bear.

Anthony Paton and all the other trustees of the late Margaret Tempest estate, for their kind approval of our representation of the illustration *Pinky Mouse and Koko*.

Everyone who acted as a sounding board and/or helped piece together the picture of *Children's Hour* – David Griffiths, Corinne Haworth, Keith Littlechild, Derek McBryde, Menna O'Callaghan, Brenda Perridge, Jan Shirley, Ian Slater and Peter Walton. I am especially grateful to Olive Ambrose of the Romany Society for her expert guidance on Romany, and to Pennant Roberts for his splendid child's eye view on the outbreak of World War Two.

The Spargo family and their dog Fizz, for providing the model for the illustration at the end of Chapter 19.

MEN Media, for permission to quote the headline from the article in the Macclesfield Express by Peter Underwood of 21st July 2004.

Sir Dennis Landau, for permission to use his phrase 'woz-been'.

Barbara Harrison and Pam Beedham, for family memories extending beyond mine.

David and Gitte Bard, for advice on swans.

Catherine Hiss, Dr Ginny Meikle, Sandra Newsome and Michèle Phillips, for sundry help and advice.

I am also greatly indebted to, and warmly thank:

Carole Baldwin, Jacqueline Richardson, Gloria Wilson and my husband Graham, for proof-reading the manuscript.

Jaz Singh, for his help and expertise on the cover design.

John Lindley, Manchester Cathedral Poet of the Year 2010 and former Poet Laureate for Cheshire, for his invaluable advice on the poems.

Marilyn Edwards who introduced me to France Bauduin, allowed her cat Gilly to pose as Mompty, provided professional advice, general encouragement and so much more, including several lunches!

Pauline Macdonald and Ronald Rae who gave me Emily Ursus Bear, a letter from Amber and their valued friendship.

France Bauduin for her skilled and beautiful drawings, her patience when I sometimes hesitated over what I wanted, or asked for changes, her friendship and, not least, for Gulliver, and now Melvyn.

Jen Darling for being a good friend and producing such great books.

In addition, I wish to thank everyone who has offered their loving support and/or constructive criticism throughout this project, particularly Angela Cooke and Jan Leavey, my sister Sheila Albury and my husband Graham.

Books used for reference and/or recommended for further reading . . .

The Nature of Alexander Mary Renault

The Wolf Talk Shaun Ellis

The Jungle Book Rudyard Kipling

Pinky Mouse and Koko Margaret Tempest

The Dog Listener Jan Fennell

Miss Garnett's Angel Salley Vickers

The Cats of Moon Cottage Marilyn Edwards

Narrow Dog to Carcassone Terry Darlington

Cat Detective Vicky Halls

The Eagle of the Ninth Rosemary Sutcliff

Wonders of the Universe Professor Brian Cox

Black's Medical Dictionary

Brewer's Dictionary of Phrase and Fable – 18th edition

Strictly English Simon Heffer

Chambers English Dictionary

Collins English Dictionary

The Oxford English Dictionary

The author also gratefully acknowledges the use of *Wikipedia* for some references.

Previous Books by Jenny Melmoth

If you have enjoyed this book and have not read the two earlier ones, you might wish to do so.

A Cat in My Lap tells the story of Jenny's early married life in Essex and her move to Cheshire. With cats at the heart of the story, this book also focuses on dogs, gardens and anecdotes of family life.

First published in hardback by Clowder Books, then in paperback by Alfresco Books.

In a funny, sad and thought provoking way, ***Dear Dear Mary*** uses heart-warming letters to tell how Amber came to live among Jenny's other cats and eventually settled happily.

Both books are charmingly illustrated by Jo Berriman.

Published by Alfresco Books.

Jenny's other books are:

St Boniface and the Little Fir Tree, illustrated by Val Hayward, tells the story of the first Christmas tree with alternate pages to colour.
First published by St Edward's Press, then Alfresco Books.

Tell You a Poem – self published

Feet First – Poems for Dance   *Footsteps – More Poems for Dance*
Both co-written with Malcolm Brown and published by Davies the Sports People.

For more information, or to order books, please contact Jenny Melmoth by email (j.melmoth@btinternet.com) or Alfresco Books (jen@alfrescobooks.co.uk).

About the Illustrator

The illustrator, France Bauduin, is an associate member of the Society of Feline Artists (SOFA). Self-taught, she was greatly influenced by her father, a professional wood sculptor specialising in animals, who first helped her develop her drawing talents.

France always loved animals and chose to become a biologist. Working in Entomology she spent many years drawing insects as a scientific artist in Quebec. Having married an Englishman there, she then moved to England and became a primary school French teacher.

In 2001 her queen, Spooky, had her first litter, which renewed her interest in art. She began in pencil, with drawings of her first two kittens, Lucky and Grippette. She then started work in colour and has drawn every kitten born in her home, plus a few cats and dogs for friends or as commissions.

She illustrated the novel *White Chin* by Marilyn Edwards, published in 2010, and is currently working on a new book with Marilyn, due out in 2013.

France lives with her husband Mark and several cats near Bristol. You can find all her drawings on her website: francebauduin.webspace.virginmedia.com